ADDICTION
AND
RECOVERY
HANDBOOK

Unmask Addiction, Unchain Recovery!

JACK ALAN LEVINE, et al.

GREAT HOPE
PUBLISHING
Coconut Creek, FL

ADDICTION AND RECOVERY HANDBOOK

By Jack Alan Levine et al.

Published by Great Hope Publishing LLC, Coconut Creek, Florida
For bulk book orders email: GreatHopePub@gmail.com

Cover Design & Layout By Scott Wolf

www.JackAlanLevine.com
www.DontBlowitWithGod.com

E-mail: Jack@JackAlanLevine.com

Neither the publisher nor the authors is engaged in rendering advice or services to the individual reader. Neither the authors nor the publisher shall be liable or responsible for any loss, injury, or damage allegedly arising from any information or suggestion in this book. The opinions expressed in this book represent the personal views of the authors and not of the publisher, and are for informational purposes only.

No Medical or Personal Advice:
This book is not intended as a substitute for the medical advice of physicians. The reader should regularly consult a physician in matters relating to his/her health and particularly with respect to any symptoms or conditions that may require diagnosis or medical attention. The information in this book, print and/or e book version, whether provided in hardcopy or digitally (together 'Material') is for general information purposes and nothing contained in it is, or is intended to be construed as advice. It does not take into account your individual health, medical, physical or emotional situation or needs. It is not a substitute for medical attention, treatment, examination, advice, treatment of existing conditions or diagnosis and is not intended to provide a clinical diagnosis nor take the place of proper medical advice from a fully qualified medical practitioner. You should, before you act or use any of this information, consider the appropriateness of this information having regard to your own personal situation and needs. You are responsible for consulting a suitable medical professional before using any of the information or materials contained in our Material or accessed through our website, before trying any treatment or taking any course of action that may directly or indirectly affect your health or well being.

Many of the various stories of people in this book draw from real life experience, at certain points involving a composite of stories. In some instances, people's names have been changed in the stories to protect privacy.

ISBN – 978-1-7356075-0-4   Paperback
ISBN – 978-1-7356075-1-1   E-Pub
Library of Congress Control Number: 2020945515

ADDICTION AND RECOVERY HANDBOOK: UNMASK ADDICTION, UNLEASH RECOVERY!

BY JACK ALAN LEVINE, et al.

FOREWORD

BY DARRYL STRAWBERRY

As a recovering addict, minister, treatment center owner, and former major-league baseball player for over 15 years, I have been using my platform to educate and inspire people to overcome the horrible effects and outcome of drug addiction. I've seen many have victory over their addiction through their faith, recovery treatment centers, twelve-step programs, as well as a variety of other available resources that either individually or combined have given people their lives back and victory over the battle of addiction. One of my greatest joys in life is to see someone break free from the bondage of addiction and go on to live the best possible life as God designed them to.

I wholeheartedly endorse and recommend this great book as a terrific resource and recovery tool. The Addiction and Recovery Handbook is truly a gift from God. It's 20 authors come together from a variety of disciplines and backgrounds in the addiction treatment world and share their experiences and knowledge. They share what works and what doesn't work and give you invaluable insight. I believe this book is a tremendous resource that will, at the very least, guide you down the path of recovery and hopefully be the tool to inspire you and show you how to live an addiction-free life.

If you are struggling with addiction yourself, this is the bottom-line truth, from those who have been there, done it, lived it, and have victory over it. This is knowledge and wisdom and information accumulated over careers and lifetimes and it is all available in one source, this book, for you to benefit from. If you are the parent or spouse or loved one of an addict, the resources and knowledge in this book will bless you beyond belief and give you insight and wisdom that will let you live your own life joyfully and happily, and show you how to best help your loved one struggling with addiction!

This book is a home run in the fight against addiction and it gets my MVP award as a Most Valuable resource tool. You should read it, then immediately share it with someone you know or love who is struggling with addiction or has a loved one struggling with addiction. Pass it on, quote it, refer people to individual chapters that have blessed and inspired you, or the whole book itself.

This book is a winner! The authors are ALL-STARS in the addiction treatment and recovery field, as well is in the game of life! Learn from them; they have what you need!

I played major-league baseball for 17 years. I was rookie of the year, eight times an All-Star, four times a World Series champion, and led the National League in home runs one year. Yet I struggled with drug addiction throughout my career. I was addicted to amphetamines and used them throughout my 17 years in major league baseball. Three times I was suspended by the league for substance abuse. I used everything you can imagine. I could shoot dope, shoot heroin, smoke crack, drink alcohol, it didn't matter. Whatever I liked to do on that particular day, that's what I would do. My pain comes from my childhood. My father was an alcoholic, he once threatened to kill our entire family with a shotgun. He beat me so I ended up with pain, but I went into baseball and I became great.

At the end of my career, I was three million dollars in debt, and for many years I was in and out of jail for criminal drug activity, solicitation of prostitutes, violation of parole, and violation of court-ordered participation in drug treatment and rehab facilities. Playing baseball and being good at it wasn't my problem. I enjoyed my success and the toys and access it brought me, but I did not consider myself a real man who could be responsible and accept the responsibility of being a husband and father, because I was in love with the lifestyle of being a drug user and womanizer. But my addiction brought me to the lowest point in my life. I came close to ending my life. My God and my wife saved my life.

In1991, I developed a personal relationship with Jesus Christ as my Lord and Savior, but still I struggled with drug addiction. It would be almost ten years later before I would truly allow God to have authority over my life and my addiction so I could live up to my potential as man, father, and husband.

In 1997 I was diagnosed with colon cancer. My mother had died at age 55 from breast cancer, so I thought I was done at age 30.

They removed a tumor in my large intestine and as result I couldn't play in the World Series that year! After finishing chemotherapy treatments, I fell back into my old habits and was arrested for possession of cocaine and soliciting a prostitute. At that point, my life became a very sad spiral downhill to the proverbial rock bottom. I left a drug rehab facility, was missing for three days, and was found sleeping behind a 7-Eleven convenience store in Florida. Yes, that was me, Darryl Strawberry, four-time World Series Champion. I was put in prison for eleven months. I will never forget the number I wore on my prison uniform "T17169." I felt so bad about life and was so depressed I refused chemo because I just wanted to die. My second marriage also fell apart during this turmoil and ended in divorce.

Eventually, I took the chemotherapy and was once again cancer free. In 2006, a few years after being released from prison, I met my third wife Tracy at a Narcotics Anonymous convention in Florida. I relapsed again and was still using drugs. Once a drug user, always a drug user. Right? But Tracy had enough faith in me and influenced me enough to convince me to grow in my faith and to get sober for real. She motivated and inspired me to apply my faith in Jesus Christ and to make the changes I needed to make. She led me back to the cross and away from the crack house, sex addiction, and drugs. Today, both Tracy and I are ordained ministers and we minister all over the country sharing Jesus to those struggling with addiction.

That was the beginning of a new life free of drugs and alcohol for me. Tracy and I got married in 2006 and started a foundation to raise awareness for childhood autism. I am still Darryl Strawberry, drug and sex addict, and alcoholic, but sober for over 15 years and can talk about it and share hope with anyone going through the same issues. I love sharing my powerful testimony about how God delivered me and that no one is beyond redemption. I am no longer Darryl the baseball player but Darryl the minister proclaiming the gospel of Jesus Christ and changing lives with my story and helping others who are dealing with alcohol, drug, or sex addiction.

Don't give up on anyone. If people had given up on me, I wouldn't be here today. My mother prayed for me and my wife pulled me out of dope houses almost 20 years ago. We're living in a time where it's very broken and lonely for a lot of young people. I've been in recovery for a long time and have never seen so many people addicted to drugs like they are today. When I see so many of these kids actually dying it breaks my heart. We have a serious problem in America today and it's going to take people like you and like me to start paying attention to our kids… if you don't talk to them, someone else will. Kids and adult users are trying escape from the pain that's deep within. We need to help kids with their deep pain inside — their hurt, habits, rejection, loneliness, parents' divorce, etc.; all this plays a big part in kids' lives. I pray parents would show more honesty and openness, more love and acceptance to their children. Parents, hug your kids. Tell them you love them and care for them.

God Bless you!
Darryl

P.S. In my book *Don't Give Up on Me: Shedding Light on Addiction* with Darryl Strawberry, I share my story of childhood abuse, anxiety, drug abuse and alcohol addiction, and provide easy-to-understand explanations and commentaries on addiction from trained professionals. The book provides a basis of coping and understanding addictions and offering hope and a path to healing. Like the book you are reading now, *Addiction and Recovery Handbook*, I pray it will be a blessing to you.

TABLE OF CONTENTS

PSYCHOLOGISTS & PSYCHIATRISTS

SPIRITUALITY

ADOLESCENTS

SHORT-TERM & LONG-TERM TREATMENT CENTERS

ACKNOWLEDGEMENTS

With great admiration, respect, and awe, I take this moment to thank all the amazing and wonderful contributors to this book. Those people, all of whom have firsthand knowledge and connection to addiction recovery, took time out of their lives and contributed what I believe to be amazing chapters to this book. Without them, none of this would have been possible.

I believe all of us share the same goal. We want to see people get well and recover. That was a motivating factor for the people contributing to this book. All of us wish you would pass this book along to people in need—both those struggling with the battle of addiction personally and the family members and friends who need a clear understanding of the problem, as well as the solution.

We have compiled a never-before-seen variety of addiction recovery opinions, ideas, and principles based on the real-life experience of what has worked and what hasn't into one volume. I think we've covered it all. I hope we have. I truly believe after reading this book you will have all the information you need to make intelligent decisions regarding your personal struggle or a loved one's struggle with addiction and, more importantly, with recovery. The chapter authors did not discuss their chapters with each other prior to writing, but spoke only from their own point of view. I think it's fascinating to see some of the themes on addiction and recovery that appear throughout the book. In my mind they confirm the validity and truth of the findings, conclusions, and opinions of our authors. Take note of these themes. They are important!

There are priceless truths, undeniable wisdom, and many great insights and ideas in these pages that will last for generations and impact the world for decades to come.

Read any chapter you want in any order you want. When you look at the table of contents, start with the chapter that appeals most to you. Definitely read the whole book, but it does not matter the order in which you read the chapters.

My belief is that man has been the same since the beginning of time. The heart of man, the mind of man, and the soul of man are the same. Yes, our circumstances, environment, and technology change, but at the end of the day who we are in our hearts defines who we are.

Addiction has haunted, destroyed, and ruined the futures, hopes, dreams, and lives of too many individuals and their families. I believe together we can break that chain and I pray we've given you the tools to begin do so in this book.

I would like to personally thank the contributors to this book. In alphabetical order the authors are: Raymond Alvarez, Graham Barrett, Dr. Adam Bianchini, Dr. Karl Benzio, Keith Brooks, Joe Bryan, Lui Delgado, Philip Dvorak, Dr. KJ Foster, Dr. Anthony Foster, Dr. David Jenkins, Douglas Lidwell, Pasco Manzo, Craig Nichols, Trinity Phillips, Dr. Jared Pingleton, Kerry Roesser, and Anonymous (Mike W. and Alice H).

Jack Alan Levine

DEDICATION

ADAM A. BIANCHINI
JUNE 6, 1962 – AUGUST 15, 2020

This book is dedicated to our wonderful brother, great man of God and front-line soldier in the long-running battle against addiction, Dr. Adam Bianchini. "Dr. B" as he was known to so many in recovery was a friend to us all.

Adam invested his time, energy and his life into serving others and helping them see the light and break free from the bondage of addiction. His chapter in this book is a critical one and I am so grateful to God that he finished it before he went home to be with the Lord. He left us (as a result of the COVID-19 virus) and His family much too early from our perspective, but we trust God and his timing and we know God has used Adam exponentially more in his life time here on earth then others could accomplish in 20 lifetimes. His life mattered and affected the outcome of so many others' lives. So many including myself are grateful for him. Adam always gave all of himself to everyone in need, often at his own expense. He devoted himself selflessly and sacrificially to helping others in need. A true model of the servant lifestyle that Jesus tells us as believers to live. One thing for certain, Adam heard, "Well done good and faithful servant… Come and share your Master's happiness!" (Matthew 25:23) as he was ushered out of this world and into the Kingdom of God. And one thing is for certain, we know we will see him again in the Kingdom.

Adam, we are so grateful for the life you lived. The way you allowed God to use you mightily to impact the lives of so many for the Kingdom of God, for deliverance from the bondage of addiction. I know your message, your heart, and the impact you had on all of us will continue to live on. The work you have done will continue to live on in the lives of so many people you impacted with your ministry, medical knowledge, time, and heart. They and their children, grandchildren, and great-grandchildren will be impacted by your selfless devotion for generations to come. As well, I believe your chapter in this book will be a living testimony to the life you lived as God will continue to use it to change lives and deliver people from the bondage of addiction for centuries to come. Well done, brother. We love you and miss you! To God be the glory!

Below is Adam's email response when I asked him to write a chapter for this book, which I believe reflects his heart so beautifully. Also, on the following pages are just a small sample of the thousands of tributes that kept pouring in when people learned of Adam's passing.

From: Adam Bianchini
<abianchini@originsrecovery.com>
Date: January 22, 2020 at 10:36:41 AM EST
Subject: RE: A book about Recovery

Been REAL busy, but, sure - anything to carry the message.

Thank you,
Adam Bianchini, MD
Chief Medical Officer
Origins Behavioral HealthCare®,
Hanley Center at Origins®

Comments & Tributes To Adam Bianchini

Philip Dvorak
In times like this, words just feel inept. We lost a dear friend and a fierce warrior for the Kingdom of God. I never met a more passionate man than my friend Adam Bianchini AKA Dr. B. We rejoice that he is with Jesus.

Betsy Bennett Gagne
Heartbreaking! Such a great man… prayers for his family!

Butch Baltimore
The church's loss and heaven's gain. He will be missed.

Carolyn Dowling-Firestine
Prayers. I loved listening to him speak.

Angie Smith Walker
Lost for words when thinking of the gratitude we have for this man of God. He has a special thumbprint on many of our hearts. Left a mighty legacy for the Kingdom that will impact generations to come. Until we meet again friend and brother!

Kathy Boler Goble
I met him in 2014, he played a huge role in my life changing!! This saddens me deeply!! My heart breaks for his family and peers! The world needs more people like Dr B!! Sending prayers!

Matt Smith
No way I loved that man he helped me so much.

Jonathan Woolf
This was a great man of God and sad to hear that passed away.

Rachel Trentor
This man helped me more than I think he will ever know. Extremely heartbroken RIP Dr. B.

Jill Sobraske LaRussa
I so hated seeing this! I loved this man, he made us laugh, cry and learn so much!! I learned so much from Him, the force He shared with us will never leave, its always in my heart. I keep learning from him! God Bless all who knew him. And we will see you again in heaven!

Robert De Angelis
Dr. B was a fierce warrior for the addicted. He brought recovery and the gospel to countless addicts and alcoholics who needed his love and compassion.

Robby Galvin
Prayers for Dr. B and his family. He is a big part of how I found my way back from the darkest points of my life. You will not be forgotten.

Donna Ireland
Dr. B was a tremendous inspiration. He lit up the halls at the Treatment Center!!! He helped so many people. I'm absolutely shocked.

Bruce Swartz
Adam had shown me how to have a relationship with God in early recovery the most incredible gift ever given to me and I'm sure to hundreds or thousands of others!

Jacob Pihlblad
Great man has helped so many of us, may he live on through us as we carry what he freely gave us. Love you doctor B rest in heaven.

Lynda Hart Lanier
I am in shock! Such a passionate, alive man of God! He helped so many and I am eternally grateful! My condolences to his family! "Well done my good and faithful servant".

Brian McDonough
I'm shocked, what a strong man, strong in recovery, strong in faith. I fortunately was a patient of his twice, and celebrated 28 months in recovery yesterday! He was very instrumental in my recovery. A pleasure to hear him speak and preach.

Janice Smothers
Adam and Jenell made the most significant impact on my life and I was forever changed through the love and obedience. I am forever grateful and will never forget. Until we meet again my brother much love and deep sorrow bye for now.

Mary Casey
So sad to hear this news. Dr. B was such an incredible man and helped me so much when I was at my absolute lowest.

Justine Irizarry
Still wrapping my head around this loss. May he rest in the sweetest of peace Grateful to have been able to learn from and love Jesus with Dr. B. He will be truly missed.

Nathaniel Carpenter
I've been clean for almost 5 years! I still hear this man's voice! Sad day.

Rich Michels
Thank you Lord Jesus for Adam

Fred McNeely
R.I.P. Dr. B! Thank you for always bringing the fire! It was people like you that made me believe that my life had purpose and was worth living. Such a big part of my life and forever in my heart… until we meet again.

Tiffany Hart
No!!!!! I loved this man! Dr. B was the truth.

Jennifer Dentzau Bucher
I'm so shocked and speechless right now. Dr. B was very instrumental in my recovery journey. I'm so grateful for the time I was able to spend and learn from him during my time at The Treatment Center in Palm Beach. He was a very passionate and caring man.

Nic Lawton
I am truly sorry for everyone's loss. It is hard to lose someone who has made such an impact in so many lives in our community.

AJamie Vogler Gregory
He was an incredible man, passionate for Jesus and I'm so thankful to have met him. My prayers are with his family and those he impacted.

Amber Mottaz
Oh my goodness what an incredible man who was on fire for Jesus. He helped so many, including myself. Rest in Paradise.

Lori Huston Marsch
Forever grateful for the healing during my darkest time in life – Dr B was the salt & light

Amy Lehosit Spell
I am just at a loss for words. God used Dr B to help me out of a life of darkness. God knew I needed a loud, strong, wise, passionate ex-athlete to help get my attention. He was instrumental at helping me understand how serious my addiction was.

Christopher Tiffanie Crowe
Soooo incredibly sad for this loss in the recovery community. That man was instrumental in myself and so many others finding freedom! My heart hurts today

Joseph Keating

Dr B will be missed. A great man. A man of God. He helped many of us. Till we meet again in heaven my brother

Wesley Hoyer

This is a huge loss as he was absolutely my favorite to sit and listen to at TTC. He was full of life and was an amazing example with his speech and passion. Sending prayers and thank you for helping me change my life.

Mary Smith Sash

I'm so sorry to hear this… he was truly an inspiration to me, prayers for his family he was a powerful speaker and man.

Tristan Canter

Wow. This is sad. Dr. B made a huge difference in my life.

Cassi Annamarie Adkins

So sad. He was the last sermon I heard at recovery church before I left soflo.

Patricia Lynch

I am so sad for hearing about the loss of Dr. B. He was such an inspiring amazing man. I am just at a loss for words. So sad to lose such a warrior.

Lynn Halliday

Such a loss for the recovery community! I'll never forget countless days being in the exam room with Dr. B while he examined patients and prayed with and over them! He touched so many! Prayers for his family and all! Sad day here on earth!

Jared Pingleton

He was one of the most cheerful and amazing Christians I have ever known. Truly a superstar in the Kingdom. I am brokenhearted but I know he is having a blast with his Savior.

Glenn Siesser

I am shocked beyond shock. Dr. B was one of the most inspirational men in my recovery which I thank God I have since shootings 2011. He was a man of God filled with love…

Kathy Verderame

Dr. B wow such a loss!! Always loved his Big Book Study! Praying for his family and friends!

Ronnie Lewis

Words can't explain the impact that this great man friendship, thoughts and teaching had on me and the many others like me. May God preserve a place in his Kingdom for him. RIP my dear friend.

Stephen Kavalkovich

I am so sorry to hear – Adam always did for others

Phil Doe

R.I.P. Dr. B. Such an amazing human. He helped hundreds of people and always was there for you.

Krystal Vermillion

I am literally at a loss for words right now! He helped me come to know the Lord and I know for certain that he is with Him now! God bless you Dr. B!

Jack Alan Levine

I am in tears! Adam was an amazing brother in the Lord and a true warrior in the fight on addiction. His life impacted so many for the better, including mine! I take comfort he is home with Jesus and in the fact it is not about how long we live that matters but about the impact we have… in that regard no one outlived Adam on this side of heaven! To God Be The Glory!

Special Thanks

Joe Bryan, the owner of the Beachcomber Treatment Center in Florida. I've known Joe for more than twenty-five years and have sent many people to the Beachcomber for recovery. That's the highest compliment I can pay him. Joe's father started the Beachcomber and Joe took over the family business. Joe is known throughout the recovery community for his outstanding integrity, his uncompromising devotion to seeing addicts get better, and for being a true friend. Joe, the truth is everybody thinks you're a great guy… and that's because you are! Thanks to Joe we have chapters from KJ Foster, Tony Foster, Kerry Roesser, and Keith Brooks.

Dr. Jared Pingleton is my dear friend, an awesome guy, and one of the most intelligent guys I've ever met—a true Renaissance man. He has dedicated his life to helping people get well and impacted countless people through his books, private practice, and positions at Focus on the Family and The American Association of Christian Counselors. Jared has been an inspiration to me and an unbelievable friend and encourager. I am blessed to know him. Thanks to Jared we have chapters from Dr. Karl Benzio and Dr. David Jenkins.

Lui Delgado is the founder of the N.O.W. Matters More Foundation, which is dedicated to helping people win the battle over addiction by providing resources and education to help those in need. I met Lui years ago and have the privilege of serving on his advisory board at N.O.W. Matters More. I love Lui because he doesn't just talk the talk, he walks the walk, as evidenced by his continual self-sacrifice to help those in need, twenty-four hours a day, seven days a week. Lui is an inspiration to me. Thanks to Lui we have articles by Trinity Phillips and Graham Barrett.

My heartfelt thanks to the three of you– Joe, Jared, and Lui for your individual contributions to the book and for opening up your contacts to make this book the best it could possibly be. You are awesome!

Raymond Alvarez. Ray, I have known you for such a long time and am so blessed to see the godly man you have grown to be. I'm not surprised as you've had the Lord in your heart since you were a young child. Your devotion to your wife, your family, and most importantly to God is inspiring to me. Your steadfastness and faithfulness are amazing traits and a wonderful blessing. You're a great guy, extremely kind and I am so glad to have your perspective in this book. Yours was rather unique as you had no experience yourself with addiction, but became a licensed counselor and learned all about addiction in your studies. Then for many years you've provided firsthand individual therapy and counseling to those struggling with addiction. I know God is using you to bless so many who will benefit from your skills and experience. I'm proud to have you as a friend and a brother in the Lord.

Dr. Karl Benzio. Karl, I'm so excited that you were willing to contribute a chapter to this book. I'm so impressed and blown away by the work you do at the Honey Lake Clinic, and the hearts of you and the staff. I know God is using you in amazing ways and it does not surprise me that He would use His faithful servant to accomplish His will. The impact you're making and the lives you are changing at Honey Lake is of priceless value. I know your clients certainly feel that way and it is easy to see from an outside view looking in. I pray God's continued blessings on you, your ministry, and your life and look forward to getting together personally and hearing more of your amazing story. Your love for Jesus shined through in our phone conversation and your concern for the gospel, its purity, and how it is represented touched my heart deeply. God bless you, brother.

Dr. Adam Bianchini. Adam, I am eternally grateful for your participation in this book. I will never forget over a decade ago hearing you make a presentation at an addiction conference. I have never been so impressed, enlightened, and educated as with the knowledge you conveyed as you shared with the audience how addiction affects the brain. It was the first time in my life somebody had laid it out so crystal clear. It was almost as if Mr. Spock had come down from the Starship Enterprise and explained it with his usual indisputable logic. As I sat in that audience of hundreds of people, many of them struggling with addiction, I could see the light going on in so many people's eyes. I thank you for your faithfulness to God and your willingness to share your knowledge and life with others. Your own personal journey and that of your family is an inspiration to me. God has gifted you greatly with an ability to communicate the intense scientific complicated things and boil them down in a manner that I and so many others without that knowledge can understand. That is just one of your many gifts. When I first had the idea for this book, asking you to contribute your chapter was the first thing I thought of, and I believe it could be the most critical of all, as it is the very foundation for understanding addiction. Your contribution to this book is invaluable and I am so grateful.

Keith Everett Brooks. What a pleasure it has been to get to know you. As we talked about your chapter in this book, I could see you have a wonderful heart and that your life is all about helping others, impacting others through your experiences, and sharing the truths you have uncovered. I know God is using you to impact many people and help many people on the road to recovery in the journey to a better life. I'm so blessed to know you. I look forward to working with you in the future and getting to spend lots of hours face to face sharing thoughts, ideas, and experiences.

Philip Dvorak is founder and pastor of Recovery Church Movement and has worked at treatment centers and churches for many years. Phil, you know firsthand about addiction as you watched a loved family member struggle for decades. I will never forget one moment in time when you were on stage at an addiction conference panel discussion. You began weeping as you were recounting all the people's lives that have been lost to overdose and addiction over the last six months when you were serving as pastor at a large treatment center in Florida. As you were addressing the audience, you said simply, "This has to stop. This has to stop!" I believe that moment in time has stuck with me and has inspired this book. I just want you to know the moment I saw you crying on stage as your heart poured out tears of grief, reminded me of what Jesus must've felt when He cried for His lost sheep. I believe we are supposed to feel this way about a dying generation who does not know the Lord.

Phil, I know God touched your heart and you are doing everything you can following God's direction to start Recovery Church. I believe this movement will transform this country and its battle on addiction. You are an amazing family man with a boatload of kids, and you manage to do it all. I know by God's grace and power you've accomplished what you have, and there's so much more to go. I want you to know that not only have you impacted my life, but so many others in the recovery and faith worlds.

Dr. KJ Foster and Dr. Anthony Foster. I'm so glad I got to speak with both of you personally and get to know you both. I am so impressed with your devotion to God and the impact you are making in people's lives. It is easy to see God working through both of you, and together you are an amazing team. I am looking forward to getting to know you both further and hearing even more of the amazing journey that your lives have been. I'm inspired by both of you as you continue to be transparent and open up to others with the goal of helping them on the path to a better life! You both are awesome. Thank you for contributing chapters. You have blessed me and I'm sure, more importantly, our readers more than you can imagine by participating in this book.

Alice H. Thank you for opening your life and soul and sharing with us the depths of your emotions, thoughts and wisdom. The impact NA has made in your life and the knowledge, hope and sobriety you have gained from it is both inspiring and awesome. Your work in the addiction field and dedication to seeing others benefit from the joy and freedom that comes from sobriety is an inspiration to me. You're a wonderful, sweet person and a blessing to all who know you and work with you. We have all been inspired and influenced by your life and the wonderful caring and generous nature of your heart.

Dr. David Jenkins. David, thank you so much for your blind faith in me and for being willing to contribute a chapter to this book just based on an introduction and a phone call. I know your chapter will have a great impact on those who read it and be a blessing, as is your life and ministry, both in the professional world at the Liberty

University campus and in your personal life. I so much appreciated getting to talk with you and hearing your heart and passion for helping others. I know God will bless that, and I look forward to meeting you in person one day soon and getting to hear what God has done and is continuing to do in your life. Thank you again, brother, for your contribution and your faithfulness.

Douglas Lidwell is the executive director and pastor of Faith Farm Ministries in Fort Lauderdale. Douglas, meeting you was no accident. It was God connecting us. You are like a brother to me. I love you so much and admire your heart and Heather's heart, and your willingness to obey God and put yourself on the front line of the daily battle as you minister to help, teach, and restore those who are the most beaten-down and destroyed, many whom the world would call hopeless as a result of their battle with addiction. But your diligence and faith, along with God's power, bring the restoring power and faith of Jesus Christ into people's lives along with practical application and teaching to give them the tools they need to succeed. Brother, you are unique, special, wonderful, and truly blessed by God.

Pasco "Pat" Manzo is the President of Teen Challenge New England & New Jersey and renowned author, pastor, and speaker. Pat, you have been such a wonderful inspiration to me personally, as you have mentored Pastor Sean and me and shared your wisdom, knowledge, and experience with us about church, ministry, addiction, and life. You are truly God's man being used on planet earth for His Kingdom. I can think of no greater blessing. What you've accomplished with Teen Challenge is amazing. I have witnessed it firsthand the reality of the program, the great staff, and the clients, as you blessed me by allowing me to visit, speak, and minister. I am not surprised that God would accomplish so many wonderful things through you as you are His faithful servant. But I also know it takes an astute business mind, a great organizer, and an amazing manager to keep the train rolling on the track! You are all of these. You and Mary Ann are so wonderful. Thank you and everyone at Teen Challenge for all you do.

Craig Nichols, Founder and Director of Washed Clean Ministries, a transitional sober home for men. Craig is a recovering addict. He's been to hell and back battling addiction personally for decades and is determined to devote his life to seeing others have victory over addiction. Craig, I've been truly blessed by having you in my life. I'm excited to see the things God is going to continue to do through you to help so many people.

Trinity Phillips. Trinity, since the day I met you many years ago, I have admired and respected you. Your gentleness and sincerity combined with the powerful strength from which you speak—based on your experience, revelations, and understanding from living life—is an incredible blessing to all of us who know you. Your faithful service as president of N.O.W. Matters More and your genuine desire to help others is not only a tremendous blessing but a reflection, I believe, of God himself. The fact that you were not an addict and yet took over the responsibilities that came with the position and became so touched by the plight of those addicted and the family members of those struggling has touched my heart in such a huge way. Brother, you are more committed than many who claim to be. And that is the best compliment I can pay you. I am proud to be your friend and to work alongside you to help people live better lives.

Kerry Roesser. Kerry, it was so great to talk with you and get to know you over the phone. I was so touched and inspired by the last two decades of your life and the commitment you made to help others get better. I know it came at great expense as you experienced the ravages of addiction in your own personal family, but you have used that to help and bless others. Sammy's life matters more now than ever as you continue to impact the world in his memory. You're an awesome woman and you have seen the struggle of addiction on many sides—as a therapist, as a sober home owner, as a mother— and yet as overwhelming as the days and weeks and years can be, you continue to have a heart focused on helping the next person at your own expense. Your self-sacrifice and dedication are an awesome inspiration, and I know your chapter will be a tremendously valuable influence and inspiration to those who read it. Thank you so much for sharing from your heart.

Mike W., Thank you brother for writing such a critical chapter on Alcoholics Anonymous and the benefits of that wonderful program. I appreciate you, your friendship and support. You are a great guy and awesome family man, but most importantly your gratitude to the AA program and your willingness to continue to plug in, as a reminder that the AA program saved your life, inspires me daily. We both know, "in order to keep it, you gotta give it away." Thank you for not just saying it but living it.

Editors: Thanks to **Caroline Mason** who did the initial editing for four chapters of this book and **Amanda Brown** who did the first edit. Thanks to my wife, **Beth Levine,** who did both the second and final edits on the entire book. Beth, your time, effort, and ability to pull together thoughts and concepts and make suggestions on ways to position the content to have it be the most effective for our readers was extremely valuable. Not only are you smart, beautiful, and an awesome person, wife and mother, but you're an amazing editor, as well. I had so much fun working with you on this book and look forward to doing other projects in the future. You're an amazingly talented woman and I am glad you got the chance to show it in this book. I could not have done this project without you. You are awesome (*and the sunshine of my life*)!

Design & Layout: Scott Wolf, I so much appreciate and I'm so grateful for the time, effort and dedication you have put into this book and all of my projects. You continue to amaze me with your intricate awesome and extremely effective design suggestions, concepts and implementation. Then to see them come to life and make the book look awesome... it's a true blessing to me! I truly don't know if you realize how talented you are... But I do! I know that I can be a pain to deal with, for many reasons... Smile! Not the least of which is my need to see everything completed and in front of me first and then change it, which definitely makes extra work for you... but I will tell you that I do enjoy very much our time working together and I cherish the opportunity to spend time with you and work on projects that I think will impact people's lives for a long, long time. You are a deeply valued friend and an incredible designer. I am blessed and privileged to work with you... keep the train rolling!

INTRODUCTION

My name is Jack Alan Levine. I am an author, businessman, and speaker, but this book is not about my professional life. It is about addiction.

I've counseled thousands of people over the years who have gone through it, and I know how torturous life can be when caught up in the pain and misery of addiction. It's an awful thing. I've experienced it in my own life, and I've experienced it as a parent, as I watched a family member struggle with addiction for years.

Whether you are in the throes of addiction yourself or seeing a loved one suffer through it, there is help. We have results and solutions for real-life situations that can crystallize this for you. Each person's situation is different, but the end result—the pain, suffering, and despair of addiction and the impact on futures, hopes, dreams, lives lost or ruined, and families destroyed—is beyond painful. It is staggering and mind boggling.

If you're like me, you know you need to be free from addiction forever, done with addiction, and not have it ruin or control your life. I know what it's like to be controlled by addiction. I know what it's like to feel as though I'm in the pit of hell, to feel that Satan's got me and he won't let go. It's a horrible feeling. When you are in the grip of an addiction, it affects everybody and everything around you. It affected me. It affected my family, my friends, my work, my health, my finances, and my marriage—every single part of my life.

Addiction is everywhere! Statistics show that at least one in every eight people is an addict. As you well know that number goes up significantly for college students. Most of those, if left untreated, will never live up to their potential, which is a tragic shame. I believe if a book like this had existed when I was a young man, I might not have wasted ten years of my life struggling with addiction. It is my goal and my purpose that others do not suffer as I did, as my loved family member did, and as so many others have, battling their addiction with no end in sight. The stakes are their lives, joy, and reason to live. That is why I wrote this book and asked so many wonderful, trusted professionals to contribute to this life-saving and game-changing platform.

I am a testimony, along with so many others, to the reality that addiction *can* be defeated. My purpose here is to give you a complete overview of addiction and recovery—no matter which part of the addiction spiral you've found yourself in—to help you see there is a way out of addiction.

I pray that we are a valuable resource and tool for you to gain knowledge and wisdom, so you can have victory over addiction and live the greatest life possible. God bless you and your family on the road to recovery.

Jack Alan Levine

ADDICTION EXPERT

THE TRUTH ABOUT ADDICTION

BY JACK ALAN LEVINE

I remember distinctly feeling as if I was being pulled down into a fiery pit by the drugs. This wasn't just a one-second flash or a dream. It was a growing feeling that took root and expanded day by day. I remember feeling like Satan had grabbed onto my leg and was pulling me down into a fiery pit. I could feel myself slipping away.

For many, many years during my drug use, I remember thinking very clearly that I could always come back. What happened was I'd party, I'd cross over the line, but I was always able to get back. In college, I could recover in a day. As I got older, it took longer. It would take three days or a week to recover. But I had *always* felt that no matter how far over the line I went, I could always bring myself back. Then I had a car accident during a drug-induced blackout and the car and I almost wound up in a lake. I would have drowned. At that point, I knew I couldn't bring myself back anymore. It was the single scariest moment in my life—not the accident itself but the full realization of what I had become. I thought I was in control. I wasn't in control. The drugs were in control and there was no way back. The pit of hell had me, and the drugs had me.

It was a horrible, awful realization. I know if *you're* suffering from any kind of addiction, the pleasure from that addiction has long since disappeared. Undoubtedly, it was there in the beginning. Whether drugs, alcohol, pornography, gambling, eating, shopping, the internet, work—whatever the addiction of choice, I know that the pleasure you got from it is long gone.

Most nonaddicts wonder why the addict continues to do these things that are so unpleasurable and destructive. They wonder why a guy would gamble away his family's rent and food money. Why would someone risk her job, her health, her sanity on drugs and alcohol? Why would a guy stay on the internet looking at pornography when he's got a wife who wants to love him? Or kids who want to play with him and hug him and who need their daddy? Why? In rehab, one of the counselors answered that question in a powerful way that has stuck with me. He said, "There's comfort in familiar pain."

Let me tell you something about my drug addiction and my gambling addiction. I love to gamble. I love to do drugs. I hated the *downside* of it. I hated the pain of losing when I gambled. I hated the coming down with drugs. But when I did drugs and gambled, I was in a place where you couldn't touch me. I was in control of the world. I was in my own world where I was the king; I was the boss. I did whatever I wanted when I wanted, and a tremendous feeling of power came with that. It was a tremendous feeling of freedom, even though it was actually an illusion. The thing offering the feeling of freedom wound up being a prison. But there is hope of escape. This is a promise from God.

"...*God is faithful; he will not let you be tempted beyond what you can bear. But when you are tempted, he will also provide a way out so that you can endure it...*" (1 Corinthians 10:13)

After God says there's no temptation that overtakes you except what's common to man, the next line is, "but with the temptation He will also provide the way of escape." I'm here to tell you: whether you're an addict yourself, or a parent or spouse of an addict, there is a way out. The only question is: will you take it or not? There is help if you want help. I believe this book is the beginning of your road to recovery and to a great life.

It's been more than twenty-five years since I took the way of escape, and my life has gotten better every day since then. I know who I am, what I am, and why I am. My turnaround began after a car accident when I asked God for help. Let me tell you a story that I hope inspires you.

Long after I'd gotten sober, I was in Lake Tahoe, on vacation with a group of friends. We had all gone out to a restaurant, and we were lingering over a wonderful dinner. The conversation was bright and engaging in a way I seldom experienced during my drug days. As we were all sitting at the table, I was telling a story about my drug-dealing days back in college. My friend's wife Yvette, a wonderfully sweet woman, looked at me, stunned. "Why, Jack Levine," she exclaimed, "I would have never imagined *you* would ever do something like that!" My reaction might surprise you. I went back up to my hotel room that night and I *cried.* Tears of joy! The story I'd told about college really *was* me—back then. Through my tears, I said, "God, thank you so much for what you've done in my life, that when people look at me today, they don't think of me as a drug addict wasting his life. As a matter of fact, it's so far removed from what I am now that people can't even believe that *would've* been me. Thank you for making that *unbelievable* change in me. Thank you that, today, I'm a new person. You've truly given me a new life."

If you're addicted, please listen to me. I know you feel like you don't have it in you. I know you feel like you've tried to get sober and failed. You feel like you're at war and you're getting the crap knocked out of you. It feels like you are starving and you have no more supplies. You've been out there forever, fighting. You're bloody and beaten. And your enemies are coming over the hill charging at you, and you feel like they're going to finish you off. But there's hope!

There's a great story about a little kid in kindergarten that makes the point I'm hoping for you to see. The kindergarten teacher gives out a piece of paper to all the kids and instructs the children, "Draw a picture. Draw anything you want on this piece of paper." The kids are happily drawing, but one little girl messes up her drawing. She tries to fix it, but that only makes it worse.

She starts crying hysterically. Hysterically! She's bawling and wailing. The teacher says, "Suzie, Suzie! What in the world is the matter?"

"I ruined it! I ruined it!" Suzie cries. "Everything is ruined! I did it wrong!" She hands the paper to the teacher, still crying uncontrollably. The teacher looks at her for a moment and then takes Suzie's first piece of paper and puts it down on her desk. She then hands Suzie a new piece of paper. "Here," she says. "Here's a brand-new piece of paper. Start again."

That's what God is saying to you today. It doesn't matter what happened before. "Here," He says, "Start again." God promises His mercies are new every morning (Lamentations 3:22-23). We should come to Him, lay our burdens at His feet and He will give us rest for our souls (Matthew 11:28-29). The best move I ever made in my life was believing God. I pray you will too.

The great news is there are resources and ways available to you right now to ensure you live a life free from addiction regardless of what or who you think God is, or if you believe in Him or not.

CAUSES OF ADDICTION

I work with people closely in many areas of the addiction rehabilitation process—physical, emotional, and spiritual—and I've learned a few things along the way.

One of the reasons people don't get help is because of the stigma associated with addiction. When they hear the word *addiction*, people often think of driving through some bad neighborhood in the middle of the night buying crack. Sometimes that's how addiction really is, but often it's not. Getting rid of the stigma is an important step. There are many schools of thought regarding the cause of addiction among scholars, doctors, psychiatrists, and psychologists, all lining up on different sides. Some say you're genetically predisposed. Some say it's your environment. Some say it's your personality. Some say it's the substance itself—that the drugs or gambling were too tempting. That discussion has its place, and I'm all for finding out whatever we can about addiction in order to help people. But from another perspective, I find the discussion rather fascinating, and here's why. (By the way, this is something I tell many people whom I counsel.) Let's say you broke your leg playing soccer. That's not good, of course. Nobody wants a broken leg. Now, let's say you broke your leg in a car accident. Okay? Also, not pretty, and not desirable. Now, let's say a guy came with a baseball bat and *clubbed* you in the leg because he was mad at you and broke your leg. Or let's say you broke your leg just tripping over the sidewalk.

That's four different ways you broke your leg. Here's my question. What could *possibly* be the difference? How could it possibly matter why or how you broke your leg? The only thing that matters is *you have a broken leg.* How it happened might be of some academic interest, or of interest to the justice system, or to history, but the only pressing question for you right now as you sit there with your broken leg is: what are you going to do about it?

Addiction is the same way. We can sit around and talk about all the reasons and causes for addiction, and that's not unimportant. Yes, there are different causes, and yes, some people are more genetically predisposed. And yes, environment can be an issue. But at the end of the day, we have someone who's *addicted.* At the end of the day, someone has *broken his leg.* So really what's the difference how you got there? The only thing that matters is: what are you going to do about it? And if you had that broken leg, would you say, "Well, you know what? I can't get my broken leg fixed because it happened in a soccer game. Maybe if I'd broken it in a car accident, it would be worthy of being fixed. But since it happened in a soccer game, I can't get it fixed." That's ludicrous. It's ridiculous. And yet it's often how we think of addiction.

Look, it doesn't matter how you got to that state. It just matters what you're going to do about it. It's not like you checked a box and said, "Hey, I want to wake up, ruin my life, become an addict, and throw everything away. I want to have physical, emotional and spiritual pain that I can't seem to recover from and live the crappiest life imaginable." I know that's not what happened, so never let the *how* you got addicted serve as an excuse for not taking action to address the problem.

I'm not a psychologist, but we know when you're a kid, you develop defense mechanisms in your mind that are very helpful and very valuable when you are a young child. Those strategies help you cope and avoid pain. They help you deal with the painful, unpleasant circumstances of your life (whether real or perceived). However, often they can hinder your recovery. As by trying to protect you from emotional pain, they can actually lead you to drug use (which can then to turn into full blown addiction) as a way to deal with or ignore that emotional pain. This happens if these defense mechanisms, which help you when you're a little child are not discarded at the proper time (when you are not a little kid anymore and when they have served their usefulness).

When you get older, those defense mechanisms you had as a child, (which are usually subconscious and have been a part of you since childhood), are no longer necessary. Like a stroller, you needed one when you were a little child, but now you can walk on your own just fine. The last thing you want to do as an adult is say, "I need to get back into the stroller to get around." But unless we adjust our perspective, unless we see, understand, and release the coping strategies we imported from childhood, we can get lost unnecessarily for our whole lives in addict-like thinking and behavior, which eventually changes our body and brain chemistry for the worse. Fortunately, therapy and/or counseling can help us recognize and bring to the surface the specific issues in our own lives. Once an addict can recognize them, he can deal with them. I believe it's the spiritual equivalent of turning on the lights in a dark room and the key to many addicts' complete recovery!

Addicts do what they do, use drugs and alcohol because of a perceived benefit. That perceived benefit is generally an avoidance of pain, or making them feel better about their present situation or providing comfort from an abuse or trauma that they do not want to think about or remember. The perceived benefit turns out to not be a benefit at all, as it leads him down the road of addiction and ruined, hopes, dreams, futures, and ultimately lives. But the addict is engaging in the addiction because they *feel* it gives them some benefit.

You need to able to be with yourself and love yourself. You also absolutely need intimacy and supportive relationships. I once heard someone break down the word *intimacy* in a way that really struck with me: "into-me-see." Intimacy. To an addict, that's *terrifying*. We won't even look into ourselves. How are we going to let anybody else in? Establishing intimacy is essential. We don't have to be perfect. But we have to be real. We are who we are, and we have to learn to be proud of that with all our faults and all our wonderful traits, as well. We need to have supportive marriages and families. And those who are single need supportive relationships and friendship groups. We also need to have a purpose. This is why employment and work resources are important, and most recovery programs can help with those things. It's important to work and derive a sense of accomplishment from what we do.

Hopefully, you'll be able to work at something you're passionate about or good at. You should strive for excellence and look for a sense of accomplishment, rounding out life with leisure activities, hobbies, and interests—different healthy ways of relaxing and enjoying your time. I know to an addict all of this sounds impossible. But I'm here to tell you, it's *not* impossible. I've been there, and I've done it, and so have millions of others. Your addiction has convinced you to believe the lies. As you recover, you're going to learn how to reprogram and recondition yourself so you can appreciate life and the beauty and joy around you.

There are many different avenues of recovery. *There is a way for you.* Would you at least go take a look? If I told you there was gold in my backyard, you might not believe me, but you would at least take a look because you'd be scared to miss it. Don't miss this. It's there if you look for it.

THE LIE OF ADDICTION

The great lie of addiction is that addiction makes you believe you are better off with the addiction than without it. For instance, if you are addicted to drugs and alcohol, the addiction has convinced you that your life is better with drugs and alcohol than without them.

In many cases, the addiction has convinced you that you need it to survive, that it is your life saver, your friend. It exists to help you. It makes you believe it gives you energy, it understands you, and is on your side unconditionally. This is a lie. The truth is addiction seeks to steal, kill, and destroy your life.

It is much like a pedophile looking to attract a child into his car with candy, dangling the candy, telling the child the candy is free and it's especially for him. Then, when the child gets close, the pedophile captures the child and does unspeakable things to him. Addiction seeks to do the same to you. It wants to gain control of your life, and, usually it does just that.

Feeding your addiction becomes the single focus, primary importance, and number-one objective of your life. We constantly think about how to satisfy, engage, and fulfill our addiction. Addiction is almost always disastrous. It causes a loss of your real identity, as well as physical, financial, relational, and spiritual consequences that are severely damaging to you and your family, friends, and acquaintances. In many cases, it leads to jail or death if left untreated.

The addiction makes the addict believe everyone is against them. They don't understand them, and they don't appreciate and love them. The addiction wants you to believe it is your friend and your defender. It's a lie! Nothing could be further from the truth. Addiction is evil. The great attribute of a good liar is they make you believe they are telling the truth. If it were obvious that someone was lying, you would not believe them. Your addiction is a great liar. That is why it is described as a cunning, baffling and insidious disease. It creeps up on you. It's like a time-release capsule. You think it's having no effect and then it knocks you on your ass, and you are not able to get up off the ground. This is the great lie of addiction.

The good news is there is truth. You can have it, but you must *choose* it. You can overcome and have victory over addiction. Your life will certainly be better without it than with it. As a matter of fact, with it you have no life at all. These are facts and circumstances that many addicts have learned the hard way, and we share them with you today as a history lesson and a reminder and a warning for everyone currently struggling with addiction. It is quicksand, and it will suck you in, drown you, and bury you. You must choose to seek the way out. There is help if you choose it and that is the truth!

THE PAIN IS THE SAME FOR EVERYONE

We know drug use or alcohol use is just a symptom of the real problem. I've worked with thousands of addicts over the last thirty years, and the one thing that amazes me about all of them is the remarkably deep amount of pain and hurt inside of them as the addiction has ravaged them spiritually, emotionally, physically, financially, and mentally. The mind-boggling fact of all of this is every addict has the same pain, regardless of how many drugs they use or how much alcohol they drink, regardless of how often they do it, and regardless of how long they have been doing it. The pain is the same.

I've seen people addicted to all different kinds of drugs: uppers, downers, painkillers, meth, heroin, cocaine, barbiturates, amphetamines, opiates, cannabis, alcohol, tranquilizers, sleeping pills, legal and illegal… You name it. But, the fascinating point is regardless of which drug they were addicted to, the pain they shared, the pain they suffered, the ravages of addiction on their life physically, emotionally, spiritually, mentally, and personally was always the same.

I will say it again. The mind-boggling fact of all of this is that it is the same pain for every addict, regardless of how many drugs they use or how much alcohol they drink, regardless of how often they do it, and regardless of how long they've been doing it.

No fixed amount of time makes you an addict. It's a mindset.

I've seen people get heavily addicted in six months and hit bottom, and I've seen others whose addiction finally caught up with them after years. Regardless of whether it grows slowly or fast, it's growing. The end result is always the same. The addict winds up a mere shell of themselves—a person who knows they are trapped, being suffocated, that the life is being sucked out of them, and that their addiction has completely overtaken their minds and their bodies.

It's as if they now live simply to feed the addiction. They know it's not a good thing, and sometimes they even wish they could find the way out, but they are so addicted and have become so comfortable in this pattern of addiction that it literally becomes the only thing they really live for. The addiction itself has overtaken them, lied to them, confused them, twisted the truth, and made them believe that only in their addiction can they find comfort from the realities of the world. When in truth the realities of the world are where they would find comfort and love, and the addiction is killing them and isolating them.

So, the bottom line is the pain is the same for every addict.

The great news is there is also hope, freedom, and a recovery program available for everyone. No one will be able to say there wasn't a way out. There is a way out for every addict. The only question is are you willing to take it?

HIGHER POWER

As an addict, I've trained myself (with the help of God and others) to think differently. I still face temptation, as do most addicts, but I want to let you see into my mind so you can see where my freedom has come from and how I maintain it to deal with temptation when it comes. So when a temptation arises, here's what I've trained myself to do. I immediately think, "You know what? This addiction [cocaine, Percocet, alcohol, placing a bet, or whatever] seems appealing right now. So let me think through the end result of that action." Already, by thinking about the consequences, I'm making headway in defeating addictive behavior.

Then I walk myself through it. I tell myself, "You'll have the cocaine, and you will definitely disappear again for three days. Once you start doing one line, you won't be able to stop, and you'll go through a quarter ounce or a half ounce of cocaine in three days. You will lose everything you have worked for in your life. You will lose your credibility. You will lose the respect of your family. You will lose respect for yourself, and you'll lose all the wonderful things you've accomplished. Not only that, you will feel like complete crap, disgusting and horrible." I remember how my mind and body felt when I was coming down from doing those drugs. So now there's some rationality happening. The thought I had about how nice that line of cocaine felt when I first did it has a counterbalance. I know there's *no question* that if I do that first line, I am going to wind up back in that situation. That is a place I never want to be again. It is not even close to being worth doing the line.

I even have a board of directors meeting with myself. This might sound funny to you, but I'm telling you, it works for me. The board consists of me and God. But sin—the devil—also attends the meeting. Everybody has a voice at the board of directors meeting.

God says, "Jack, you don't want to do that. That's bad for your life. I have good blessings in store for your life. Trust Me and all will go well with you."

So, I say, "Okay, God, that's great."

Then Satan, who is the embodiment of sin itself, speaks up and says, "Jack, God's an idiot. What you want to do is party. You need pleasure now. You *need* to do these things. You need to gamble; you need to use drugs. You can steal; you can cheat on your wife—anything you want. Go for it! You know it's okay. God will forgive you, so you can do whatever you want."

I say, "Okay, that's interesting. You've had your say." Then, of course, I say, "God, I'm with you. I know you're right, and I know how much pain I suffered by believing the devil before."

Then we vote.

But here's the thing. Sin has no vote. He has a *voice*. He gets to speak, but he has *no vote*. God and I vote. We vote *yes* to God, to the good things of life, the good things of the world, and the wonderful life He's already given me.

I'm sharing this with you because I want you to understand that whatever those urges are toward behavior that isolates and destroys you, I'm calling it sin because that's how I relate to it. But whatever you call it, the point is, that voice may not *ever* leave your head. "Hey, come use drugs… Come gamble… You need to isolate yourself… This is your relief… I'm your buddy… I'm the object that always gives you relief and pleasure."

That voice and desire may never go away entirely. That's okay. He can speak all he wants, but he has no vote. He doesn't have control of my life anymore. For example, I'm a lifelong Yankees fan. Here comes a friend's voice telling me how great the Red Sox are. You know what? He can talk himself blue. He can cite every statistic of every Red Sox player from the beginning of time to the end of time. He's not changing my mind. It really doesn't matter what he says. I'm not becoming a Red Sox fan. *I'm a Yankees fan.* I know who I am. I know which team is my team. In the same way, you need to unshakably know whose team you're on. The old adage is simple. If you have two dogs and you feed one and starve the other, the one you feed becomes strong and the one you starve eventually dies. Which will you feed… your spirit or your addiction?

I know not everybody reading this believes in God, and that's up to you. If you don't believe in a higher power, you shouldn't let that fact dissuade you from trying to find help. But I will tell you this, God was absolutely essential to my recovery, and I believe He can be to yours as well. The reason Alcoholics Anonymous and Narcotics Anonymous tell you to seek a *higher power* is because internally you feel estranged from it. You feel separated from it. You know in your heart that you have that yearning for fullness. There's a void, an emptiness in the life of every person who does not have a spiritual relationship with their Creator.

If you disagree, I can't force you to believe the way I do. But in counseling thousands of addicts, I *know* that emptiness is there. The relationship with the Creator I'm talking about is not a fearful one. You shouldn't have the attitude, "Oh my gosh, I'm going to do something wrong and there's a guy up there just waiting for me to screw up so He can slam me with a baseball bat!" That's not how we think of our own kids. I love my kids. I love them so much I don't want them to screw up. Now, at times I may have to discipline them because they screwed up. It's not because I'm waiting gleefully to nail them but because I love them and I want them back on the right path to blessings, happiness, and peace. That's exactly how God is with us. God loves us and wants us to have all the blessings of this abundant, wonderful life He created for us.

Why Not Go?

In order to begin that recovery, the addicted person needs to understand that, with the help of loving, helpful friends and a suitable recovery program, the seed of renewal resides within every suffering person. It's not embarrassing to need help. There's nothing to be ashamed of in needing help. We all need help in a lot of areas.

We need teachers to help us learn. We need doctors to help us when we're sick. We need mechanics to fix our cars. The question is where to get the right help. Many years ago, I was the editor of a magazine called *Back Pain Magazine*. This was after I had back surgery myself, and it was a pretty specialized publication, as you can tell from the name.

What I learned from running that magazine was there were a lot of different ways to treat back pain. *A lot of ways.*

Here's what I found. If I went to the surgeon, he would say, "I can heal your back pain. I need to operate on you." If I went to the chiropractor, he'd say, "I can heal your back pain. I need to adjust you." If I went to the doctor, he'd say, "I can heal your back pain. Just take these drugs." If I went to the physical therapist, she'd say, "I can heal your back pain. I need you to do these exercises." The acupuncturist? "I can heal your back pain. I need to stick a few needles into you." The yoga instructor says, "I can heal your back pain. You need to meditate." The reflexologist, says, "I can heal your back pain. I just need to massage your toes." And on and on and on.

So, through that job, and through my own experience, I learned there were many different treatments for back pain. Believe it or not, most of them worked—but not for everybody.

Some treatments worked for some people and other treatments worked for other people, but none of them worked for all the people. In the right circumstances, nearly every one of these treatments could be quite effective for *someone.*

The same holds true in addiction. There are different ways to treat addiction. The reason I share this experience with you is because I want you to understand that there may be one voice or one group talking the loudest and with the most authority saying, "This is what you need to do." That's not necessarily the case. It may be a very good idea, but just because they're talking the loudest and with the most authority doesn't mean they have the best system or solution for *you.*

Perhaps it worked for *them*, and something else will work better for *you* or your loved one. There are many different ways of going at this. We just need you to *get better!*

What I learned as the editor of *Back Pain Magazine* applies to addiction recovery. It doesn't matter which way you gain victory over addiction and live a life of freedom. It just matters that you do it! If you want to go to New York from Florida, there are several different ways you can do it. You can fly, take a train, ride a bus, or drive a car… You can even hitchhike, go on horseback, or walk. Some of the methods take longer, and some of them are much more efficient than others. I guess it depends on how motivated you are to get there, how quickly you want to get there, and what you are willing to pay. They will all get you there!

The important thing to remember is resources and methods are available to you right now to ensure you live a life free from addiction. It doesn't necessarily matter which one: a complete surrender to God, a thirty-day rehabilitation program, a twelve-step program like AA (Alcoholics Anonymous), NA (Narcotics Anonymous), GA (Gamblers Anonymous), therapy or counseling, intensive thirty-to-sixty day inpatient programs like at the Beachcomber, long-term rehab programs like Teen Challenge and Faith Farm (ninety days to one year), intensive outpatient programs, like the Celebrate Recovery program and many others. There are many good options. Like back pain, not all work for everyone and some work better for some people than others.

THE KEY TO YOUR FREEDOM

I have to fly a lot for business, but I really do not enjoy flying these days. It seems the skies have gotten very turbulent. And, I really hate turbulence! I hate that feeling of bouncing up and down on the plane like a knuckleball, and the large drops. Once I was sharing this with a friend of mine who was a pilot in the Vietnam War. He looked at me and laughed and he said, "Jack, if you understood turbulence, you wouldn't be afraid of it." Then he proceeded to explain to me how turbulence in the air is really like turbulence at sea. The boat goes up and down in the waves but you know the boat is not going to sink. It's just a bumpy ride. He explained to me how the air pockets in the sky had that same effect on airplanes. I have to tell you, it did make me feel much better because I really understood how it worked. I truly believed that we weren't going to crash just because of turbulence. It gave me great peace of mind and helped me enjoy flying much more, even with the turbulence.

It's the same thing with addiction. If you understand addiction and what it does and why, and how it works, you will be less afraid of it. And, certainly, if you understand recovery, what it does, how it works and why, you will be more excited and encouraged to embrace it and have it work for you.

Many people don't do things because of fear of the unknown. So, instead they just stay in the knowledge, or I should say lack of knowledge they have. Scared to act, even when those actions would be beneficial to their life and health. We want to eliminate this issue for you. We want to educate and inform you about addiction by teaching you why addicts think and behave like they do, the effects of the addict on the family, and the most effective paths to recovery. This gives you a working knowledge of addiction you can apply in your own life, or in the life of an addicted loved one.

More importantly, when you understand not just why addicts think and behave like they do, but also see the paths to recovery and what you can do to take control of your own life or to help an addicted loved one take control of theirs, it will be an eye-opening and wonderfully empowering experience for you.

It all starts with knowledge. Knowledge is the key to wisdom. When you have knowledge and understanding, you will find great peace and comfort. In this same way, you can achieve your goals. Imagine trying to put together a model airplane without instructions or assembling a car engine without instructions. You probably couldn't do it. Yet, when you follow the instructions step by step, carefully and accurately, you can complete the task and accomplish the goal. It's the same with addiction.

MAKE THE COMMITMENT

In life we have to make choices, and our choices have consequences. It seems that when we are determined to get something done and turn our attention to it, we get it done. It usually means accepting the challenge, picking up the gauntlet, and making the decision to go forward. We usually do that when the results or benefits of what we are going to get become more valuable to us than the price we pay or commitment we make. If you sign a contract to buy a house, you are committed. If you buy airline tickets to take a flight, you are committed. If you sign up to join the Army, you are committed. If you put food in your mouth and swallow it, you are committed to eating it.

So, what commitment are you going to make to the rest of your life? If you take a trip from Florida to California, you commit by getting in the car and pulling out of the driveway. You are on the way. Plans may change along the way. There may be twists and turns, changes and challenges to your plan as you go. Road conditions, weather, health, and other factors could impact your journey as you continue on to your destination. However, none of these conditions and circumstances should change the fact that you are committed to getting to your destination. A life of recovery is the same way. You begin the journey and then continue to move forward regardless of what comes your way.

When athletes like football, baseball, or basketball players play the game, we expect them to give their best efforts during the game. In other words, we expect them to be committed to playing their best. Your recovery journey is the same. You play the best you can, give it your best effort, and leave the outcome in God's hands. You just do the best you can. We often look at athletes and judge them based on the effort they gave and not so much on the results of the contest. Many great players have been hailed as heroes because of their individual commitment and effort, even if their team lost the game. The most frustrating thing is seeing an athlete (or a person) not giving one hundred percent effort. When athletes or players don't give one hundred percent effort, we have words for guys like that—lazy, slacker, stiff, bum, loser, the list goes on. So, it's not so much about the result of one game or one season as it is about the effort. I know God will bless your effort more than you can ask or imagine.

I believe that's the challenge for us in recovery. We must make a commitment to begin the journey. Your individual journey starts with change. A commitment to engage in any of the proven ways of recovery would be an awesome start (e.g., coming closer to God, a twelve-step program, a thirty-day rehab facility, out-patient therapy,

Celebrate Recovery, counseling, therapy, in-patient rehab, long-term care). The bottom line is you need to make the commitment to begin the recovery journey. When you commit to something, it means that you are going to do it. You attempt to do your best at whatever you said you were going to do.

I pray that today you have the desire to make the commitment to beginning your recovery journey. I pray you have the desire to cast off the lifestyle of addiction, to break free from that bondage, and to seek treatment for this disease and begin your new life. It starts with a commitment to the recovery journey!

So, don't delay. The choice is yours. No one can make the commitment for you. It has to be your decision and your commitment. I can tell you one thing. I believe you will never regret it, and I believe it will lead you to the happiest life you could ever imagine. Your life is not over. Your addiction has not defeated you. Far from it. Your new life begins now with your commitment. As in a marriage, as in accepting a new job, as in getting behind the wheel of the car, the journey begins when you commit to getting started and then begin to walk in and live that commitment. In the case of recovery, it is always worth it!

AVOID MAKING THE MISTAKE

It's so easy to put things off, especially things that are uncomfortable or things we believe may cause us short-term pain. Yet, if you were dying from a heart attack, you certainly wouldn't put off going to the emergency room and getting life-saving heart surgery. Why? Because even though there is short-term pain involved, the long-term result so far outweighs the short-term pain that you would run to it immediately.

I remember having a hernia and knowing I would need hernia surgery. I was so excited about the hernia surgery. I knew it would hurt and there would be some pain and soreness through the recovery process, but I was so anxious to get rid of the hernia pain that a week or two of short-term pain seemed like a small price to pay in comparison to being able to get up to play ball again, hold my young son, and do basic things without pain.

And I was right. It was a small price to pay! Addiction is the same way. Often we put off beginning our recovery journey because we are scared of the short-term pain of addiction withdrawal and the perceived suffering we may go through. We live the saying, "There's comfort in familiar pain." Even though in our minds we know there's a better way of life, and we know it's a small price to pay to get there, we still use the fear of the recovery process as an excuse to cling to the old way of life that is killing us! Our addiction is still controlling us and destroying us.

Don't make this mistake. Don't let addiction suck more life out of you or take away more years of your life. Don't let it take away more time with your family, your joy, your peace, your happiness and the life God intended for you to have.

Addiction is a lie. It's a trick and that is exactly what addiction does. It lies to you. You need to address your addiction issues now. Yes, there may be some short-term discomfort and even a little pain and suffering, but with medical detox programs, these are minimized to a great extent.

Of course, you have emotional and psychological issues that need to be worked through and a new recovery lifestyle that needs to be learned and established. But these things are a blessing. You have to take a test to get your driver's license, but it is worth it. You have to go on some dates to win over a boyfriend or girlfriend, but it's worth it. You have to exercise to keep fit, but it's worth it. Why? Because the end result is worth the short-term sacrifice. This is the same truth about addiction recovery... Don't miss it!

AM I HOPELESS?

Our lives are a journey and a gift from God. We are to look at them as we would chapters in a book or scenes in a play. Yes, in a chapter in our lives, we suffered from addiction and the spiritual, physical, and emotional problems that our addiction caused for us and our loved ones. But now we will have so many more awesome, exciting, and happy chapters on our recovery journey. Can you imagine a football player practicing and complaining to the coach that the opposing team was hitting him? Well, of course, they're hitting him, that's part of the game. That's why players train and practice, to get tougher and stronger so they can withstand the hits of the opponent in the game and win.

So, yeah, we have some pains and problems in our life, and addiction hurt us when we suffered through it. But we rise above that with faith, hope, and excitement, as we look forward to our recovery journey and the beginning of the rest of our life—a life focused on faith and hope, and certainty that we have value as an individual, that God loves us and God has a specific purpose for our life.

We need to stop thinking about our lives in terms of accomplishments and start to think of them in terms of a journey. Imagine a ride at Disneyland. The question wouldn't be, "How long did the ride last ?" The question would be, "How did you enjoy it?" We want to be able to enjoy our lives and enjoy the journey. Yes, we face some hardships and trials along the way, but just like an army boot camp recruit, who is training to get tough so he fights well to win the war, we can use our addiction as a training ground. We use it as an inspiration point. We use it as a turning point in say, "Yes I suffered through this, but God is letting me use it to help others and see the purpose in my life."

God has shown me and millions of other addicts that we can have a recovery journey of faith and hope. God promises if you seek Him with all your heart, you will find Him. (Jeremiah 29:13) So, rest assured that even though other people may have deemed your life not of great value, and even if you yourself have deemed your own life to be not of great value, the good news is you are not the final judge. God is the judge, and He has deemed you extremely valuable. He created you in His image and He created you to live an abundant life here on earth and forever. So, take that step of faith. Do not lose your hope. We lose hope when we believe tomorrow could never be better than today. So, don't lose hope. Get on the road to recovery. You are far from hopeless.

Just take that first step on the journey. If that is a step of faith toward God, just ask God to help you and admit you can't do it by yourself. He will not let you down. He will help you and restore you better than ever. Try it, please. What have you got to lose? If you're like me, your addiction has stolen everything from you that mattered already.

What have you got to gain? Everything! How about your life back and better than ever, better than you could have ever imagined it? That's the power of God. Let Him use it on you as you begin *your* recovery journey. And that, my friends, is the path, the map, the key to a happy, joyful, and peace-filled life. You deserve it. God wants you to have it. The ride doesn't end at your addiction. That's like thinking school ends at sixth grade, dinner ends with a roll and butter, or a football game ends after the first quarter. Nope, you'd miss the best part if you left early. So keep going. Hop on. The ride is just starting!

MEDICAL DOCTOR

How Addiction Affects Your Brain and Your Life

By Dr. Adam Bianchini

Clearing Controversy / Clarifying Confusion

In his contribution to the book *Alcoholics Anonymous*, Dr. William D. Silkworth described the alcoholic illness according to the medical knowledge of the 1930s. His description of alcoholism, although devoid of the detail available by today's modern scientific investigation techniques, was impressively accurate describing the abnormalities in the body and brain due to chronic exposure to alcohol. He also skillfully outlined the resultant aberrations in thinking and behavior associated with alcoholism. The past eighty years of scientific pursuit and achievement has ratified and more deeply explained what Dr. Silkworth and the cofounders presented about alcoholism from their collective experience. Despite millions of recoveries based on their understanding and approach, today much confusion and controversy still exists around addiction causes, mechanisms, and cures. There is also, believe it or not, repudiation of the concept and approach of the twelve-step model initially put forward in the "Big Book." of Alcoholics Anonymous.

Although addiction has been plaguing humanity since the discovery of fermentation, insight into its mechanisms and solution has remained a mysteriously elusive challenge for millennia. Much of this enigma revolves around its unique underlying cause and its multidimensional manifestations, around which whirls of debate and opinion continue. Many assert that addiction is simply a deficit of character or weakness of the will, while still others claim moral deficiency or sin to be the root. The explanations are as numerous as the individuals who purport them. Opinions regarding the solution to addiction are as varied as the explanations for it.

The definition of addiction, adopted from the American Society of Addiction Medicine Board of Directors in 2011, reads as follows:

> Addiction is a primary, chronic disease of brain reward, motivation, memory and related circuitry. Dysfunction in

these circuits leads to characteristic biological, psychological, social and spiritual manifestations. This is reflected in an individual pathologically pursuing reward and/or relief by substance use and other behaviors (asam.org 2011).

Later revised in 2019, it stands today:

Addiction is a treatable, chronic medical disease involving complex interactions among brain circuits, genetics, the environment, and an individual's life experiences. People with addiction use substances or engage in behaviors that become compulsive and often continue despite harmful consequences (asam.org).

We have little doubt the controversial debate surrounding the origins and treatment of addiction will continue into the future. The unique nature of addiction is likely the single most important contributor to the ongoing mystery. Although addiction is a disease or illness, it differs from other ailments that torment humanity, in that it manifests differently as three separately contributing parts. Other diseases may have one or two parts, but addiction has three—physical, mental, and spiritual. Most disease processes can be understood and treated along one of these manifestations. Diabetes, for example can be both explained and treated as a physical abnormality. The cells in the pancreas responsible for producing insulin, or the receptors in the body that respond to the insulin become abnormal, thus producing the disease. Treatment is aimed at increasing the body's insulin or its response to the hormone while decreasing the carbohydrate load in the diet.

Other diseases can be understood and treated by one of two separate manifestations. Depression, for example, can be understood and treated by either the physical or the mental manifestation. From the physical perspective, depression can be described as an imbalance of neurotransmitters within the brain. Antidepressants can be prescribed to rebalance the neurotransmitter concentrations, thus relieving the depression. In addition, depression can be understood as an emotional response to past unresolved trauma or similar issues in one's past accounting for the maladaptive coping mechanism of hopelessness. This can be treated by psychotherapy or counseling to develop healthier coping mechanisms, thus relieving depression. Addiction, on the other hand, has all three manifestations listed above. Anyone who has experienced withdrawal can well describe the physical presentation of the disease. The emotional irregularities and mood swings of the post-acute withdrawal period and the craving and mental obsession are examples of the psychological or mental aspect. Lastly, the unstoppable moral and value decline during the progression of addiction points directly at the spiritual nature of the illness.

This newer understanding of addiction, presented in 1939, ushered in the description and solution of alcoholism, so well explained on page 64 of the "Big Book." "...for we have been not only mentally and physically ill, we have been spiritually sick. When the spiritual malady is overcome, we straighten out mentally and physically."

ACCURATELY ASSESSING ADDICTION

So, is addiction genetically predetermined, or is it a deficiency of moral character? Is addiction a weakness of the will, or is it the result of bad company or poor choices? Is it a medical illness or is it sin? The general answer seems to be, "Yes." All of these things, and more, seem to play a potentially significant part. To avoid the confusion, which can be caused by the complexity of addiction, let us identify some key concepts to more accurately understand addiction from the medical perspective.

1. The brain is the most complex and sophisticated creation in all the universe.
2. Chronic exposure of mood-altering chemicals changes the brain anatomy and physiology.
3. The brain attempts to compensate to restore balance (homeostasis).
4. The changes in the brain, although initially experienced as positive, bring about negative effects.
5. The process progresses through stages (Use/Abuse/Dependency/Addiction).
6. The brain eventually becomes *hijacked* via the reward circuitry and pathways.

7. These changes contribute to the priority shifting that occurs during addiction progression.

8. These brain changes cause alterations in perception and attitudes, as well as behaviors.

9. Addiction needs treatment most effectively via a multidisciplinary approach.

10. Successful treatment must employ methodology to restore altered brain function.

1. The brain is the most complex and sophisticated creation in all the universe.

Weighing in at approximately three pounds, the average human brain contains approximately ninety billion neurons and approximately the same number of supportive cells. Interestingly, there are about four hundred brain-specific genes within human DNA, which, in cooperation with the rest of the genome, amazingly blueprint this amazing creation! Lastly, one cannot fathom the enormity of the number of cellular interconnections, which allow for the communication among the brain cells and their target organs so as to control the function of the body by the conscious and unconscious brain.

Considering the enormous complexity of the brain and its array of vital tasks, it is inconceivable that one would willfully and repetitively pour poison on it! But that is exactly what happens during addiction. Alcohol, for example, is a direct toxin to all cells in the body. Other drugs interact with the receptors of brain cells, thus altering function, but are not in themselves toxic on a cellular level. Many of the symptoms of addiction and withdrawal can be traced back to the changes in the central nervous system by the long-term use of these substances. Either way, it takes little imagination to see that the chronic exposure of the brain to mood-altering chemicals will negatively impact the brain over time.

2. Chronic exposure of mood-altering chemicals changes the brain anatomy and physiology.

It is the age-old adage of the cucumber and the pickle. For those who have not heard this one, let's have a little fun. So… if you take a cucumber and put it in a jar of vinegar, what do you get? Answer—you get a wet cucumber (not a pickle)! Now, what do you get when you take that same cucumber and put it back in the jar of vinegar for a bit longer? Answer—a _really_ wet cucumber. (Not a pickle, again!) But if you were to take that same cucumber and put it in the jar for a _long_ time, eventually you will get that pickle you've been looking for! And no matter how you try to squeeze the vinegar out of the pickle or evaporate the vinegar out of the pickle, there simply is no way of getting that pickle to turn back into a cucumber. It is the same with the alcoholic or addict brain. After sufficient exposure of the mood-altering substance (vinegar) to the brain (cucumber), well, you get the idea. Moral of the story—you can turn a cucumber into a pickle, but you can't turn a pickle into a cucumber.

A more serious portrayal of this process can be described as the crossing of imaginary lines. This analogy can be easily identified by anyone who has battled addiction. During the _honeymoon_ phase of addiction, all goes seemingly well for a time, as the person takes a drink or drug with impunity. But there invariably comes the day when an unseen imaginary line is crossed. Despite decisions to only have a couple, or to do it for a short time, these well-made plans fail, as more is taken or the substance is used for a longer than expected time. After this goes on for a while, yet another, more ominous, unseen imaginary line is crossed, and now even when well-intended promises are made to not consume the substance, these resolutions break down and give in to the craving or mental obsession. This _process_ can be abbreviated as follows:

A person takes a drink. / The drink takes the drink. / The drink takes the person.

Recent scientific discoveries have shown this phenomenon in brain cells via the electron microscope. Intracellular changes have been observed in brain tissue of experimental animals who have been made chemically dependent. This recently discovered observation has opened a new avenue of research. What if treatments could be developed to prevent or reverse these intracellular changes? Could this possibly prevent or reverse addiction, or could this at least minimize its symptoms? These are some of the exciting areas of current addiction research on the horizon.

Fortunately, from a functional standpoint, the brain changes do seem to, at least in part, be amenable to some reversal. For example, SPECT imaging can show functional brain impairment due to addiction for twelve to eighteen months following the last ingestion. However, normalization can be observed with continued recovery thereafter. There is an important caveat here. It is vital to understand that the brain recovery possible does NOT mean that the addiction is cured and gone completely. It means the disease is in remission and the symptoms are gone. In other words, if you took that same person with the now-healed brain and restarted the exposure to the mood-altering substances, the disease of addiction, previously in remission, would now restart and progress with great rapidity.

From the family's perspective, the altered brain physiology is seen in behavioral changes that are many times out of character in the addiction sufferer. These changes in behaviors are often the first signs present in the addiction process. Some examples are weight loss, mood swings, fiscal irresponsibility, dishonesty, avoidance behaviors, and intermittent signs of intoxication (slurred speech, pinpoint pupils, drowsiness, memory loss, falls, loss of balance or coordination).

3. The brain attempts to compensate to restore balance (homeostasis).

The physiology of every biological system in the human body makes an effort to maintain balance with its environment. All biological systems have a preferred set point at which optimal operation is attained. The easiest example to explain this phenomenon is body temperature. The optimal body temperature, ensuring optimal efficiency and operation is, of course, 98.6 degrees Fahrenheit. This number is interestingly exact and precise—so much so, that the body will make great efforts to maintain this exact parameter. If the temperature rises even 2 percent, one has a low-grade fever, feels sick, and perspires to achieve evaporative cooling, thus restoring the desired temperature level. If the temperature deviates the same miniscule percentage in the opposite direction (cooler), one shivers and makes great efforts to retain heat and increase temperature. This effort to maintain balance at a certain set point is called homeostasis. It is important to know that the body makes extreme efforts to maitain homeostasis, as it is critical for survival and well-being.

Regarding the brain, one of the more commonly affected areas of homeostasis is activity or arousal. The brain, for survival purposes, operates at a predetermined activity level to maintain safety in a potentially hostile environment. Many mood-altering drugs are classified as depressants (alcohol, benzodiazepines, sedative-hypnotics, barbiturates, etc.). This means they depress the activity of the brain. The brain's homeostatic response is to increase activity, compensating for the unexpected decrease in function. Over time, this internal adjustment can be seen in the phenomenon known as *tolerance*, where it takes more of the substance to accomplish the same effect. The usual reaction of the addict is to increase the amount ingested, which, again, over time, leads to more tolerance.

This process also explains the withdrawal experience. As the consumption of the substance is interrupted, the brain's unchallenged compensatory homeostatic response is experienced by the sufferer. Insomnia, anxiety, panic attacks, and seizures can occur as the brain's compensatory mechanisms are very strong.

Opiates are a double-edged sword in this regard, as they cause analgesia (pain relief) and euphoria (sense of well-being/*high*). The brain needs this pain information to keep the body safe. (The quick removal of a hand from a hot object before injury is sustained, for example.) Therefore, the brain makes great effort to become more sensitive to the pain warning system now interrupted by opiates. This increased pain sensitivity, over time, is called *hyperalgesia*. It is the magnified experience or sensation of pain caused by chronic opiate ingestion. In fact, many instances of chronic pain are actually caused secondarily by the pain medicine being used to treat the initial pain syndrome. As opiates are stopped, the sufferer will experience heightened pain sensation as well as dysphoria, both of which are powerful motivators for continued use.

Lastly, stimulants (amphetamine type drugs, cocaine) cause a depressed or decreased activity response by the brain, leading to a lethargic, unmotivated state with difficulty concentrating during the withdrawal of such substances. Although the withdrawal syndrome from these substances is more psychological than physical, the desire to experience the energy and euphoria from these substances is powerful. Cannabinoids and hallucinogens elicit a more complex compensatory response from the brain, which can result in psychosis, dysphoria, and mood instability.

4. The changes in the brain, although initially experienced as positive, bring about negative effects.

By accidently touching a hot stove, most everyone learns at an early age that the red, glowing element on the stove is not a lollipop or a play toy. Considering how drugs and alcohol *burn* much more than a hot stove, how is it, then, addiction sufferers keep going back to the drugs and alcohol time after time, despite learning not to touch the stove? The answer is simple. There isn't a moment of pleasure when touching the stove. The *high* experienced during substance use, however, is the *bait* that keeps the addict hooked. After time, they will be willing to suffer significant and longstanding pain and consequences for the brief moments of *feeling good*.

The irony of this insanity lies in the brain pathways. The same reward pathways that ensure survival and the propagation of the species are stimulated during the mood-altering process. The *pleasure center* in the reptilian brain drives the instincts. Under normal conditions, the system works well enough. For example, we get hungry, and we are motivated to put effort into obtaining food. We eat and are satisfied. The drive is turned off for a while. However, when these centers are stimulated by mood-altering substances, the *off* switch doesn't work nearly as well, unfortunately. Simply put, this is because the stomach *was* made for food, but the brain *was not* made for drugs. Thus the desire and addictive behavior continues despite life-damaging consequences, devoid of the restraint of effective negative feedback.

5. The process progresses through stages (Use/Abuse/Dependency/Addiction).

Although some become addicted early in their experience with the substance, most people are trapped by addiction over a period of time. This is the insidious nature of addiction. It is patient and cunning. This progression can be seen through stages of *Use, Abuse, Dependence, and Addiction.* During the *Use* stage, there are often no signs or symptoms of addiction. Unless there is a co-occurring psychiatric disorder, there frequently exists little or no noticeable problem. During the *Abuse* stage, issues revolving around in-toxication can arise. Many facets of one's life can be affected at this stage. Legal issues (DUI, domestic violence, or illicit drug possession) or economic issues (loss of employment or fiscal irresponsibility) may occur. Intermittent exacerbations of underlying psychological or psychiatric disorders may occur at this phase, as well as challenges among interpersonal relationships. These can be solitary, episodic, or repeated depending upon the severity of substance abuse and the substance characteristics.

With the emergence of the *Dependence* stage, the above-mentioned potential complications can continue, increase in frequency, and become more severe. Many times, negative health consequences can be seen as the cycle of intoxication and withdrawal accelerates and intensifies. Increases in medical care utilization can occur, especially if prescription drugs are being abused. Domestic strife often increases as the secrecy of the addiction becomes threatened and hiding behaviors increase. Work or school performance can decline rapidly at this stage. Physical symptoms can also increase in variety, frequency, and severity.

Often a fine line separates *Dependence* from *Addiction*. Often-times this simply manifests in the crossing over from legal and appropriate means of obtaining and ingesting the chemical to alternative substances, alternative means of ingestion, or increases in illicit activities. In many cases, the differentiation between dependence and addiction can best be made by an addiction professional, and,in general, can be a moot point overall, as treatment is warranted in both situations.

6. The brain eventually becomes *hijacked* via the reward circuitry and pathways.

As the reward pathways are continuously and repetitively stimulated by increasing amounts and frequency of substance use, abnormalities among the neural pathways and nuclei begin to develop. These abnormalities reinforce the pleasure-seeking stimulation more and more until it spirals out of control. For example, as tolerance begins, more substance is consumed to gain the desired effect. The negative experience of withdrawal further perpetuates this process. Over time the brain adjusts by compromising its normal homeostatic set point. This *new normal* reset may happen several times during the course of progressing addiction to the point where unexpected or abrupt discontinuation of the substance can lead to death. This is the case of DTs, or delirium tremens.

At this point in the addiction process, it is as if the brain now needs the very substance it was once fighting against to maintain normalcy. The instinctual drive of the pleasure center powerfully interacts with other centers in the brain to adapt to this new lifestyle. In fact, the acquisition and the ingestion of the substance become as important as breathing in the life of the addict. He or she cannot live without it. Once this has become firmly established, the sufferer has reached the place where the battle cannot be fought alone, and they need help. However, the brain is so deceived that it is more often the case that not only do addicts not want help; they deny they even have a problem! At this dreadful point, oftentimes the substance is in control of one's life instead of the individual. This is the bondage of addiction.

3

7. **These changes contribute to the priority shifting that occurs during addiction progression.**

Another amazing phenomenon that occurs during the addiction process is the changing of life priorities more and more toward addictive activities. It may start out as weekend *partying* and slowly progress to a more regular activity. It may begin with *taking or leaving* the substance and progress to *liking* the substance more and more. As time passes, this regular activity may mature into a daily habit, and as one becomes dependent, the need for the substance increases. As the need increases, so do the surrounding behaviors, attitudes, and activities. Soon the substance becomes the most import priority in the addict's life—more important than one's job, health, family, freedom, and even one's life. For many, all of one's money and time are spent in addiction activities.

8. **These brain changes cause alterations in perception and attitudes, as well as behaviors.**

The brain can be viewed as a super-computer, which is used as a tool to perceive and interact with our environment. As it is poisoned by addiction, its ability to function is hindered. We use our senses to perceive our reality and use our complex, higher functioning brain to interpret and respond to those perceptions. When the brain is altered, so can the judgments made based on those perceptions. Also, the perceptions can themselves be altered, as well. It is not surprising then that bizarre responses and behaviors, as well as delusional thought processes, can ensue. This is becoming much more common with the increased use of amphetamines and the more potent cannabinoids now available in our society.

Many patients describe a significant personality change, which had occurred over time, as a result of their addiction. Family members often concur that the patient is not the same person they used to be. A common request from both patient and family is to *get their life back* or *get their loved one back*. It is also common for people to abandon their spiritual practices and ideology, other times acting in contradistinction to such principles and philosophies. Many times an addiction sufferer's life becomes exactly what they once swore it would never be.

Devoted parents drive their children while intoxicated or in a blackout or take them to dangerous parts of town; faithful spouses and partners resort to infidelity to support their habit or otherwise entertain themselves, and loving children steal from their parents or grandparents. These behaviors are frequently seen as the evidence of spiritual bankruptcy or moral degradation accompanying addiction. This value compromise can be one of the painful and shameful consequences of addiction behavior.

9. Addiction needs treatment most effectively via a multidisciplinary approach.

Unless you are an insurance or pharmaceutical company, it is painfully obvious that all cases of addiction, being progressive and fatal if unabated, need aggressive treatment. Most cases are so advanced and serious at the time of presentation that they require inpatient detoxification and stabilization. Successful treatment requires a long-term, multidisciplinary approach, utilizing a sequential and gradual step-down in levels of care as the patient improves. Addressing comorbidities (simultaneously occurring medical or psychiatric conditions) in conjunction with the *substance use disorder* (technical term for addiction/alcoholism) by the appropriate health care professionals is imperative. Inpatient treatment is preferred as the patient cannot control or stop their use of the substance, so guarded supervision is almost universally necessary. This also provides for the coordination of intensive medical, psychiatric, and clinical assessment and treatment simultaneously. Differential expertise (nursing, medical, clinical, psychiatric, psychological, nutritional, holistic, etc.) facilitate the administration of care and treatment according to the variety of symptoms and conditions associated with addiction. Since addiction is a three-fold malady, it might be prudent to utilize a three-fold (at least) approach!

10. Successful treatment must employ methodology to restore altered brain function.

The brain, being so sickened by addiction, is the root of so many of the symptoms suffered by the addict and their family. Selfish, hurtful words spoken in anger, dishonesty, and untrustworthiness all come forth from a sickened mind. Unfortunately, no medication or alternative treatment exists that will immediately reverse these pathological brain alterations. Most commonly the time involved in addiction recovery treatment processes gradually restores the brain to health. Proper nutrition, healthy sleep hygiene, counseling and therapy, and, of course, twelve-step facilitation with involvement in a faith-based or spiritual support network are all components conducive to brain healing. The treatment of co-occurring medical and psychiatric illnesses increases the chances of success. Recovery seems to take the course of acting one's way into better thinking, instead of thinking one's way into better acting.

It seems prudent at this juncture to spend a moment explaining MAT, or Medication Assisted Treatment. As many have heard, this is being touted as the hot, *new thing* in the fight against opiate addiction. The term, MAT, as it is used today, describes a treatment model where a less dangerous substance is substituted for a more damaging, abused chemical. Known in the scientific community as the Harm Reduction Model, this approach differs from the formal Abstinence Model in several ways. The Abstinence Model, which has long been the ultimate goal of substance use treatment, aims for the removal of substance use from the patient. The Harm Reduction Model aims for the replacement of the substance by the patient to a potentially less harmful substance.

While it may seem obvious that abstinence is better than replacement with respect to substance use, two scenarios may justify the compromise. First, many patients are not willing to embrace abstinence as a goal of recovery, especially if they are averse to spirituality or the Twelve Steps. Second, many also chronically relapse, and the risk of overdose death is extremely high. In these cases, addressing the potentially imminent lethality of the addiction by decreasing the possible risk of overdose becomes the more tangible, achievable goal.

Some advocate that the risk of overdose death in opiate SUD (substance use disorder) is so significant that all opiate use disorder patients should be placed on Buprenorphine. The hope is that replacing the heroin or other synthetic opiate with this drug will decrease overdoses and fatalities. Perhaps, it might even provide more time for the patient to contemplate abstinence. The Harm Reduction Model takes into account that the best treatment option (Abstinence Model) may not be suited for or accepted by all patients at all times. It consists of substituting the drug of choice— usually heroin—with a medication with a reduced risk of lethality (Buprenorphine or Methadone). The treatment is aimed at reducing a symptom (death or overdose) rather than eradicating the disease (addiction or substance use disorder).

There are three different types of MAT strategies:

1. Agonist Therapy describes a medication that stimulates opiate receptors (E.g. Methadone).
2. Partial Agonist Therapy describes a medication that *partially* stimulates the opiate receptor (E.g. Buprenorphine).
3. Antagonist Therapy describes a medication that blocks opiate receptors (E.g. Naltrexone). Both one and two above are opiate medications while three utilizes an opiate blocker and is a non-opiate.

Although this approach and rationale may be appropriate for some patients, it is important to note that agonist and partial agonist treatment come with many significant potential drawbacks. Understanding these drawbacks is important for both providers and patients. First, Buprenorphine and Methadone are both opiates, which will continue to affect the brain in the negative way all opiates do when administered chronically. These side effects include chemical dependency, tolerance, sedation, depression, anxiety, hyperalgesia (increased pain sensation), and anhedonia (the inability to experience pleasure). Second, the side effects involving other organ systems can continue, as well, including constipation, nausea, urinary retention, muscle cramps, immunosuppression, and hormonal imbalances. Third, detoxification from these longer acting medications is a longer, more discomforting process. Last, MAT is not a guarantee against relapse. In fact, there is a significant risk of both opiate relapse and relapse to other chemicals, such as Benzodiazepines and alcohol. This includes the subset of patients who will misuse Buprenorphine from the outset, having no desire to avoid other opiates entirely.

Another underestimated but important issue is that MAT allows the unabated progression of the disease, which, in so many cases, results in a dark, internal emptiness that only fellow sufferers can understand. This includes deepening depression and anxiety, as well as hopelessness and despair, which can block a later pursuit of recovery or cause one to consider even darker alternatives. Also, during this time, many relapse into their previous opiate addiction or start additional mood-altering substances, leading the patient to worse consequences than ever imagined. Because of these very common side effects and related issues, abstinence therapy still remains the gold standard of treatment for substance use disorder, as it allows the brain to heal from the deleterious effects of chronic opiate administration.

KNOWING NEUROBIOLOGY

When considering the neurobiology of addiction, an oversimplified approach is necessary due to the inherent complexity of the brain anatomy and physiology. Although many tracts and pathways and all neurotransmitters are involved with some facet of addiction, suffice it to say that the most important and predominant neurotransmitter is dopamine. This is the main transmitter in the pleasure center nuclei, namely the nucleus accumbens and the ventral tegmental area. These areas send connections to various parts of the brain via their dopaminergic pathways. This, basically, is where the pathophysiology of addiction begins in the brain. As previously stated, overstimulation of these nuclei and their resultant influence on the areas of the brain downstream affect the changes during addiction.

When a mood-altering substance is ingested, it reacts with

receptors in the brain specific to its biochemical classification. Opiates stimulate mu, kappa, and delta receptors in certain areas of the brain while alcohol and benzodiazepines mediate their effects primarily via the GABA receptors. These responses then stimulate the dopamine-rich pleasure center and the cascade begins.

The interconnection between the pleasure center and other areas within the brain, as with all of the central nervous system circuitry, is vast and complex (See *Figure 1*). Again, eventually the majority of neural pathways, either directly or indirectly, will be affected by the addiction cycle just as a virus within a computer will eventually affect all of its major functions. Also, while dopamine is the most significant neurotransmitter when considering addiction, it is important to note that pathways of every neurotransmitter (acetylcholine, norepinephrine, serotonin, GABA, etc.) become involved (See *Figure 2*). While it is beyond the scope of this chapter to describe the entire impact of these numerous pathways, several important interconnections will be discussed.

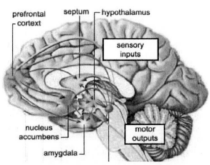

Figure 1

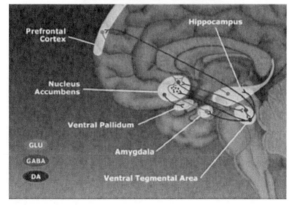

Figure 2

Stimulation of these reward pathways promotes a sense of well-being and calmness, contributing to their attraction to a susceptible individual. Prolonged stimulation of these reward pathways leads to an unbalanced preference for the sensation, which is a powerful motivator to continue the addiction. Through other connections further perpetuation of the addiction occurs.

The Prefrontal Cortex

Dopaminergic fibers arise from the pleasure center and directly inhibit the prefrontal cortex. The prefrontal cortex, nicknamed the *executive center* of the brain, is responsible for judgment, rational thought, planning and impulse control. This area of the brain contributes to the ability to live a civilized, rational life, making decisions considering both complex and future implications before acting. Continuous inhibition of this area of the brain, which can be seen on SPECT images, leads to irrational, impulsive behavior, often absent of future or safety concerns. This explains why, as addiction progresses, less thought and action is aimed toward future goals and more impulsive and dangerous behaviors involving instant gratification are observed. Emotional outbursts, erratic behavior and poor overall planning are commonly seen. This can progress to the point where little or no care is given to one's personal hygiene, social appearance, health, or personal safety.

From a treatment perspective, prolonged supervision and support are needed to improve overall compliance and success because of this pathological process involving the prefrontal cortex. The lack of impulse control heightens the relapse risk during early recovery, as does the decreased ability for positive, forward-looking recovery planning. Guidance and encouragement from family, sponsor, counselor, and support network can be invaluable to relapse prevention at these stages.

Hippocampus

The hippocampus is the structure that is most responsible for short-term, long-term, and spatial memory. It is part of the *limbic system*, located bilaterally underneath the parieto-temporal cerbral cortex. Dysfunction in the hippocampus due to addiction can be acute (temporary), during a blackout, for instance. It can also be chronic (permanent), as in Wernicke-Korsakoff syndrome (*wet brain*). These issues arise from the direct effects by the substance on the structure. However, some of the effects mediated by changes in regulating pathways due to addiction process are far more interesting.

The phenomenon known as *euphoric recall* is a selective memory process by which the reward pathways train the hippocampus to preferentially remember the pleasurable aspects of substance use while neglecting memories of the negative consequences. This positively reinforces the substance consumption and associated behaviors. These changes can be seen even after the discontinuation of substance intake. This is commonly seen clinically as differential reports of the same incident being given by addict and family. The family describes a horrific event while the addict relates only a minor issue or none at all.

The treatment for this issue can be described as Repetitive Reality Therapy, which is a form of Cognitive Behavioral Therapy (CBT). Supports of the individual, including family, counselor(s) and sponsor, break down the actual events over and over to combat the sugar-coated delusion of the patient. Over time the sufferer will have to face the fact that everyone else perceives and understands what happened one certain way, and they all cannot be wrong. They will also come to realize that this handicap in perception is due to the deleterious brain changes brought about by the addiction cycle.

It is important to note that it is common for these altered perceptions to accompany and reinforce the mental obsession preceding relapse. An important interventional modality in these instances would be to target these erroneous memories with the more accurate negative consequences of relapse. This usually needs the support of more objective individuals, but with experience and time it can be accomplished by the individual. However, early on in the recovery process, environmental cues or emotional stresses can frequently trigger these false, fond remembrances of active addiction. Being aware of this potential and soliciting support as soon as possible during these episodes can avoid relapse.

Some of the saddest consequences of chronic addiction are seen involving the hippocampus. While reversible short-term memory loss can happen early on in addiction due to the intoxication process of the substance, irreversible short-term memory loss can also occur over time. This, unfortunately, is more commonly seen in the older population and can mimic dementia. Formal neuropsychological testing can assess and quantify this complication.

Amygdala

Located just anterior to each hippocampus lobe bilaterally are the amygdalae (amygdala—singular). These are likely the second most important structures involved with memory formation and recall, concerning the processing of associative or emotional memory—emotional responses, which become associated with past events. It is commonly understood that learning and memories can be established through cues perceived from the environment by our five senses. Associative or emotional learning is a strong potentiator of past memories, being associated with powerful emotions—the stronger the associated emotion, the stronger the impact of the memory.

Because of this unique function, the amygdala is also involved in motivation by reinforcing favorable recall of those memories associated with past reward. Thus, the hijacked reward pathways influence the amygdala to be motivated toward behaviors that increase the likelihood of a reward (the euphoria caused by the drug) and to be more apathetic or much less motivated toward behaviors devoid of such reward (recovery-based activities). Anyone who has raised teenagers has experienced this differential motivation. Adolescents can text their friends or play video games until their fingers turn blue, but it takes an act of God for them to do their chores, for example!

By continuously encouraging and reinforcing recovery behaviors, the amygdala learns a different positive reward associated with the spiritual and community connection of the program. These pleasant, positive memories reinforce positive, recovery behaviors while supplanting old, negative motivations. In the early stages a recovering addict/alcoholic needs much encouragement and guidance, and occasionally firmer admonishment to remain engaged in the recovery process. Later, the motivation comes internally from the retrained amygdala!

As previously mentioned, the above descriptions of brain structures affected by addiction are a simplified explanation of a short list of brain pathways and nuclei. More complete descriptions of other parts of the brain can be found in more scientific resources. Also, as addiction research continues, our understanding of the involvement of the brain changes during addiction will become more widespread and detailed. Hopefully this will advance treatment options for those who suffer.

Also, the above sections have focused on the brain as the target organ. Obviously, addiction affects every organ system in the body, and a detailed analysis is beyond the scope of this text. Cirrhosis, pancreatitis and other gastro-intestinal pathology, including diabetes are very common side effects of addiction. Dangerous cardiovascular effects, such as atrial fibrillation, myocardial infarction, congestive heart failure, and hypertension can be life-threatening complications. Emotional health can also suffer during addiction. Anxiety, depression, panic attacks, and delusional disorders can be common, as well as the more physical ailments mentioned above. As can be imagined, no organ system is immune to the onslaught and ravages of addiction, and successful addiction treatment can avoid death and unimaginable suffering for the addict/alcoholic and their families.

Works Cited - Bianchini

"American Society of Addiction Medicine." *ASAM Definition of Addiction*, American Society of Addiction Medicine, 2011, www. asam.org/Quality-Science/definition-of-addiction.

"American Society of Addiction Medicine." *ASAM Definition of Addiction*, American Society of Addiction Medicine, 2019, www.asam.org/Quality-Science/definition-of-addiction.

Silkwood, Dr. William D. "The Doctor's Opinion." *Alcoholics Anonymous.* 4th ed., Alcoholics Anonymous World Services, Inc, 2002.

THERAPISTS, COUNSELORS, & PHDS

THE BOTTOM LINE ON ADDICTION AND RECOVERY

BY LUI DELGADO, CAP

The hardest part about treating addiction is that there isn't one solution or system of care that works for everyone. Addiction is a disease of the brain, and the brain can be impacted and affected by all sorts of individual experiences, traumatic effects, culture, and family issues. Everybody brings in their own individualized set of complications and personality. You and I can experience the exact same lifestyle and have the exact same trauma, be from the same family, live in the same culture, and yet respond completely different to all of it. There are so many factors involved.

Many little factors make our brains unique, although there are only a certain number of personality types. We can all relate to a certain number of things in each personality type, but these individual factors make our brains different. Those individual factors have so many different variables that support success or sabotage success.

A lot of people living successfully in remission from addiction feel that the only way to get sober is the way they found their sobriety. Although this thinking is very subjective, it feels valid when your own personal story is laden with difficulties and struggles along the way. The more relapses and denial experienced prior to sobriety only further supports this line of thinking. It makes it even more difficult to not think that if everyone would just do what I did, then they too can experience this gift of recovery.

These personal experiences of success lead to a belief in the process of recovery that got them there. That belief further develops into faith in that process. This faith fuels our passion and is what creates programs and systems of recovery. The benefit to all of this is that this provides us with many choices in finding our own path to success. People who found their recovery in mutual-aid groups using sponsorship, step-work, and a belief in a higher power are justified to feel that the system works. Those who found their recovery in a church or house of worship, identifying their higher power directly as God, are equally justified and have proven to support the development of faith-based programs all over the United States. These are simply two systems out of many, but I think the point has been made.

One common factor in all systems is the separation of age groups. I'm not convinced either way if it's easier to get sober young or old. I can make a case for both. Young people have the ease of not having the years of habitual behavior, but they do have the issue of invincibility. They view life as a one-time experience full of adventures there to be had to the fullest and they don't fear death. They don't fear homelessness because they only need a place to crash. They also don't tend to have a spouse to lose or children they want to come home to. These are just some things they just don't have to deal with. Older people may have the wisdom, but they also have the years of habitual behavior. Doing something over and over for a long time makes it much harder to break out of that lifestyle. Not only do they have a disease, but they have a lifestyle full of people, places, and things all associated with their substance use and very little remaining that doesn't include or accept that. Habit, lifestyle, and disease all mixed together can be quite a task to overcome. It may be difficult to teach an old dog new tricks, but potty training a puppy isn't always that easy either.

Developing a new lifestyle regardless of age requires consistency, and consistency requires repetition and practice. Much like how we learned our multiplication tables through consistency and repetition. You didn't just do them once and that was it. You've been adding and subtracting and doing multiplication and division for a very long time. It makes very difficult math problems simple if you break them down to the simplest forms. It's the same with recovery or mental health issues. If you break it down to the simple mathematics, knowing I still have to get up, get dressed, comb my hair, brush my teeth, and as many in recovery say, "Suit up and show up and not pick up." As long as you do the work and move forward, eventually we have faith that a miracle is going to happen. Eventually you're going to begin to feel the confidence and power within you at work. The point is that those things are standards. Those things are constants. If you ask anybody, regardless of what method they used to get clean and sober, what is necessary? Well, consistency is necessary.

You must also develop an understanding that life is not just about you. If you stay within yourself, how can you benefit from the experiences of others. You may not care about them at first, but listening and practicing focus on common factors can help you learn how to use their struggles and victories to find your own path to success. During this process you may find yourself relating to others more than you anticipated and connecting with them. Caring for them and happy for them even. Connectivity is key to long-term success in recovery and remission. After all, focusing on yourself only is most likely a defense mechanism that may not be necessary in this new life you have chosen to accept. Any personality disorder that involves the difficulty of being teachable is going to make you struggle more. For instance, ADD (Attention Deficit Disorder) is very difficult, and a lot of addicts tend to be ADD. There's a common argument over which came first—ADD, ADHD (Attention Deficit Hyperactivity Disorder), or addiction? When you're easily distracted, meaning you're impulsive and you do things very impulsively, you see the next squirrel and you go to it. This makes it very difficult to practice something over and over again, be consistent, and be patient. But those things are important in recovery.

During the recovery process, you also find that recovery is easier when you also process any mental health issues, trauma, and any significant relational issues you may have. These issues left untreated will most likely sabotage your personal growth and the internal peace you seek. I don't need to tell you how those little whispers inside can become loud fits of rage with just a little spark of something seemingly insignificant to others. The same substances that initially worked to medicate you through difficult times may not work anymore because they aren't sustainable. It really doesn't matter which came first, the mental health issues or the use, because they both need your attention. Either left untreated will keep you from enjoying all of the benefits of recovery and keep you at risk for relapse.

We now understand the brain so much better than before and, therefore, can set it up much better for success. We have found that the use of substances creates shortcuts for our managing certain processes, and this tends to harm normal development. For instance, if you have anxiety and you use substances to reduce anxiety, your brain never learns how to deal with anxiety naturally. Instead it begins to rely on the substances you use, even though it only seems to reduce the anxiety when under the influence. Instead I suggest you seek out natural methods whenever possible and consult with a physician that treats addiction and anxiety. Also, learning a little about anxiety and accepting it at low levels may be helpful. You need a little level of anxiety and stress because that makes you go to work. Motivation isn't just pushed by passion. It's pushed by stress and anxiety. You require a little bit, but some people are in such a way that they have no tolerance for it. They feel their anxiety is such a disorder, so they give it too much power and weight, and therefore become paralyzed.

No one personality type succeeds more than the others. As far as having a Type A personality or being a timid person, it doesn't matter. It's more a factor of you how you view yourself, rather than how successful you can be in your recovery. We do see better recovery numbers with high-level professionals, but one reason is the enabling completely goes away once the doctors, attorneys and pilots get caught since there is such a high level of expectation, and the punishment is so severe from their own professional regulating bodies. Not to mention the quality of care they can often afford.

Also, they have practiced doing things that they don't want to do for years. That's how they got through their education. They had to learn things they didn't want to learn and accept things they might disagree with because that is how you get through the educational process. They've spent a lot of hours in places with people they don't really want to be with because they want that ultimate goal. Plus, they have proven to have the commitment and perseverance to make it through very tough situations because they want the end goal.

So, the same personality type that projected them into being an attorney or doctor has some positives they can latch on to, but there are also negatives. The negatives are the unfortunate situation of possibly being narcissistic or having a God-complex. In many cases this trait makes it more difficult because even though they might yes you to death, they may not believe you. They may walk through the process, do the process, appear to be healthy, and appear to be doing very well. They may not be using the substances that will get them in trouble. However, just like many other people with substance use disorders, they may suffer transference. This can now be in the form of something more acceptable within their circle—gambling, sex addiction, spending, power hungry stuff, collecting. These things may go unrecognized or untreated until much later, if ever, because these behaviors may not be a disqualifying offense to whoever or whatever is watching.

OBSTACLES TO RECOVERY

Self-esteem is a big obstacle to the treatment of addiction. A low self-esteem can prevent you from reaching out for help. You may not feel deserving of help. People also sometimes feel they got themselves into a situation so they are the only ones who can get themselves out of it. This may sound like ego, but it's often fed by low self-esteem and insecurity. After all, who has failed you more than yourself and that is a hard reality to accept.

The ego getting involved is a big killer. Things like grinning and bearing it, manning up, and all those things that you have been raised hearing can start working against you. The internal thoughts that say you haven't been strong enough, smart enough, or capable enough can and will work strongly against you, as well. Remember, this is a brain disease. This brain disease goes deep inside your psyche and uses all of your fears and insecurities against you. That's how it stays strong. It keeps you psychologically questioning yourself and doubting yourself, and then you stay reliant on something that feels so decisive, like drugs and alcohol, because those substances make decisions easy for you.

Oftentimes people sit back and do whatever the drug tells them to do. If the drug says sleep, they sleep. If it tells them to run around the neighborhood until four o'clock in the morning, they run around the neighborhood until four o'clock in the morning. If they want to do something that's a criminal activity or morally wrong, they allow the substance to say it's not. *Everyone does it, so who cares?* That's a judgment.

If it's something that is against your faith/religion and your God, the drugs tell you, "Do it anyway." The drugs tell you that to control you. They tell you things like, "You're going to let other people control you? You know religion is used as a form of control." So, they respond, "Oh, no, I'm not going to be a sheep. I'm not going to be controlled." No matter what the question is, drugs say you can put everything off until tomorrow. That's comfortable for a lot of personalities.

At one time, you could control it. You picked it up, put it down, and you didn't use it again. Because of that, you tend to always have that in your memory. You believe you can put it down any time. Many addicts have a period of being clean at least for a day or two, a week, a month or whatever. They feel they have done it before so they can do it again. Addicts think, *I know what I need to do. I just need to do it.* However, since it hasn't happened yet, you can only call that a theory. You have to allow yourself to understand that most of the ideas you have are actually just theories. Just because it feels and sounds like a fact, doesn't make it a fact.

Our own personal bias is also a huge obstacle. We all have a level of biased thinking. This can complicate our recovery because it makes it more difficult to listen and learn from others with different opinions or observations. Just like me being a Mexican-Puerto Rican influences what boxers I like, what music hits the heart strings, and what foods I prefer. I'm biased. When an individual is biased toward what they think works for them, what methodology is more comfortable for help, and what recovery program they prefer, it puts them at a disadvantage to listen to options that may be life-saving.

There's Help and a Hope!

There is access to treatment available for most who want it, but they may not like it. For instance, people say that they are willing to do whatever it takes, but they may not want to go to treatment or mutual help meetings. I know of a year-long faith-based program. I tell the client that they can go there for free. They may say, "I don't want to go to a religious program." A minute ago, they were dying and willing to do whatever it took, but now they have doubts and want to negotiate. That's exactly how complicated this disease is. It makes us negotiate life-saving measures due to it not being what we want.

In reality we, as a society, just struggle with truly accepting addiction as a life-threatening disease. To give an example, four people I've known have had brain cancer, severe brain cancer. All four of them immediately had brain surgery. What did that feel like when they were in a physician's office? That physician said, "I'm going to operate on your brain. I'm going to cut your brain open. The surgery is dangerous and there may be some brain damage but without surgery you will most certainly die." They didn't need time to decide. They immediately said yes. Whereas, people with addiction can go to multiple treatment providers, rehabilitation facilities, doctors, or have lost their homes, their families, and their jobs. The doctor says, "I need you to go to counseling or at least some meetings." And the client says, "No that doesn't work for me." They can go to meetings, which is less invasive than brain surgery, but many refuse. As a society, we just don't treat it like the medical problem it truly is. We treat it like a decision or behavioral issue.

Even people who claim to understand, are in recovery, or have recovered from this, tend to view it like a behavioral issue sometimes. We have all heard how someone "doesn't want it enough." Programs that kick people out for using, being disruptive, or being *noncompliant*. All three of those things are exactly what qualified them for programs in the first place. It is up to us, the treatment community, to develop a system for that and train staff to understand that.

Insurance companies may even cut off funding after repeat relapses, even though relapses are known to be part of the disease. Relapses are not part of the recovery or remission, but they are definitely part of the sickness and disease. Just like cancer comes out of remission, diabetes complications can occur, and heart disease or high levels of cholesterol can be persistent, so do complications related to recovery. Yet, I do not know anyone who was told by a physician that their failure to regulate their cancer, blood sugar, blood pressure, or cholesterol was a form of non-compliance, that they don't want it bad enough, and therefore will not receive any more help from their insurance for the treatment. As a matter of fact, there are even physicians who charge patients cash for addiction treatment even though they accept the client's insurance for any other form of medical care. If you find yourself in that position, find a new provider ASAP.

To effectively treat this problem, you must *know* that its life threatening. This knowledge is very specific. It's similar to when we drive down the street and *know* cops are always on that road doing a speed trap, so we slow down. Since we don't see the cops but know that they are usually here we may go five miles faster than the speed limit. You feel pretty safe. That's one kind of knowledge. That's the kind of knowledge in which you don't see it or fear it, but you believe it's there. Then there's the other type of knowledge. The one similar to driving down that same road and you actually see the cop with a radar gun aimed at you. Now you may not only go the exact speed limit but maybe even slower. You don't feel safe doing any different. There are differences in those two types of knowledge. One is true knowledge and the other one is the kind of knowledge that we walk around with, arrogantly, all too often.

We *act* like we know, but we really don't know. We just know there's a high level of probability that it's true. This world is based on probabilities, but we tend to use them when they're to our advantage and not when they're to our disadvantage. When they're to our disadvantage, we tend to rationalize that nothing will happen to us because we're different. We like to play outliers when it benefits us. We use the probabilities to our advantage when it's for a purpose. I would like to say that recovery changes this, but I must admit that this is more of a human condition I'm using to make a point. It's a flaw I for one have become accustomed to identifying and even laughing out loud to myself when I catch myself believing my own arrogance.

THE TREATMENT INDUSTRY TODAY

I don't think the treatment industry typically works well together. This becomes a problem for the client. That is why we have to fix the way we work together. We have many pathways to recovery, but each feels *their* way is *the* way. If they played together a little more and didn't confuse the client with certain biased, opinion-based comments, then the client could know that each of these *could* be effective and *are* effective.

What I mean by that is there are programs that put priority on one aspect of your care and they may speak negatives about other methods or programs that differ in approach. Some programs use medications and others do not feel that you are in recovery by being on medications. Some programs say God and others say higher power. Some programs require mutual-aid meetings and others allow you to choose your own groups that you wish to attend. All of this is okay, as long as we respect the others. If a program is well-intended and offers help by using methods that are not harmful to the client, we should all be good right? Well, that's just it. Since so many of us in the business of recovery are also in remission, we take it personally. When you deal with death as much as we do you tend to take it very seriously.

Unfortunately, we tend to offer opinions based on our own understanding or experiences about Medication Assisted Treatment programs, Methadone clinics, faith-based programs, or mutual-aid meetings to our clients. We need to remember that any and all of these methodologies are useful and have saved many lives. I only mentioned the most common of the time, but believe me I could continue with gender specific, age specific, specialty groups, and on and on.

If the programs worked well enough with each other, they would be able to discern which types of individuals fit with their program and which types fit other programs. There are multiple pathways to recovery. We are saying that now. We realize it's wrong to say there's one way to recovery for everyone. That frustrates a lot of old-school programs. A lot of old-school people were in recovery and got sober by being told how to act. It just is what it is. No coddling, no babying, no soothing, just here's the tissue.

I can see why the programs don't work together. We don't have the full answers because of the way we get science. That is the biggest hindrance. We get science through research. Who does research? Universities and pharmaceutical companies. If the pharmaceutical companies are not doing the research to find cures or find the right treatments, we don't get those answers. If the universities are not putting the dollars in to do the research to find new alternatives or understand the ways to get better, we won't get better. So, what drives those things? Money drives all those things. What are the barriers in the treatment industry? The barriers are money from a federal standpoint, money from the pharmaceutical standpoint, money from a social aspect, and money from the universities. If we dumped as much money into addiction as we do into heart disease and cancer, I believe without a doubt we would have a cure.

Take cancer and diabetes, for instance. Even though we have

information, we all still eat foods that could hurt us, we still go in the sun, which can hurt us, as well. We still do all the behaviors that cancer loves and feeds upon, yet nobody's blamed for getting cancer. We don't go to a person with skin cancer and say they were dumb for being in the sun. We don't go to diabetics and say they're not smart for eating sugar in the first place. We don't do that medically because we have put so much money in those disorders and illnesses, and we trust the medical models. However, the treatment industry is only just now accepting medical models. Old-school models have been the standard—the faith-based community and the mutual-aid programs. They had success for the suffering before the medical models. Medical models gave people a lobotomy. Medical models put everybody into institutions. The medical models are most definitely necessary and we are lucky to be in a time where more money and emphasis is being placed in our space. Unfortunately, it's because those same medical models failed us through loopholes in prescribing other drugs and how that all played out, but that's not a discussion for this moment. We all know what happened.

Today, it's hard for people in the recovery community to trust in medical models. The last big entry into this space was via Methadone. For whatever its worth, Methadone was apparently successful despite any of our opinions on how individual services use it. The purpose of Methadone was to reduce crime, and they were supposedly successful in reducing crime. That's all it was meant for. It wasn't to treat addiction. It was to transfer addicts to something we could manage, so we could help them get back to some form of productivity. It is successful for what it was meant for.

Then came the Buprenorphine products. Suboxone is the most common of the time and used to move you from heroin or an illicit opioid to a regulated opioid agonist medication that is more manageable. We know how to cover up those opioid receptors that are craving some attention, and it's a cleaner option than heroin or street opioids. During a time when we have too many loved ones and friends dying from overdoses, often under the use of fentanyl, we need some solutions. No solution seems to be quicker than to simply be given a medication once the effects of your street drugs are wearing off and then follow back up with a physician that should be wrapping you up with some other programming that can help you live a life of recovery. It's successful in what it's meant to do.

The other medication in the Medication Assisted Treatment model is Naltrexone. In the oral form, it is very subjective. A doctor can prescribe you a level and you may take it or may not take it. It involves a lot of choice. 30 good decisions in 30 days. Anytime a person has to make that many consecutive good decisions to stay on track that can be difficult. Especially since this one is an antagonist instead of an agonist like Methadone or partial agonist like Buprenorphine. This in simple terms means that you don't feel it because it doesn't create an increase in dopamine stimulation. In simpler terms, there's no *mmm good feeling* attached at all. Similar to how vitamins are good for you, but you don't feel them. Compared to an energy drink that you do feel. The injectable form of Naltrexone is Vivitrol. Vivitrol is medication administered by your health care professional once a month. That form is very successful. It is success-ful and a good option because it is a non-opioid, not addictive, and there aren't any withdrawals whenever the client chooses to discontinue using it. Since it doesn't have a street value to it because it doesn't have any *high* or *mood-altering* effect, the only way to learn more about this option is to consult a physician that prescribes it.

People focus on addiction being this one thing. You have it, and you have it forever. No, it's two things. It's *physical dependence* and *psychological addiction*. Physical dependence is temporary, but the psychological addiction appears to be permanent. I say appears to be because I still believe that we can find a cure. The physical withdrawal symptoms of dependence are short-lived after last use. The psychological connection we have developed to our use and everything that comes with it is much harder to manage for long periods of time. When you use something like Vivitrol, you've beaten the physical dependence part and we can focus on the psychological part, which is very necessary.

Many people just don't believe in it because they don't *feel* it and they're used to feeling something. You smoke pot and you feel something. You drink and you feel something. You do opiates and you feel something. But with vitamins you don't feel anything. You just spend a lot of money to urinate a different shade of yellow. All of a sudden, people want to give you a medication that makes you feel nothing. It's very difficult for addicts to believe in anything that doesn't come with a feeling. How are you supposed to believe that it's working for you? Other than the decreased cravings you may experience. You must have faith that it's working. But you don't have faith in yourself. You lost that long ago. You don't have faith in God. You don't have faith in family. Now you're trying to use a muscle you no longer have when you don't have faith in anything. How are you supposed to have faith and trust in *something* when you don't have faith and trust in *anything*? That's the problem.

On Easter, I watched monks who had masks on to protect them from the Corona virus, which was running rampant at the time. Why would a monk have a mask on? What happened to faith? The monk believes in science too. We have to rely on science. Science is crucial. Math is crucial. The big fight between science and faith is incorrectly placed. Both exist and both are equally as important. You can't believe in numbers and think life is in a random order. There's a meaning to the numbers being placed in the way they are. They fit together so well and create so nicely.

The point, right now, is things are not working. The barrier is not in the pharmaceutical companies. The real barriers are in treatment. You have your own disbelief that it can work for you and doubt you're going to make it. There is this unfortunate thought within everybody's head that they are done, terminal, and the world would be better off without them. That pity party we sit in is hard to get out of. Very difficult. Nobody wants to admit to being a victim. If you call someone a victim, they may freak out on you and destroy your office, but a victim mentality is very easy to step into. That learned helplessness does exist. We can see it when they test on rats and other animals. It's no different. Conditioning exists.

All those things we've learned with Pavlov's dog, all that's true. Not one addict out there won't tell you that before they score, they were already feeling high. They are already feeling the effects and the excitement. That's Pavlov's dogs. Why not use that same science and research to cure addiction? That's why I am relying on the medical community to step up. We still have physicians that have never had any studies in addiction or addiction treatment. Can you imagine how much better our methods and treatments would be if they actually started doing more research and education within medical schools? Our criminal justice community has stepped up much faster as evidenced by drug courts, diversion programs, offering treatments, and re-entry programs. It is time for the medical community to join the fight.

BALANCING THE FOUR QUADRANTS OF LIFE IS THE KEY TO RECOVERY

Four aspects of the addict's life need serious attention—the psychological, the physiological, the spiritual, and the physical. No one is more important than the other. I think you're only in a bad spot when you try to fix one and not the others. When all four are fed you have balance. Any lack of balance will cause you to seek out another way to regulate that balance and that isn't always good.

The *psychological* is dealing with the psychological issues that create that self-doubt—the traumas that you've experienced, the way you have interpreted those traumas, and any ill effects they've had on you. The way you interpreted your childhood, your family of origin issues, your failures and your insecurities must be addressed.

Physiological means the things you must do to keep your organs and tissues functioning, alive, and well. You still must not put certain things in your body. You still must nourish the body and give it what it requires. If you require a certain medication for stabilization, you need to take it. You still need to drink water, eat the proper foods, and balance that system for it to work properly.

Spirituality means you must acknowledge that you're not the only one in the world. You're not the creator of all and the doer of all, and you're not always right spiritually. You have to believe in others and then believe in the connectivity of human beings, animals, and plants because we're all connected in one way or another. We're just a few little molecules different than everybody on this planet. You must face the spirituality of understanding you are just another piece of this long chain of generations, and you are simply here to do your part.

Physically, you must move the body around. It's a machine that requires movement and exercise. It just needs to be used because if any parts of this body are not used, it starts to decompensate and eventually becomes unable to perform basic functions.

For example, if you start doing poorly physically, you start feeling bad psychologically about yourself. You start eating poorly because you're depressed, and then you struggle spiritually in regard to why you are even here in the first place. They all relate. At that point you are just hating the world and miserable. All four of these need to be treated together. It's really simple. We look at earth, water, wind, and fire. These four things are true, and they all are in balance with each other. Fire requires oxygen, and all things nourish each other to work in unity. We believe that about the four elements on Earth. But for some reason, when it comes to us, we think we're different. We're not. We need all four of our elements to be in complete balance, as well.

When I say you need a chemical solution for a chemical problem, I'm strictly talking about the chemical part. I still think you need the spiritual solution for the spiritual problem, you need the physical for the physical problem, and psychological for the psychological problem. You need to address all four. I call them the four quadrants, and you must address all four quadrants for balance. I believe balance is the true cure. Most people don't have balance. When you're off balance, you tend to look for ways to regulate. Your body and your brain are always self-regulating. We can't see what's happening on the inside. We can only see what we're doing out on the outside. You have to physically try to self-regulate as much as you can but in a healthy way.

A lot of things are legal but can still be harmful—sugar, caffeine, nicotine, alcohol. The largest contributors to heart disease are alcohol and poor eating habits. Those things are legal. The biggest contributors to diabetes are sugar and poor eating habits, but those things are legal. The biggest killers we have in our lives are legal things. Illegal drugs are a problem because they work really well and really quickly initially. If someone wants to get sleep and takes a sleeping pill, it knocks them out and they go to sleep. The next time they need to get to sleep, what do you think they're going to do? They're going to take a sleeping pill. Many people out in the world aren't addicts but take sleeping pills because they believe without them, they can't sleep. This exact concept applies with other drugs.

Imagine telling people that sleeping pills will now be illegal. For you they work. So, you ask, why should it be illegal for everyone? The answer is because one person can't deal with it, or a group of individuals can't use it. That doesn't seem right! This is how I feel about marijuana, alcohol, opioids, and chemicals. I don't care what

it is. A group of individuals are using just about every substance
out there in a way that's not disrupting their daily life, or the way
it's disrupting it is not annoying enough to quit. Therefore, I don't
believe that government should get involved with that. I just think
the government should get involved with *understanding* it.

The more we understand and diagnose it from that aspect, the
more I think we should at least get better education and better
knowledge. The problem is that it becomes a war of what's true
versus what's not true. I can always find something on the internet
to validate my thinking. If I want to validate that marijuana is okay
for me, I'm going to find many websites and many successful people
who smoke pot. I'm going to be able to show you that you can be a
professional athlete, very successful, and rich never having graduated
college and smoke pot every day. I'm going to find a lot of evidence
for that. So, why spend all of our research, time, and energy trying
to discount that?

Some truths we just need to acknowledge and accept. I would
love if the communities that actually push for legalizations could
just be honest and acknowledge the issues they can cause. All I want
them to say is, "Look, at the end of the day, we know pot could be
medicine, but we don't really want it in medicine form. We just want
to get high. We just want to smoke and get high." That's honesty,
but that's not what they're saying. They're making it seem like it's the
next biggest thing out there and actually better than opiates for pain.
No, it's not better than opiates for pain. If it was, doctors would have
you smoke pot instead of taking an opiate prior to surgery. Let's see
how well you do in surgery. That is not a reality. I don't get involved
with the legalization part, but I do want the honesty part. I don't like
to over dramatize either. If you talk to somebody and they say if you
smoke pot, you're going to move on to other things. Well, there's
no cause and effect there now, there is correlation but not causation
effects.

In other words, I don't know many people who have done heroin,
crack cocaine, or other similar drugs who didn't smoke pot at some
point. But that not a causation. There's just a correlation between me
searching for something to feel differently or to escape whatever my
situation is. I was searching for something to make me feel whole,
secure, or good about myself. There's a lot more evidence to suggest

that than science saying, "You move on from one drug to another drug to another to another."

At the same time, me using something brings about the culture. I start doing something, and I bring the culture of use now. Therefore, you're going to tend to try other things. When you're involved in a culture, that makes a subculture. If I'm smoking pot, I'm probably going to try dabs, I'm going to try other forms of THC. I'm not just going to try marijuana one certain way. If I'm drinking alcohol, I'm probably going to try vodka. I'm probably going to try whiskey. Those are just the realities of the situation. If we would actually talk truth like that and just understand things like that, our truth and our understanding would be a lot more realistic than the fear tactics.

One of the biggest problems in our industry is that we don't have an X-ray machine. We don't use brain scans. In a perfect world, we would brain scan every child at the youngest age possible without doing them damage before they eat any harmful chemical. It would be fantastic. So, that at some point in their life, when their behaviors become maladaptive, risky, and they start using substances, we can scan them again. We could show them the effects on their brain.

I remember as a kid, I went to the doctor when my arm was hurting. They showed me an X-ray, a little line that was a hairline fracture. They needed to put a cast on me. There was no conversation. I didn't argue that it was just a small fracture and I would be okay. I had a cast almost all the way up to my shoulder. I had to bathe with a plastic bag. It was on my right arm, which is my dominant arm. It was horrible having to go with that cast all the time. Why did we do that? Because they had an X-ray machine and they proved to me that I needed it.

People with a brain injury or brain cancer have an MRI. When X-ray technicians can show you the clot or the cancer, you can see it, so it's really hard to be in denial. I think science needs to get to a point where we can all physically see ourselves before harmful substances and after. Therefore, we knock denial right out of the box. Then we can also see proof and see treatments based on how healthy that brain is later. Imagine a pharmaceutical company coming out and saying, "If you take this medication, we can prove it works. Here's the brain before the medication and here it is afterward." It would sell millions and trillions. Nobody's doing that because they're not repairing the brain like that. We haven't gotten there, but that is exactly where we're heading.

I believe the Elon Musk of addiction has been born and is out there. He or she requires funding and knowing it's possible. We cannot go around saying it's impossible. We have to believe it is possible. I can't even name an addiction research group out there that's as big as the cancer groups that collect money. How many cancer groups can you name? St. Jude's, The American Cancer Society, and the list goes on and on because we put so much money and research into it. Yet we haven't found the cure for it. I think addiction is much easier to find the cure for because we at least know that when it knocks on your door, it looks a certain way. It looks like cocaine, heroin, or alcohol. We at least have something we can look at and find correlations, but with cancer you don't have that. It's an invisible enemy. Whereas with addiction, it's not invisible. It's right there in front of you. You see it when it's walking into you.

THE TRUTH OF TREATMENT

The truth of treatment is required. First, you have to discontinue the use. You have to stop aggravating it. You can't treat the disease if you continue to build upon it. You can't stoke the fire, help it burn, and then try to put it out at the same time. We first have to snuff out the fire. Then we can go back and evaluate, to identify how it started? It's no different than what our fire departments do after a fire. When the parents tell me, "I think he's using this," I don't care about the why. In that moment that reason doesn't matter. The reason is not what matters, it is the fire itself. All I've got to do is put out the fire.

Then the next person will deal with it and take it a little further. Just like in a fire, after all the fire is gone, they'll walk around the rooms in the building, trying to find the hotspots and looking for things. After they find something, they'll educate, going to the building owner and discussing the cause.

We do the exact same thing with addiction. We see a fire, evaluate what helped cause the fire, go back, evaluate and then educate the person who had the fire. For the future, this is how fires are started. With addiction, we try to do that. However, since we sound so judgmental toward the addict in the way we do it, we take away all the reality that thousands of buildings didn't catch fire. That doesn't mean your building won't catch fire. It's just a safety measure. I'm not saying that because you're smoking pot you'll move onto heroin. I'm just giving you another safety measure. You have got to relate it to analogies that make sense. You can use so many analogies, and any good counselor or therapist can do that.

TOP REASONS FOR FAILURE IN RECOVERY

I think the top reasons for failure in recovery are reservations, distraction, and feeling good. Here's what I mean by reservations. Something was recommended for you to do, and you didn't do it. You had a reservation about it. When you have reservations, you tend to believe you are fine where you are. You say, "So, I reserve the right to not have to go to meetings because I got this."

Next, we get distracted by life and whatever happens. We were going to therapy groups, we were going to twelve-step meetings, we were doing something, and then we had to go to dinner with our spouse the other day, so we didn't go to a meeting.

The minute you're feeling good, you don't do your medicine. That's normal. Many people stop taking the medicine once they feel good. How many people don't take all of their antibiotics? The doctors tell them to take all of them, but once they stop coughing or sneezing and are no longer feverish, they stop taking their antibiotics. It's hard to take something when you don't feel a need to take it. So, in mental health, we deal with that all the time. Schizophrenics constantly go off their medication once they feel good. And then boom, back to schizophrenia.

We predict that when we start a habit it has really sunk in. Has it really sunk in yet? No, it has not become part of your life so deeply, and it's easy to fall out of it. For instance, people who are real athletes work out. They just do it. When they don't work out, they don't feel good, and they know they have got to get back to the gym. It's not really hard for them. They start going back to the gym to get back in the routine. For people who have never really developed that and aren't athletes, it's almost impossible to ever get comfortable with that. It just does not happen. They start an exercise program multiple times in their life but never really get into the routine. We need to understand that's how recovery is for us. We are those people who have never really been doing these recovery things.

Moreover, if we stopped doing it, it will be really, really difficult to start going back to it. We get distracted by life and start getting back into our old routine. Well, the old routine wasn't helping. It wasn't fueling recovery. So, we just get distracted by life and fall back into old routines and habits. Then we're so far removed from all the stuff that was actually saving us because, at the end of the day, we still think it's a behavior and a decision without giving credence to it being something deeply embedded within the brain.

THE FAMILY'S ROLE IN ADDICTION

We get in trouble with addiction when we have a family member primarily dealing with an addict or living with a loved one who is an addict. It's a tough situation for the family member. They must have their own understanding of what this disease really is because it will come at you hardcore. They should watch the movie *The Exorcist*. Know that before that demon was exorcised, that person used every bit of information they could to try to hurt feelings, distract, anger, and fight loved ones. The disease of addiction will do exactly that.

This disease grabs your loved one and turns them into the disease's possession, somebody they are not, and it'll attack you with your sense of how you raised them. It'll attack your insecurity about whether you did the right things as a parent. You may think your divorce caused it. It'll make you blame yourself. That's why parents of hardcore addicts many times divorce. It's hard to stay connected in a relationship through all that because it's a traumatic experience.

A family dealing with an addict is going through chaos and trauma. The people in that family need to treat their chaos and trauma right then. Immediately. A lot of times a loved one will send the addict to treatment or to therapy, but they won't do it for themselves. They absolutely need it for themselves because they need to stay stabilized. If they get off balance, they're not going to be useful at all.

I always tell the family members to please get the help they need for themselves because it will tap into everything. You will blame yourself. You won't be able to help it. That's why the family members often overcompensate financially and give. That's why they parent out of fear. You cannot parent out of fear. You can't say, "If I do this, they'll go out and die". The reality is, whatever you do or say they will use anyway. You should do the right thing regardless. You have to have faith that the situation is not in your hands. Regardless of your belief about whether it is in your hands or not, the situation is not in your hands. Stop acting like you are in control of the situation. You haven't been in control for a very long time. Why are you trying to control it? You can't. If you could control it, you wouldn't call me.

You can take preventative steps and reach out to people. At what point should the family members reach out, and how should they reach out? How does a family member know at what point the addict needs help? Certain things are obvious signs that action should be taken. Certain things are not. If your child is using heroin, cocaine, crack, anything that can kill him on the first try, you take action. Other things are less obvious—drinking, smoking pot, or maybe experimenting with little things. If that's the case, it will be harder for you to take action.

Also, there are two different kinds of parents—ones who take preventative action when their kids are little and others who take action after the problem has already presented itself. First, the best time to act is when they're itty bitty little kids. You can teach them causation and correlation with things like sugar and caffeine that they will ingest and use in their lifetime. Show them and teach them an understanding of these things, which are considered minor drugs. Then, as they get a little older, you can move on with the education and teach them more. Tell them about the next level of drugs. Educate them again and again, not with fear tactics, but just plain and simple understanding and truth.

If you are a parent reacting out of response to a crisis, they're already using, and you can feel free to go full-bore as soon as you can. Sometimes, other people will say you are overreacting. The key is to do what you have to do so you can live with it. I think any parent should react to the level they can live with. If you feel that if you don't respond to this, the worst-case scenario may happen, and you're not going to be able to live with yourself, you need to respond and react to it. Do not wait and then regret what you should have, could have, or would have done. That is the worst thing to do. I would rather you overreact and let a professional tell you to calm down. The professional will say, "I know you thought it was cancer, but it's not. I know you thought he had AIDS, but he doesn't." I would rather you go that route and get all the testing done than to not do it all because you think the worst can't happen to you. You may think you drank a little bit or did it when you were young and you were okay, so they are going to be okay. No, it doesn't work that way. Our victories don't transfer to our children, and our losses don't transfer to our children. However, blindness to a situation does transfer to our children if we ignore it and fail to have the conversations.

Conversations are the cure. You must have conversations from the time they are young, and you must have them from a place of love. I think every parent and family member going through this comes from a place of love. When you're confident, you're communicating. If you push somebody, they're going to push back or try to stand firm. That's normal behavior. Nobody likes to be pushed. Don't go aggressively and push. When you go into a conversation, go into it with love, keep that love the whole time, and come out of it thinking I love you. I love you, but I don't like the behavior. They could be cursing at you and everything, but you need to still hold true to your message of love.

You can show them that while their behavior wasn't acceptable, you know what's more important—the fact they're suffering from this and using right now. Never have a conversation when they're high or intoxicated. Wait it out. Wait to talk to them when they're sober. Just don't let them sleep in your house at night, and then as soon as they wake up, they're off again. Don't keep on letting them come back home if they're just using your house as a safe place. You feed them and you give them a bed, you give them electricity, you give them safety, but then all day long, they're out there getting high or partying. You need full-force action. At that point, you need to call a professional who knows how to deal with this. Give them the exact information you're dealing with and let that person analyze it. Rely on the professionals who do this for a living. They can hear out your entire story.

Go to whichever professional source you can access first—a counselor, therapist, psychiatrist with addiction experience, a mutual-aid meeting, or a church. Don't go to a family member or a person who is emotionally attached to the situation. If they're emotionally attached to you as a friend or you as their parent, they will side with you regardless. They will get upset at the other person or speak out of emotion toward the other person because you're the friend, the loved one, or the family member.

You should go to someone who is emotionally unattached. They will hear you out very clearly and try to help you in that way. If you are more comfortable going through a church, go to a church and ask for a church figure who deals specifically with addiction. Ask who has the most knowledge with that specific area within that church. If you're going to a counselor, find the one with the most experience.

In other words, don't go to the counselor that has twenty different areas they specialize in. Find the counselor who specializes in two or three things with addiction as one. If you go to a doctor, don't go to the doctor who specializes in everything. Even if you are comfortable with your doctor, ask for a true specialist in addiction. Ask who they would refer you to. Ask who they would send their loved one to.

Do You Need to Hit Rock Bottom to Recover?

I don't believe you need to hit the level of *rock bottom* to be considered *in recovery* or in need of help. I think there's only one bottom and that's death. When we're better, later on in life, it's easy to look back and say, "I hit bottom." It's similar to looking at the stock market. You don't know where the bottom is until it doesn't hit that anymore. Your fifty-two-week low is only your fifty-two-week low because it never hit that again. You don't know when you're at your bottom until you're no longer hitting that bottom.

The best way to look at a bottom is, is it bad enough for you right now? How comfortable are you on the path you wanted to walk? Here's the problem. A lot of the time you're walking down a path, and it's a gradual move toward that bottom. You got off the path just a little tiny bit. When you take that years down the road, all of a sudden that little bit leads to a lot of deviation. Now you're a mile or two off the path. Sometimes you can't even get that chance to turn around.

You hear many stories of people cave hiking or diving, and they wind up at a dead end and can't find their way out. That's a reality of life, depending on the situation. Just because you went in doesn't mean you can get back out. The path becomes hidden, and you lose your way.

Pilots can even lose a sense of up and down, and therefore crash planes because up became down and down became up. They lost their orientation. If these realities exist in diving, and they exist in piloting, they also exist in regular life. Science has already shown us they exist, meaning they can exist *in me* at any point in time. I can lose my orientation and think I'm moving forward when I'm actually walking backward. It's really important to understand that it's easy to get off the path and not to be moving forward.

The best thing to do is stop completely. Just stop and reevaluate the entire thing. Look all the way around, take everything out of your pockets, meaning take everything out of your soul, and just put it on the table and discuss it with somebody who's willing to discuss it. I promise you, at least one thing you pull out you won't want to put back in your pocket.

I use an analogy for this concept. Every night a guy goes home, pulls everything out of his pockets and puts it in the same place. The next day, before he goes out, he doesn't put everything he pulled out of his pockets back into his pockets. Sometimes he might have a business card that was important for his pocket yesterday, but it's not important today.

Take the time out to look all the way around at what's going on in life. You must expose everything and be willing to talk about it with the counselor. The counselor must talk about everything, even things you don't find problematic. They'll talk about your job, your social life, your personal life, and your love life. They'll discuss your aspirations, your childhood, your brothers, your sisters, and your parents. They will say things such as, "Tell me about living in Florida. What do you think about it?" They'll talk about everything because they don't know. They're looking at everything you pull out of your pockets. It's your life. Once you stand still, pull everything out of your pockets and evaluate it, then you can redetermine which direction to go.

DIFFERENT PATHS TO RECOVERY

There are many ways to recover. There are twenty-eight-day programs, long-term programs, one-year programs, mutual-aid meetings, all types of counseling, and out-patient therapy. I think the twenty-eight-day in-patient programs, like the Minnesota model, is ineffective as a total, all-inclusive and complete treatment program. I think twenty-eight days is something that was created a long time ago for insurance coverage. There's no science backing it. No study or research indicates that twenty-eight days does anything but initial stabilization.

In today's way of recovery, you would use a twenty-eight-day program to simply get out of your current situation, take a break, stabilize a little bit, breathe, and reevaluate. A twenty-eight-day program is great for taking a little break from your life. Take a time-out, disconnect, unplug from all of your daily responsibilities. Use the time at the twenty-eight-day program to get with your therapist and other professionals and start letting everything just kind of set. That's your first real therapy or treatment. When you go to detox, all you're doing is medical stabilization. When you go to a twenty-eight-day program, you'll get some mental health stabilization. That's not long enough for full stabilization, but you'll at least get the substances out of your body so you're medically stable. Once you're relatively psychologically stable, we can start to diagnose what's really happening.

The next step for a patient after a twenty-eight-day program is a PHP or an IOP. PHP is partial hospitalization, and IOP is intensive out-patient. At this level of care, you may be living in a different place. You could either be living at home or at a residence owned by the treatment center you did the twenty-eight-day program with, but you're not having to go to treatment every day, all day anymore. This level of care allows you to have moments when you have freedom of movement and choice. Little by little, slowly, you're being brought back into the reality of the world, which allows you to go to the store if you want to go to the store, but you're doing enough programming so you still have a high level of responsibility of where to be and what you're having conversations about.

Now, because you're interacting with the real world, you're bringing different conversations into the groups and into those counseling sessions, you're starting to say things such as, "Yesterday, I was sitting on the back porch, and I couldn't help but notice a liquor store across the street. I didn't even notice it before. I didn't even know that when I was sitting there looking at that sign, I felt like it was calling to me." Or, "I didn't even have the draw or the pull to it like I normally would when I see that sign." Whatever story you bring back, the fact is you're starting to experience some choices while you are still in treatment.

In the out-patient program, a PHP or an IOP, you're most likely living with other people who are also in treatment. You start making decisions and working on sticking to those decisions that are a bit more serious. If you're going to take time out of your life to do this type of treatment, don't make it a time to try to attack your family by staying negative. Don't spend time saying this is not going to work or trying to prove to them it was a mistake. Utilize it so you never have to do it again. If you never want to do it again, try to maximize the time you have in there. Stick to the people who are taking it really seriously and being positive about it. If it works, you'll never have to go into this type of program again. If it doesn't work, the likelihood of returning to such a scenario is very high. Next time might even be a harsher treatment program. If you really want to shut everybody down and have everybody shut up and no longer think they need to try to control you, be as positive as you can in the program and get through it.

I don't put time on recovery. I don't put a number of days on it. I don't really say that forty-five days, sixty, or ninety will work because time is irrelevant to me. I think as long as you're alive, you're moving forward, and you're doing what you need to do, you can sit with the professional you've already entrusted and discuss time with that professional. Now going into it as if it's a jail or a prison, thinking you have got to go to jail for ninety days, that's a different mentality. I don't like to go there. I think if everybody got healthy in ninety days, I would say a ninety-day time frame was better than a thirty-day time frame, or a longer time frame, but that's not true. It's just not the way it works.

Instead of setting a date that may or may not be met and feeling down if you don't meet it, leave it open-ended. Don't set a date for your recovery because you might start using it against your family to your own disadvantage. You might say something along the lines of, "I told you I'd go to treatment for thirty days, and now it's been thirty days. I'm out of here." What if you were doing good? Why are you fighting it? Don't think you go to treatment for thirty or sixty days. Leave it open-ended and just keep on going. Let yourself move forward and get better. Additionally, allow yourself to be rewarded for getting better. Don't make it boring and tedious. If you are being rewarded and are able to identify that reward, having to buy into that reward will help you move forward better.

There are much longer programs than twenty-eight, thirty, or ninety days. There are year-long programs. A year is a great measure of time because a lot can happen in a year. If I'm at a year-long program, and I'm isolated from the world I currently live in, it's too sterile. There's a big difference between being sober a year in a program and being sober a year out in a world with the birthdays, ups and downs, celebrations, and holidays. If I experience life out here for a year with support, and I'm getting better, I'm going to build up a lot of natural tools that are actually more useful than if I'm in a sterile environment for a year. If I'm in a sterile environment for a year, and I have a year clean, my brain is a hell of a lot more stable. However, it's going to be much harder to now get back out into the world.

From being in that sterile environment for a year, your thinking may become institutionalized. In other words, you now require someone else to tell you when to wake up, how to wake up, what to eat, and when to eat. You require the structure you had there, so you appear to fail when you leave that structure. Those programs tend to say their clients had a year clean, which makes for a great success rate. Their clients were in that sterile environment. That may not happen outside.

That same environment doesn't follow the patient out to the real world. I tend to say those programs are really good to use when you really need to get out of your life for a while because your life is that destructive. If you are going to die outside of a program, get away for a year because at the end of the day, they can't lock you in anyway. If you want to leave, you can leave. They're not locking it down. It's not going to hurt you to commit to it.

The point is, those programs do have a value when you're out there living on the street and you've been living on the street for a long time or something along those lines. Then, you will probably need to learn the structuring they're going to teach you. If you no longer know how to wake up and eat, take care of yourself and shower, and eat foods that are nutritious, that kind of structure can be really good. Again, it's just based on where you're coming from and what your needs are. Just because you finish that program and you've stayed sober a year in one location, compared to another doesn't really give me enough information.

There are mutual-aid meetings, like AA and NA. Their meeting rooms (and the organization itself) are supposed to have no opinions on outside issues as they only care about and focus on recovery. That's the most beautiful part. Those rooms are filled with individuals who can absolutely relate and understand because they've been there and done that. All that. The problem with the rooms is that they're full of humans who, unfortunately, are at different levels of thought. Different personalities show up, and some people have opinions that are a little more far-reaching than what they're asked to do.

For instance, and not just in the rooms (AA and NA), but even therapists, counselors, and sponsors should never give you financial advice. A recovery therapist, counselor, or sponsor should never give you marital advice. They can talk to you about it and provide options but shouldn't give finite advice unless that therapist was hired for marriage reasons, then they can give you marital advice. The same concept happens in the rooms, but, in the rooms, people are trying to give all kinds of advice. People there are giving medical advice, marital advice, and other advice reaching way farther out than they should. Instead, they should stick to what they need to do.

The positive of the rooms is, the people who do know what the rooms are meant for stick to it and do what they are there to do. Those are the principles and the purposes of the rooms themselves. They will relate everything to the reading (The AA "Big Book" and other selected materials), and then they'll recommend any other information to a professional outside of them. If it's a medical issue, you need to go ask your doctor about that. If it's a therapy issue, you should go talk to your therapist about that. The people in the rooms should not be trying to give the answers themselves. That signifies a healthy room. If the rooms themselves didn't exist, millions and millions more of us would be unhealthy. Luckily, the rooms do exist and a lot of people are healthy just from that alone.

Many issues need to be taken up with a counselor or therapist, and there are different ways to counsel. One problem with a therapist or counselor is they have to measure the level of severity of what they're dealing with. If they're dealing with somebody who actually requires a higher level of care and trying to do it as an out-patient counselor or therapist, they're not only doing it incorrectly, they're actually harming the patient. Use the other professionals in the community—residential programs, detox programs, other types of therapists and counselors, as well as physicians.

The most important role of an out-patient therapist or counselor is to know or evaluate if a client is at the right level of care. That's really important because a lot of people, especially in substance abuse, require a higher level of care, but they're not getting it because the therapist is not making that referral. The therapist has given them homework assignments, thinking the assignments sound really good. The client is yessing them to death and they believe them. They drug test and therefore as long as the client does what they need to do, they'll be okay. No. The disease is very, very hardcore, and it doesn't just activate once every seven days. A lot can happen in a week. As long as that person is able to do relatively well and move the ball forward in outpatient therapy, then sure.

I come from twenty-six years of outpatient programs. I don't think a ballpark number of therapy hours work for everyone. There is no standard, and no length of time is guaranteed to give the patient or the counselor a good idea of what the patient's core issues are. If regular education has taught us anything, it's that everybody learns differently. The problem is we must understand what a patient's daily life is like. They will be going back to a lot of things, especially when in out-patient care. As an example, the younger the client, the more frustrating it will be to go back home. It will be more frustrating because the adult figures are constantly asking questions and the young figures are never answering the questions to the full degree the adults expect.

An adult asks you how a school day went, a child says, "Okay." That sounds like a decent answer for a young person. The problem with that is the young person is thinking, *why did you ask me that question? What kind of dumb question is that?* The adult will be thinking, *I'm a caring parent, and I want to know if there's anything happening.* You deal with those type situations when dealing with out-patients. This is why I can't put a time on it. I think first you must build a rapport, which is a completely individual thing and case by case, so if there's a crisis, you get called. If there's an issue, they rely on you. If you give advice or a suggestion, they will put a little bit more weight on that advice or that suggestion.

Other categories of treatment exist, but many of them are very outdated. There are therapeutic treatments. The therapeutic communities that used to be really big in the northeast are not very meaningful anymore. In outbound types of programs, people go out in the woods for an extended period of time. They have their value and their use, but statistically they are not used enough to make them something we should be too concerned about. I think a lot of new stuff will be coming forward. As long as they come from an evidence-based model, you'll find them in treatment centers today. The problem is that we use the term *evidence-based* now all the time.

Sometimes pretty outrageous things work, which just further proves there is no one way to do it. If a person is, for the most part, able to stay clean, sober and just every year or so, they just fall back into it, they may require a little bit more finesse in their programming. They could need something completely different. Again, I would go back to the three most common reasons people fail in their recovery: distraction, reservations, or just not feeling good. A person stops doing what they normally do, so you keep on throwing those three things in front of them, put some questions around those three things, and you'll find one of those three things is typically coming up.

Everybody has the lizard brain. We call it the lizard brain because it's actually all lizards have. All of us have that exact same brain that lizards have, and it is pure instinct, purely fight or flight. That's it. Hungry, not hungry. That's it. All of us have that. Well, when you use drugs or alcohol, instead of thinking from your frontal lobe, you tend to think from the middle part of your brain, that instinctual lizard part of your brain. You go right to the impulsivity of what you want to do. Unfortunately, that doesn't involve thought.

When you tell somebody, "Hey, didn't you think about what you were doing? Did you think about what was going to happen? The consequences?" They'll say, "No, what I did was fine. I did think about it. I didn't care. I just wanted it." That's what we're talking about. That's what addiction does. Addiction changes the way your brain operates. So, you have to stay away from drugs long enough.

That's why those therapies like NLP (Neuro Linguistic Therapy) and EMDR (Eye Movement Desensitization and Reprocessing) help because they help reprogram the messaging and where the messaging goes within the brain. Then your thinking involves more of the frontal lobe, which is where your reasoning, learning, and listening resides. You need more of that instead of where the impulsivity and the reactions come from.

I would consider any of these things acceptable. However, I come from a time before we had all those options. At the time when I got clean and sober, all we really had were institutions or jail, going to the military, or going to the rooms. Back then, if your sponsor said just hang back and clean out the ashtrays, and that's how you're going to get clean and sober, that's what you did. If that worked, realistically, I could write a book and say cleaning out ashtrays got me sober. If NLP or EMDR work, likely the essence is trauma. We're finding trauma in almost all of the people who suffer hardcore relapse issues.

If that is the case, you should be doing something that's *trauma-based* in therapy. Therefore, it is a little bit more of an issue you're dealing with because now you're not just dealing with addiction, you're dealing with what actually changed the way you process relationships. The trauma changed the way you process fight or flight instincts, and those instincts are your core, your lizard brain. If something has affected the way your lizard brain operates, you better treat it or else you're always going to run to the drug or alcohol because that's the way you reprogram. You must treat it.

CAN YOU BE IN RECOVERY AND STILL BE ON MEDICATION?

Many addictions are relatively acceptable for everyone, so people don't fight those. People don't get this caught up in a work addiction. For instance, the only people who hate work addictions are family members. The work addict is able to say, "I might not be home, but how do you think you have that car that you're driving? You went to that school and look at that house you have." There is so much validation and social applause in a work addiction and that's okay. A work addiction only affects family whereas a drug addiction can affect not only family but the addict and many other life aspects. The work addict may suffer high blood pressure and suffer physical conditions, but it doesn't matter because they have chosen financial success over emotional health.

I would consider people free from addictions in many instances even if they are on other medications or substitute medications. Recovery is very personal. Medications are very personal and depend on the situation. I think you can be considered clean and sober or in recovery even though you're on an approved medication. The diagnostic criteria come from using outside medical advice. If you're supposed to take two a day, and you take four today, that's different. If you stick to two a day, you're doing it as prescribed, then clearly, you're not using it as an addict. It may be a substance that can have some questionable components to it or may be socially unacceptable. However, it might be that many people in recovery never see this as acceptable. I believe that is a tragic shame.

That's one of the biggest problems. A lot of people in recovery pretend to be speaking for the AA and NA rooms or speaking for recovery as a whole, but they *don't* speak for recovery because recovery is very personal. If you are working with your physician, and your physician puts you on a medication, for example a benzodiazepine, most treatment centers will not allow it. Of course, addicts don't like benzodiazepines because they're very addictive. Examples of benzodiazepines are Xanax, Valium, and Klonopin, and a lot of people in recovery would have an issue with those medications.

However, if that person suffers from a generalized anxiety disorder and their physician puts them on that, or a psychiatrist who understands addiction, they should go in that direction. If they went to a specialized physician such as a podiatrist, an optometrist, or a general practitioner, and they are prescribed a benzodiazepine, I would question that. I would suggest a professional who not only deals with an anxiety disorder but also one who has the additional professional specialty of dealing with addiction. In that way, if there's any other alternative, they'll prescribe that instead.

A lot of people use replacement drugs in recovery—Suboxone, for example. Replacements in general should only be a concern for the individual who's using the replacement. Medication-assisted treatment is absolutely necessary because it brings science into our treatment world. Everything else is very subjective and can be complicated because it has human error attached to it. Whereas, once you deal with something that is at least science-based, things are easier to measure.

Nobody should look at someone else who has to be on a medication, or feels they have to be on a medication, and question if they're achieving the life goals they want. For instance, the problem with me is using heroin. I no longer go to work. I'm no longer a productive person in my home. I ignore my family and then I get on something like Suboxone. Then, I go back to work and my family says, "Wow, we're glad to have you back." Why shouldn't I be on that Suboxone? It all becomes very subjective. You don't think I should be on it because it's a mood-altering substance or because it's still opiate-based. Yet I got the goals I wanted from it and, in that way, there is significant benefit.

So, who am I to question this situation for any individual or even question how long they should be on it? Not only did they get the results they wanted, but they realized that finally something else is working. They then develop a fear of getting off of it. If in therapy, they are dealing with this fear, maybe there is hope to reduce use of it completely. Those substances and medications are not bad, especially if a person is using them as prescribed. However, anytime you have to put something from outside the body into the body, the natural elements within your body cease to work as hard because your internal body becomes dependent on what you're putting into it. So that part alone, spiritually, inside of a person starts feeling a challenge. If you're an individual and your life has become stabilized, you don't have to feel weaker, or less than, or not fully in recovery because you are on these medications. I think people need to be very careful about making such comments.

I lost somebody I cared a lot about, a young man I helped, and he had six months clean, but he was on Suboxone. He was going to mutual-aid meetings every day, going early, staying late, doing everything we asked him to do and doing service work. He was back in college, taking care of his financial obligations, helping his mom because he lost his dad. Well, in the meetings, he was continually told by individuals that he was not sober and not in recovery. That really, really, bothered him a great deal because he already had self-esteem issues. Remember, many addicts already have self-esteem issues or issues that make them people-pleasing. So, when certain people made comments to him, he felt hurt by that and started making tougher decisions, which led to him giving me a call on a Thursday night.

It was eight something at night and he was crying. He was saying, "Look, I can't do this." I asked, "What's going on?" He said, "Well, I got off my Suboxone and I threw it away. People were saying I wasn't sober, and I couldn't deal with it anymore. So, I threw it away." I asked, "Why did you throw away your Suboxone? Brother, if you were going to do that, we should have done it correctly. We could have talked to the doctor. We can still talk to the doctor. Let's meet with him and if you want to titrate down, we'll do that, but you can't just get off it like that." He was just completely torn up and I said, "Listen, why don't we do this. Come see me in the morning. We'll talk about it, and I'll get you an appointment immediately with the doctor. We'll figure this thing out."

So, we made an appointment for the next day. Next day came, but he didn't show up. His mom called me in a panic. She was in New York, and he was down here in Florida. Mom called me because she couldn't get a hold of him and wondered what was going on. I knew he was in a bad way last night. So, I said I'd do a wellness check on him. I did a wellness check and he was dead. They found more than ten bags of heroin in his house and he had overdosed.

He threw away his Suboxone, but somewhere in the night, the withdrawals got to him so badly, the disease got to him. Because he no longer had the Suboxone in his system, he ended up doing heroin and he died. So, what we do know is if our clients take the Suboxone, they're not dying. They may be on something of reliance, but they're not dying. Whereas, when you buy heroin, you never know what you've got. You never know what you're getting, and death is always a concern. Now we don't have him to help anymore.

I felt those individuals who kept telling him he wasn't in recovery actually killed him. I went on a rampage to everybody around, saying, "Stop telling people they're not in recovery because you don't even know. You don't even feel guilty that you killed him because you don't even know you killed him." I think it's very personal. We should leave that to the professionals who are treating them. I understand some physicians out there don't really know what they're doing when they prescribe Suboxone, and that is a problem. But that's for each individual to keep in mind when they search for a physician with a reputation of understanding recovery. That's how you use those medications safely.

What I Care About

My goal and purpose in life is to fight the disease of addiction. So, all I care about is the disease itself. I don't care whether a substance is legitimized by government, an individual, a family, or a person's faith. That's irrelevant. If a substance, once it gets into your body, creates a chain of events that causes harm to you individually, to your family, to what you truly want out of life, that's the problem. That's what I focus on. You had this goal. You had this thought process of who you were and who you're going to be, and you put the substance in your body, which completely disrupted that. That's the problem. That's what I focus on.

ADDICTION'S EFFECTS ON THE FAMILY

BY DR. KJ FOSTER

Watching my son slowly killing himself with drugs was hands-down one of the most painful experiences of my life. Anyone who has had someone they love addicted to drugs, or has been addicted to drugs themselves, knows that the illness of addiction sucks the life out of your very soul, and turns your loved one into a shell of their former self. Sometimes the illness will cause them to become a monster, emotionally erratic, and erupting at the smallest upset. The illness of addiction, over time, depletes the afflicted individual of all their life force, all their strength, and all their power. With my son, I could see it in his eyes. Blank, dark, no light. When I looked at him, I knew he was in there somewhere, but the addiction had completely taken control. He was overpowered, irrational, and deep in denial.

I don't care if you're the mother, father, sister, brother, friend, child, or spouse. When it's someone you love, watching your loved one *killing themselves*, and seemingly not being able to do a damn thing to stop them or help them, is as frightening and painful as it gets. Aside, of course, from the actual death of your loved one, which is part of the overwhelming sense of fear and desperation felt by most family members. A fear that their loved one might actually die, and most likely will die, if they don't stop. A fear that is being experienced by millions of people around the world, right now at this very moment, as you're reading this book. Perhaps by you or someone you know. That's how prevalent and pervasive the illness of addiction is in this country, and the world.

"But what do I do?" "How do I get him to stop?" "I've tried everything!" "What if he dies?" These are the questions I asked everyone and anyone who'd listen, and the thoughts and fears that were constantly running through my mind, when my son was addicted. They are the very same questions, thoughts, and fears I hear echoed by the family members I work with today, as the family program director at a nationally-known treatment center for alcoholism and drug addiction. Questions, thoughts, and fears I help them to navigate as family members in recovery.

Yes, you read that correctly, family members in recovery. What most people don't realize, and have a hard time accepting, is that the *entire family* needs recovery and rehabilitation, not just the person experiencing the addiction. This is a key concept, and one of several key components, that helped my son (and me) to successfully recover.

You see, in our family, our substance abuse issues fed off each other for several years, ultimately resulting in addiction with both of us. Essentially, I have my son and his illness to thank for my own successful recovery from codependency and alcoholism. In fact, my son and I not only recovered, we are both better, stronger, and more powerful now (individually and as a family) than we ever were before our addictions occurred.

I went back to school as the result of my recovery and became certified in addiction, relapse prevention, and trauma. I earned a Masters' in Mental Health Counseling and a PhD in Counselor Education. I specialize in relapse prevention and family recovery through family resilience training. My son is a successful musician with his own record label and production company. Our lives are infinitely better as the result of our addiction experience and it's my passion and my mission to provide hope to other families. I've worked with thousands of families over the past 10+ years, helping them to overcome addiction and become better than ever before.

Yet, in order to achieve that result, the result of a successful and powerful recovery, a recovery where you're not only recovered, but you're thriving and living your best life, I've learned there are a few essential requirements. Aside from the key concept of each person in the family being in need of their own recovery, there are also three critical components that will help you achieve success and one issue, above all other issues, that will make it all so much worse. However, before I go on to share the three critical components and the one thing that will make it worse, let me expand a bit on this concept of family recovery.

Let me see if I can paint a picture for you. We have a client in treatment – doesn't matter what the age, gender, race – doesn't matter who it is. Picture anyone you want. Perhaps you know someone struggling. Imagine that person. I'll use Emily as my example. Emily comes into treatment for a severe substance use disorder. She can't stop drinking. Emily is motivated and committed to recovering. We provide her with all the knowledge, skills, and tools for a successful recovery. Emily spends 28 days in treatment. Oh heck, let's make it 90 days. It wouldn't really matter if it was a whole year. When Emily discharges, *if* she returns into a family system that has not had any recovery or rehabilitation, no experienced change, the likelihood that Emily will relapse is significantly higher than a scenario where Emily's family has participated in gaining their own knowledge, skills, and tools for change. The dynamics of the family are such that Emily will likely fall right back into old patterns of behavior within that dysfunctional family system if no one else in the family has changed or is working on their own recovery. Addiction doesn't happen in a silo. It happens within the context of a family.

And this is the concept, a key concept, that's hard for families to understand, and certainly hard for many to hear. Because they don't view themselves as being sick or in need of having to recover. In fact, the idea of having to *do* anything else may be incredibly over-whelming. Especially if they've already been taking on the responsibilities of their loved one who is struggling with the addiction. The frustration and anger may be such that they don't *want* to do anything and even *resent the idea* of having to do anything else that they perceive as being for their loved one, as opposed to what it really is, which is for themselves.

But the truth is that the entire family, each person in the family, has been impacted by the addiction, and each person in the family needs to focus on their own growth and recovery in order to effect change. The truth is that the more each person in the family is able to do that, the greater success their loved one is likely to have with their own recovery success.

So, when family members ask me, "What can I do, KJ?" or they say, "I'm willing to do anything to help and support my loved one, just tell me what to do." I tell them that the best thing they can do to help their loved one is to help themselves and focus on their own growth and recovery. The more each person is focusing on self and taking responsibility for themselves and their own change, the more successful the entire family will be in effecting change for themselves *and* their loved one.

Once this is established, people will then of course want to know how they can go about their own personal recovery process. "Where do I go; what do I do?" This is where the three essential components come into play. Based upon my personal and professional experience, I have found that the three components for gaining rapid resilience and effecting positive change for recovery are 1) a *mentor*, 2) a *tribe*, and 3) *spirituality*. These essential components apply no matter what your recovery issue and no matter who you are (individual with the addiction or family member).

Let's start with the **mentor**. A mentor is someone who has achieved what you're seeking to achieve. As the family member of someone who is struggling with addiction, you will want to identify someone who has a family member, and a family for that matter, that has successfully recovered. For example, as the mother of a son who was recovering from addiction, I found other parents who had children who had successfully recovered. One in particular, helped me through some of the most difficult times with my son. If you're the spouse, then finding other spouses who have successfully recovered will be most helpful. Then the goal is to follow what they did to recover. This is the formula for all success. Find someone who has achieved what you are seeking to achieve and follow their path to achieve the same result. If you're finding it difficult to identify someone, a counselor or therapist who specializes in your specific addiction issue would also be highly effective.

Another component for achieving a successful and powerful recovery is participating in a support group of individuals who are on the same path. I call this the **tribe**. These are your people. The people who are going through or have gone through what you are going through and can help you through their own experience and knowledge. Sometimes I'll have family members say, "Oh, I have great friends" or "My family is a great support for me." Your friends and your family, unless they are all going through the same experience or have gone through exactly the same experience, which is unlikely, are not going to be nearly as effective as participating in a support group of individuals who are facing, or have faced, exactly the same issues that you're facing. This is also where I don't dictate which support group. There are a number of different support groups that are specific to the family, including some that are online. It's about picking one, getting involved and starting to build relationships with the other members of the group.

The final component and I would say the most important to a successful and thriving recovery, is **spirituality**. Spiritual practice is what is going to take you from a place of powerlessness to fully empowered, and better able to handle any situation that comes your way. Whether that's your loved one's relapse or, preferably, the many changes and growing pains that you'll both experience as the result of their successful recovery. And this is where many people fall off the rails, so to speak. I believe that spirituality is one of the most misunderstood concepts. So many people equate spirituality with religion. They view them as one in the same, when spirituality is not singularly represented by or synonymous with religion. One can be spiritual and not be religious, just as one can be religious and not practice spirituality. I was the latter, until I began my recovery journey and discovered the true nature of spirituality.

First of all, in terms of a definition of spirituality, I believe the following definition taken from the Oxford dictionary, is an appropriate definition, especially relative to addiction recovery. It states, "Spirituality is the quality of being concerned with the *human spirit* or the *soul*, as opposed to material or physical things." I use this definition when I teach on the topic of spirituality and it's a definition that seems to resonate with most.

For me, spirituality became so much easier to understand relative to something I call the *spiritual trinity*. This refers to spirituality in terms of beliefs, practices, and experiences. Beliefs are exactly that, what we believe. Do you believe in God, nature, the universe, a Higher Power, energy, Divine Spirit or no God? Next, how do you practice your spirituality. Religion is a way in which many people practice their spirituality. For others it can be through artistic endeavors, yoga, relationships, music, nature, or other sources. And finally, there are our experiences, which serve to shape our beliefs and dictate our practice, or lack of practice. Our experiences, also have the potential to dramatically change our beliefs, as well as our practice.

Let's examine spiritual practice a little further, since that's what I'm really talking about relative to successful recovery. It doesn't matter to me what you believe. Everyone has a right to their own personal beliefs and I can't control your experiences nor can you, for the most part. But what does matter is that you are consistently and persistently practicing spirituality. Okay, so what does this mean?

One of the best books I've ever read when it comes to understanding the true nature of spirituality and spiritual practice is called *Power versus Force* by Dr. David Hawkins. Dr. Hawkins' research introduces a logarithmic scale to calibrate the relative energy of different attitudes, thoughts, feelings, situations, and relationships. Dr. Hawkins' research indicates that all energy levels below 200 produce weakness within the individual, and are destructive of life in both the individual and society at large; in contrast, all levels above 200 provide strength, and are constructive expressions of power. An example of some of the attitudes, thoughts, and feelings that operate below 200 (weakness) are anger, hate, anxiety, grief, guilt, blame, and shame. Conversely, some of the attitudes, thoughts, and feelings that operate above 200 (strength) are acceptance, courage, compassion, willingness, forgiveness, optimism, trust, love, joy, and peace. As one advances in the evolution of their individual consciousness to higher energy fields, the process (strength) becomes self-perpetuating and self-correcting, so that self-improvement becomes a way of life. This phenomenon can be commonly observed among twelve-step groups who constantly work toward overcoming negative attitudes, such as anger, self-pity, and intolerance.

The lower regions of consciousness (below 200) anger, hate, anxiety, grief, guilt, blame, and shame are where addictions live and thrive. One can be fixated at any of the lower levels. Almost all of these energy fields, and the behaviors associated with them, have given rise to specific support groups. One must reach an energy level of 200 (courage) in one's own inner development to be healable. Lingering within the fields below 200 entails real danger of becoming so deeply rooted that one cannot escape. History, however, has noted that this is not always so and there are many who have suddenly broken through to higher levels of consciousness (spiritual awakening). Yet, that said, for individuals to make any real progress, it is unlikely to occur alone and generally requires a mentor, spiritual teacher, counselor, or, in the case of a twelve-step program, that would be a sponsor.

How can you begin to practice the spiritual principles that will give you more strength and power? Practicing these spiritual principles (courage, willingness, compassion, forgiveness, understanding, etc.) will help you gain strength and resilience.

Now, this leads me to the one major issue that serves to make it all worse. That one issue is *shame*. Shame exists within the lowest energy field possible and often serves to perpetuate powerlessness. When you or your loved one is in a state of shame, you/they are at high risk for relapse. I say you or they, because I'm referring to acting out in ways that are destructive to life and relationships. This is essential for family members to be aware of because often family members will shame their loved ones without even realizing they're doing it. It's especially common relative to relapse. Family members get frustrated when their loved one relapses, they get angry with them, may even accuse them of not trying, being a failure, or even calling them names, rather than understanding that relapse is a part of the very nature of the illness, and is a common struggle for most people before they ever achieve a successful recovery. I relapsed countless times before I achieved a successful recovery. My son did, as well. This doesn't make it any easier, but the danger is that you can absolutely contribute to making it more difficult for your loved one, based on your reaction to their relapse.

I can tell you as someone who has personally struggled with addiction, that the guilt and shame is felt intensely. Even if your loved one doesn't appear to be experiencing any shame. Even if they don't look like they feel bad. It's there. Sometimes it even manifests as arrogance. But I can tell you that having a loved one pile more shame on top of the shame that is already there is literally like feeding the addiction a steak. You're making it more powerful!

This also happens when family members treat their loved one as if they *are* their addiction and not as someone who has an illness, a powerful and potentially deadly mental illness that requires understanding and compassion. In case you're wondering what the difference is between guilt and shame, the easiest way to differentiate between the two is that guilt is about behavior and is external "I've *done* something bad" versus shame, which is about self and is internal "I *am* something bad" or "I'm defective" or "I'm unworthy." Guilt is good and can actually help motivate someone to get treatment. Shame, on the other hand, is toxic and destructive, and will most certainly contribute to relapse and make it extremely difficult to recover. Teaching family members to identify their own shame and how to speak to each other without shaming is key to moving up the scale and gaining more resilience and more strength for a successful recovery.

Consider what follows as my personal *family* recipe for a successful and powerful recovery: It starts with each person in the family focusing on their own change, growth, and recovery. Hands off your loved ones' recovery. Stay in your own lane, with your hands on your own wheel. Don't try to reach over and drive your loved one's car. If you do, you both are more likely to crash. Allow your loved one to be responsible for their own recovery. It will give them the self-esteem they so desperately need. Add a mentor, find your tribe, and start your spiritual practice. Replace any judgement and shame with compassion. Your anger is based in fear, your fear is based in love. Focus on the love. Be relentless in the pursuit of your own recovery and be gentle with yourself and your loved one, along the way. Recovery is a journey that involves the entire family. May God bless you and yours.

Understanding Codependency

By Dr. Anthony Foster

The word *codependency* has many reported beginnings. Although there may be some argument about where the word first started, we generally believe it originated as part of Alcoholics Anonymous and its sister organization, Al-Anon.

In 1951, Lois Wilson, wife of AA founder Bill Wilson, helped to start Al-Anon, a twelve-step recovery program for the families and significant others of the alcoholic. Al-Anon has its beginnings and ideals in AA and was begun to address the suffering family members who, like the alcoholic, felt their lives were out of control. Al-Anon states that, "Al-Anon is a mutual support group of peers who share their experience in applying the Al-Anon principles to problems related to the effects of a problem drinker in their lives. It is not group therapy and is not led by a counselor or therapist; this support network complements and supports professional treatment."

As treatment for alcoholism and drug addiction evolved in the 1970s, providers began to realize the need and importance of a program for the families. Further, since drug addictions and alcoholism shared more similarities than differences, beginning in the early 1980s, various drug treatment programs adopted the term *chemical dependency* as it better reflected the similarities between alcoholism (alcohol addiction) and other drug addictions. This created a more commonly used diagnostic term.

Treatment for all chemical/drug addictions coalesced into a unified treatment paradigm, *chemical dependency*, which today is categorized as *substance use disorder*. To fit in with the changes, *co-alcoholism*, the term previously used for family member of alcoholics, was updated to *co-chemically dependent*. Being too much of a mouthful to say, it was shortened to *codependent*.

The term *codependency* has been around for decades. Although it originally applied to spouses of alcoholics (first called co-alcoholics), researchers revealed that the characteristics of codependents were much more prevalent in the general population than they had previously imagined. In fact, they found that if you were raised in a dysfunctional family or engaged in an unhealthy or dysfunctional relationship of any kind, you could also be codependent.

Today, codependency is not limited to alcohol and drugs, but is used in many ways to describe relationships, almost always in disapproving way. The real question is how does one know when they're in a codependent relationship? To what extreme are each of us codependent? It is important to understand that every one of us is codependent to one degree or another. According to Melody Beattie, generally considered the foremost authority on codependence, and author of *Codependent No More*, "A codependent person is one who has let another person's behavior affect him or her, and who is obsessed with controlling that person's behavior."

SYMPTOMS OF CODEPENDENCY

The following is a list of common symptoms of codependency. You don't have to have them all to qualify as codependent, nor is this an exhaustive list.

• *Low self-esteem*—Feeling that you're not good enough or comparing yourself to others are signs of low self-esteem. The tricky thing about self-esteem is that some people think highly of themselves, but it's only a disguise. They actually feel unlovable or inadequate. This is usually manifested in a large ego. Underneath, usually hidden from consciousness, are feelings of shame. Guilt and perfectionism often go along with low self-esteem. If everything is perfect, you don't feel badly about yourself.

• *People-pleasing*—It's fine to want to please someone you care about, but codependents usually don't think they have a choice. Saying "no" causes them anxiety. Some codependents have a hard time saying no to anyone. They go out of their way and sacrifice their own needs to accommodate other people.

• *Poor boundaries*—Boundaries are sort of an imaginary line between you and others. It divides up what's yours and somebody else's, and that applies not only to your body, money, and belongings, but also to your feelings, thoughts, and needs. That's especially where codependents get into trouble. They have blurry or weak boundaries. They feel responsible for other people's feelings and problems, or blame their own on someone else. Some codependents have rigid boundaries. They are closed off and withdrawn, making it hard for other people to get close to them. Sometimes, people flip back and forth between having weak boundaries and having rigid ones.

• *Reactivity*—A consequence of poor boundaries is that you react to everyone's thoughts and feelings. If someone says something you disagree with, you either believe it or become defensive. You absorb their words because there's no boundary. With a boundary, you'd realize it was just their opinion and not a reflection of you and not feel threatened by disagreements.

• *Caretaking*—Another effect of poor boundaries is that if someone else has a problem, you want to help them to the point that you give up yourself. It's natural to feel empathy and sympathy for someone, but codependents start putting other people ahead of themselves. In fact, they need to help and might feel rejected if another person doesn't want help. Moreover, they keep trying to help and fix the other person, even when that person clearly isn't taking their advice.

• *Control*—Control helps codependents feel safe and secure. Everyone needs some control over events in their life. You wouldn't want to live in constant uncertainty and chaos, but for codependents, control limits their ability to take risks and share their feelings. Sometimes they have an addiction that either helps them loosen up, like alcoholism, or helps them hold their feelings down, like workaholism, so they don't feel out of control. Codependents also need to control those close to them because they need other people to behave in a certain way to feel okay. In fact, people-pleasing and caretaking can be used to control and manipulate people. Alternatively, codependents are bossy and tell you what you should or shouldn't do. This is a violation of someone else's boundary.

• *Dysfunctional communication*—Codependents have trouble when it comes to communicating their thoughts, feelings, and needs. Of course, if you don't know what you think, feel, or need, this becomes a problem. Other times, you know, but you won't own up to your truth. You're afraid to be truthful because you don't want to upset someone else. Instead of saying, "I don't like that," you might pretend it's okay or tell someone what to do. Communication becomes dishonest and confusing when you try to manipulate the other person out of fear.

• *Obsessions*—Codependents have a tendency to spend their time thinking about other people or relationships. This is caused by their dependency, anxieties, and fears. They can also become obsessed when they think they've made or might make a *mistake*. Sometimes you can lapse into fantasy about how you'd like things to be or about someone you love as a way to avoid the pain of the present. This is one way to stay in denial, discussed below, but it keeps you from living your life.

• *Dependency*—Codependents need other people to like them to feel okay about themselves. They're afraid of being rejected or abandoned, even if they can function on their own. Others need always to be in a relationship because they feel depressed or lonely when they're by themselves for too long. This trait makes it hard for them to end a relationship, even when the relationship is painful or abusive. They end up feeling trapped.

• *Denial*—One of the problems people face in getting help for codependency is that they're in denial about it, meaning they don't face their problem. Usually they think the problem is someone else or the situation. They either keep complaining, trying to fix the other person, or go from one relationship or job to another, and never own up the fact that they have a problem. Codependents also deny their feelings and needs. Often, they don't know what they're feeling and are instead focused on what others are feeling. The same thing goes for their needs. They pay attention to other people's needs and not their own. They might be in denial of their need for space and autonomy. Although some codependents seem needy, others act like they're self-sufficient when it comes to needing help. They won't reach out and have trouble receiving. They are in denial of their vulnerability and need for love and intimacy.

• *Problems with intimacy*—By this I'm not referring to sex, although sexual dysfunction often is a reflection of an intimacy problem. I'm talking about being open and close with someone in an intimate relationship. Because of the shame and weak boundaries, you might fear you'll be judged, rejected, or left. On the other hand, you may fear being smothered in a relationship and losing your autonomy. You might deny your need for closeness and feel that your partner wants too much of your time. Your partner complains that you're unavailable, but he or she is denying his or her need for separateness.

• *Painful emotions*—Codependency creates stress and leads to painful emotions. Shame and low self-esteem create anxiety and fear about being judged, rejected or abandoned, making mistakes, being a failure, feeling trapped by being close, or being alone. The other symptoms lead to feelings of anger and resentment, depression, hopelessness, and despair. When the feelings are too much, you can feel numb.

Below are some additional indications that you might be codependent. You may want to self-assess your significant relationships for your own knowledge.

• *Do you feel responsible for other people's problems?* Codependent people feel the need to solve others' problems. They feel that others' problems cannot be solved unless they are involved. Often intuitively, they feel the person they're helping cannot make good decisions or take the right actions to fix their problems. My wife, who also has written a chapter in this book, likens it to one driver reaching across a lane of traffic to steer the other person's car for them.

• *Do you offer advice even when you haven't been asked?* A codependent person views his advice as vital and continues to provide it, whether it's been asked for or not. It becomes natural for the codependent to *butt in* to every problem of the other individual, showing the value of their relationship, thereby artificially inflating the codependent's self-esteem.

• *Do you expect your advice to be followed and followed to a tee?* Codependent people often struggle with boundaries. They expect their advice to be followed completely and get angry when it's not followed. They value their own opinion and expect that the other person in the relationship does, too.

• *Do you feel underappreciated in your relationships?* Besides becoming angry when advice is not followed, the codependent also gets angry over the amount of effort they've put in to helping the other person and the fact that no level of appreciation seems to be enough. Don't forget, this is all done with the idea that the codependent is just trying to help.

• *Feeling unloved, the codependent tries to please others so they will be liked or loved.* There is a purpose to the codependent's helping others. They expect to be appreciated, even loved. If that doesn't occur, they feel taken advantage of and develop resentments. Many times they don't act on the resentments, just losing relationships because a perceived slight for something that was never asked for in the first place.

• *Codependents have a tendency to take everything personally.* A codependent sees everything as a reflection of them. Any slight or comment that implies less than perfection is taken very personally. Their lack of boundaries causes them to always want to be in control so they can create the sense of the codependent being perfect.

• *Codependents often feel victimized.* Though they are often resentful and angry, codependents have little self-knowledge or self-awareness that they have caused their own unhappiness. It's done through their need to control others and constantly get positive feedback, once again projecting that everything about them is perfect.

• *Codependents are incredibly manipulative in their control of others.* Under the guise of helping others, codependents will sometimes use guilt and shame and any other available methods of manipulation to get what they want. As the codependent makes a habit of controlling and manipulating, he often becomes unconscious of his actions. This is the height of feeling in control of every situation and person.

- *Codependents struggle with being honest with themselves and cover up others' bad behavior.* Often codependents will rationalize and justify their own and their loved one's behavior so that they can maintain control and manipulate those around them. This self-dishonesty is usually unconscious and manifests itself in their belief of their own lies, distortions, and exaggerations.

- *The codependent often feels unwanted, unlovable, and a sense of rejection.* An extension of creating the perception of everything being perfect leads a codependent to negative feelings about how others feel about them. Their low self-esteem and fear of not being needed creates this sense, which leads to distrust and an unwillingness to share their feelings in an honest manner for fear of being exposed as a fraud.

As described above, codependency is characterized by a person engaged in an unhealthy, dysfunctional, one-sided, relationship where one person relies on the other for meeting nearly all of their emotional and self-esteem needs. It also describes a relationship that enables another person to maintain their irresponsible, addictive, or underachieving behavior.

Do you expend all of your energy in meeting your partner's needs? Do you feel trapped in your relationship? Are you constantly making sacrifices in your relationship? Then you may be in a codependent relationship.

Researchers also found that codependent symptoms got worse if left untreated. The good news is they're reversible. This chapter is not written as an answer to your codependent issues, but more as a method of identifying if you are in a codependent relationship. Reversing the symptoms are a much more in-depth proposition and can be found in the reading of *Codependent No More*, Melody Beattie's seminal book on the subject. The first edition was written in 1986 and remains the bible of controlling and reversing codependence. The book describes detachment, not being a victim, living your own life, acceptance, communication, and learning to live and love again, among many other possible improvements. It even discusses twelve-step programs, so for those of you who have attended Al-Anon meetings, don't be surprised if releasing yourself from codependence looks a lot like what you're hearing in meetings. *Codependent No*

More is much more than what you receive by attending meetings. Used properly, the book can be for the codependent what *Alcoholics Anonymous* became for alcoholics—a how-to guide to survive and recover from a seemingly hopeless state of mind and body.

A Therapist's View

By Raymond Alvarez, LCSW

I started in the field of substance abuse treatment quite by accident. At that time, I had two young kids and I was providing in-home family counseling, driving from client to client and meeting with families during late afternoons, evenings, and weekends. I wanted a job that I could drive to, spend all day at one office location, and then drive home at the end of the day to spend time with the people I love the most. I had applied to jobs all over, submitting applications online, networking, and trying to figure out what I could do and what I wanted to do. I got a call from a *behavioral health* facility offering me an interview. During that first phone call I honestly had no idea what *behavioral health* meant, but I quickly came to learn that this term was used to describe the field of substance abuse treatment.

While studying to receive my Masters' in social work at Florida State University, we had to complete two semesters of internships. Having an interest in working with adolescents, I followed the faculty's suggestions and completed an internship with the Juvenile Drug Court program for one of the semesters. In the four short months of my internship, I began to learn a lot about addiction, but never caught a real interest in pursuing this field. I remember one of my earliest lessons came from a seventeen-year-old client who told me in a very straightforward way that only juveniles can. "No matter how many times you tell me about consequences, and why I shouldn't do it, I'm still going to do it. I have to make my own mistakes." As I completed my internship and said good-bye to the staff there, a seasoned staff member told me, "Once you start working in the field of substance abuse treatment, you will always come back to it." Of course, I did not believe him until I got that phone call.

I was fearful getting into this field. My view of the alcoholic was the stereotypical older male with long mangy hair and beard, missing teeth, leathery skin, holding a sign and a cup on the side of the road. I feel a sense of embarrassment now looking back on my naive opinions and judgmental stereotyping. As I have come to know many people suffering from substance use disorders, I have come to realize the amazing talent, persistence, dedication, creativity, and intelligence of men and women who have been ensnared by the disease of addiction—people of every ethnicity, age, socioeconomic class, religion, and family background. I have worked with clients who have owned their own multimillion-dollar businesses, and I have worked with the indigent. I have worked with an eighteen-year-old who was addicted to hardcore illegal substances after a sports injury at age sixteen, and I have worked with a seventy-three-year-old alcoholic who been drinking since he was a teenager. I have worked with people who have grown up in homes full of dysfunction and chaos and others who grew up in homes with two loving, supportive, and available parents. I have worked with pastors, church secretaries, and pastors' kids. I have worked with men suffering with military combat trauma, and women who have been abused and neglected. Those in the field understand how true this statement is—"Addiction does not discriminate." Nowadays, I enjoy working with a population with such diversity, resiliency, and ingenuity. I marvel at the speed and depth of change as this marvelous group of people change their behaviors and their lives.

One of my first big hurdles coming into the field of substance abuse treatment was that I have never been addicted to substances. In fact, in today's culture I am about as rare as a unicorn simply because I have never smoked a cigarette or marijuana. Many of my clients would ask at our first meeting, "Are you in recovery?" I would answer them truthfully and say "no," which was quickly followed by their next question, "Well then, how can you help me?" or, "Why should I listen to you?"

Many people who are attempting to get help for addictive behavioral patterns struggle to keep an open mind and do not want to hear from others who do not have the same *street credentials* they do. However, this is simply a barrier to test the genuineness of the counselor/therapist, friend, or loved one who is trying to help. People do not ask their cardiologist if they have survived a heart attack, and people do not ask their oncologist if they have ever overcome cancer. The root of this question is simply this: "Are you willing to understand *me* and the *struggle* it is to change my persistent thoughts and engrained behavioral patterns? Or are you going to be like everyone else and tell me to *just stop it?*"

I have had to reassure my clients that I was willing to enter into the most messed-up parts of their lives, without judgment, and walk with them until they came out the other side. It is about developing trust and relating as a human being. All of us have tried to change something in our lives and struggled. Have you ever failed at a diet plan? Have you ever broken a New Year's resolution? Have you ever told yourself, "I really need to start doing…" and delayed so long it never got done? We are human and change is hard. If the person struggling with a substance use disorder understands that you care about them, that you will not judge them, and that you will support them through the good, the bad, and the ugly, then and only then, will they begin to allow you to help them. And so, the process of healing can begin.

How can we help? What is the best way for someone to get sober? My short answer is through Alcoholics Anonymous (AA) or Narcotics Anonymous (NA), spirituality, and if needed, therapy. Let's explore a little deeper through my journey in the substance abuse treatment field. For the first seven years in the field I worked for two large behavioral health facilities that were abstinence-based and twelve-step oriented. It did not take me long to fall into a similar mindset. I believe that the programs of AA and NA work. I have seen the positive results of these programs and I have seen the incredible transformation people have experienced as a result of these programs.

ALCOHOLICS ANONYMOUS

A measurable healing and palpable freedom from addiction can occur by following the twelve-step program. Many people have doubts and objections to the AA and NA programs. However, these people generally do not have a lot of experience with either program. One of the best reality checks I was given as a counselor occurred when I had been working in the field for a couple of years and one of my clients asked, "Have you read it?" referring to the AA "Big Book." I was making a presumption and taking the word of others instead of reading it for myself. When I actually read it for myself, it strengthened what I heard about the program. For those who aren't sure, try it for yourself! Read the text, go to meetings, obtain a sponsor and follow their recommendations. Best case scenario, you experience the freedom of sobriety. Worst case scenario, you are educated about alcoholism and have a support person on your side.

The book *Alcoholics Anonymous* has much wisdom for the person suffering from a substance use disorder, but it does not stop there. It can be helpful to the employer, the friend, the spouse, and even the treatment center worker, as it was to me. In the book, specific chapters are geared toward the wives (At the time the book was written, the overwhelming majority of those suffering from alcoholism were men. Now the chapter title might read "To the Spouses."), to employers, and to the family as a whole. If you are unsure if you have a drinking problem or an addiction to drugs, read the book. If you love someone who you think might have a problem with substances, read the book.

In order to have an intelligent conversation with those going through the struggle, we need to have some firsthand education on the subject matter, and no better or more comprehensive book exists than *Alcoholics Anonymous*. Some of the most interesting things I learned through the book have been: understanding alcoholism and addiction as a disease, the importance of abstinence, the need to address spiritual deficits to treat substance abuse, and a fuller picture and understanding of what it means to be sober. The AA program and the Twelve Steps are simply one vehicle to get a person from where they are (stuck in their addictive behavioral pattern) to the freedom that is available in recovery.

The other main component of recovery is spirituality. For five years, I worked in a facility where clients could choose a treatment track that was distinctly Christian. Those who developed and supported this *faith-based* approach to treatment understood the importance of addressing spiritual maladies in order to achieve long-term recovery. The "Big Book" states it quite clearly, "What we really have is a daily reprieve contingent on the maintenance of our spiritual condition." (*Alcoholics Anonymous p.85*) Many of the clients I worked with held to a faith perspective that if God is all powerful, He alone could deliver them from their addictions. Like these clients, I too hold to the belief that God is all powerful and *can* completely deliver people from their addictions, bad habits, and all the rest. However, just as God allows doctors to provide physical healing through medicines and operations, I believe God also allows therapists and sponsors to provide healing through counseling and the Twelve Steps. I encourage people to use the best of AA and the best of their faith practices to extend their platform of recovery. The diagram below is an example of how both faith and AA can work together to help achieve long-term sobriety. (See *Figure Below*)

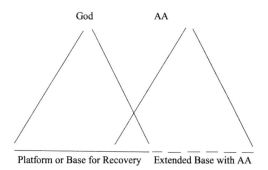

Platform or Base for Recovery   Extended Base with AA

SPIRITUALITY

Christianity and AA/NA are not mutually exclusive and, in reality, are best used together to achieve sobriety. What happens for those who are relying solely on God is *not* that God cannot live up to His name, power, or ability, *but is* the fact that we walk away from Him, outside of His will, by choosing our own desires and the things that are bad for us. By adding AA/NA and including the great benefits of the Twelve Steps, the platform of recovery (bottom of the diagram) is extended by the length of the dotted line. So, when a person walks away from God, or is struggling with their concept and understanding of God, they can still stay sober. The hope is that they can use the best of both worlds. God, the church, and the Holy Bible are great tools to help someone who is struggling with addiction, but they do not have to be the only tools for the Christian. Similarly, AA/NA should not be the only tool used by the person seeking recovery. As the AA program itself professes the importance of continual spiritual growth, involvement with God, the church, and the Holy Bible can be extremely helpful.

How do we access spiritual power? First off, we need to recognize that we did not create this entire universe, nor do we sustain it. We have so little control over the things. Although we may be able to control the rate at which our hearts beat and our lungs breathe, we cannot *make* these things happen. We do not control the formula of chemicals in the air that are mixed perfectly to sustain life. These things are controlled by a Higher Power. I choose to believe in the God of the Bible who is the Creator and Sustainer of all things. This holy and powerful God exists in three persons, God the Father, Jesus Christ the Son, and the Holy Spirit. When we humble ourselves and recognize that we are not God, this is the first step in our spiritual journey.

Next, we need to trust and believe that God is all powerful. Anyone who can create a universe as complex and beautiful as the world we live in can take care of any problem we have. Understand that God *can* (and wants to) restore all things is the second step in our spiritual journey. Next, we need to learn about Him and we can do that through reading about Him in the Bible, talking to Him in prayer, and spending time with Christians who are trying to become more like Jesus. When we learn about the amazing love and the promises God has for us individually, we begin to see joy and peace in our lives. We begin to have a desire to do good things because of the mercy and grace God has shown us in our lives.

THERAPY

The last component of recovery is often therapy. I know it probably sounds strange for a therapist to say that not all people need therapy, but it is true. Not all people need therapy. Sometimes people can get a little off track and fall into the traps of addictive behaviors or become physically addicted to a substance after choosing it as a shortcut coping mechanism.

However, sometimes people use alcohol or drugs to deal with some serious pain and suffering, and in those cases, talking it over with a trained professional can be beneficial to break free from the addictive patterns of thought and behaviors. Some people are afraid of therapy for one reason or another—maybe due to their cultural beliefs or practices or maybe just individual pride. But therapy can help to provide an objective look at your situation from the outside and give you clear direction on how to move forward toward your goal. Going to AA meetings and working through the Twelve Steps with a sponsor can be therapeutic. Attending church or a small group, reading the Bible, and praying with other Christians can be therapeutic. But sometimes these things should be coupled with seeing a therapist to address what was happening in your life when you started using substances, as well as what has kept you using substances. Please do not be afraid to ask for help or be ashamed by the stigma of *going to therapy*. It takes strength to be humble and insight to know that you cannot do it on your own.

In addition to these three main points of healing and recovery, I have developed a method of targeted behavioral changes that address specific areas negatively impacted by the use of substances. While counseling men and women through detox, post-acute withdrawal symptoms, and grief and loss over the abrupt discontinuation of their substance of choice, I have learned that addiction affects all people in similar ways. Despite the vast differences in age, culture, family background, or financial history, these six areas have been drastically impacted in negative ways and should be addressed as a person works toward achieving long-term sobriety. Some of these common effects of ongoing substance use include a disconnection from their spiritual practices, physical health problems, difficulty concentrating and remembering, isolation, increased feelings of guilt, depression, and despair, and lastly financial ruin. I have found it helpful to give the problem some definition by dividing the problem into these six categories so we can create a targeted solution. Taking them one at a time, ongoing substance abuse will negatively affect you:

• *Spiritually*—Regardless of your amount or style of spiritual practice, when you are consistently under the influence of drugs or alcohol you cannot connect with God or any Higher Power. Many people feel ashamed, unlovable, or judged and therefore stay as far away as they can from the church and Christians. If you once had a routine of attending church, reading the Bible, daily prayers, most likely as your addiction increased, your faithfulness to those routines decreased. Some people were able to keep their routines, but admit they were no longer effectively engaging their inner spirit and/or their ministry was increasingly less productive/fruitful.

• *Physically*—All drugs act as a poison in our bodies and therefore the more a person uses these toxic substances, the more health problems they will have. From the minor incidences of lack of hygiene to chronic and life-threatening conditions, using substances can eventually lead to the person with a substance use disorder neglecting their health. The person abusing alcohol might suffer from GERD (Gastro Esophageal Reflux Disease), type 2 diabetes, high blood pressure, and in extreme cases, cirrhosis of the liver. Or the person abusing drugs might struggle with dental problems, deviated septum, collapsed lungs, abbesses, Hep C, or HIV.

• *Socially*—Addiction thrives on secrecy and hiding becomes part of the addictive process. The person with a substance use disorder is naturally going to lie to cover up their addictive behaviors because if it is exposed and brought into the light, it is threatened and could be eliminated. As an addiction progresses, the person becomes more and more averse to social situations in which their addiction might be identified and questioned. The person abusing alcohol who used to drink with all his/her friends, may now be drinking more and more by themselves because even the other heavy drinkers cannot keep up. The person using more and more drugs does not want others to ruin their high or may become paranoid about getting caught. They may skip family meals, holiday gatherings, or avoiding going away on vacation, knowing it will be more difficult to obtain their substance of choice. Many clients describe a shrinking geographical circle that centers around their home and their supply.

• *Cognitively*—When under the influence, most people do not realize their own impairment. However, those around them notice this quite easily. As people recover, the most common statement in this area is, "I'm finally coming out of the fog." Neuroscience research confirms this, stating that during the first ninety days of sobriety, a person's brain is healing and returning to its most functional level. We can track the high correlation between drinking and poor decision-making by rates of arrests while people are intoxicated. Over the years I have heard so many people tell me that when they were using, they acted in ways that they would *never* act if they were sober. By a person's behaviors, they show they are not thinking correctly.

• *Emotionally*—Joy disappears, laughter (if present at all) is on the surface, and the endless cycle of chasing the feeling of *numb* begins. Many people using substances are trying to avoid their feelings, the memory of trauma, the stress of their day-to-day lives, and reality, choosing instead to create a false emotion through their substance that produces unnaturally high amounts of dopamine and serotonin and shortcuts the natural processes of these neurochemicals. The rates of involuntary hospital admissions and suicide attempts are significantly higher in populations of people who are using and abusing substances. Using substances leads to feelings of anxiety, guilt, shame, and depression. Many people get to the point where they don't necessarily want to kill themselves, but feel so bad they just "didn't want to wake up in the morning."

• *Financially*—This area is one my clients insisted I add to my list. Regardless of how much money you had to start with, addiction will rob you of large percentages of this money. A coworker of mine would have clients add up all the money they spent on alcohol and/or drugs in the past year. The numbers were staggering! This exercise allowed clients to recognize how much money they could save, what material possessions they would be able to have, or things they would be able to experience if they were not spending this money on alcohol and/or drugs.

P.E.A.R.L.S.

If you have experienced an addiction in your life, or know someone who has, you can most likely recognize some, if not all of these symptoms. As a therapist, I want to help my clients find answers to these problems. I have come up with an acronym, PEARLS, to address each of these problems listed above.

Pray—To address the negative effects of substances on you *spiritually*

Exercise—To address the negative effects of substances on you *physically*

Attend an AA meeting—To address the negative effects of substances on you *socially*

Read—To address the negative effects of substances on you *cognitively*

Laugh—To address the negative effects of substances on you *emotionally*

Save—To address the negative effects of substances on you *financially*

The acronym PEARLS can be used to remember these six areas. So, let's explore this list again and see how engaging in these solutions can benefit someone in the recovery process:

• *Spiritually—Pray*. Prayer is key to a recovery process. Just as there are large differences in people and personalities, we can expect there to be large differences in the type, amount, and posture of prayer. But taking this on in a very general sense, most people will agree on the importance of prayer. In its most basic form, it is a time of focused thought (meditation) and communication with a power that is greater than ourselves. If the person struggling with substance use disorder understands they cannot stop on their own, they need to ask for help from a power that is outside of and stronger than they are. They might ask God for help in the morning and thank Him for help in the evening. A simple place to start would be practicing *gratitude* in the morning and evening.

• *Physically—Exercise*. Exercise is important for a variety of health reasons. I recognize that this will look different for different people. Whether you are going into a weight-lifting gym and bench pressing three hundred pounds or taking a twenty-minute walk, you should be making regular attempts to care for and strengthen your body. The act and commitment of exercise demonstrates to yourself that your body is important and your health matters. When you can obtain this routine and pattern of thinking, why would you be willing to put toxins into your body, which you are actively trying to take care of and improve? Medical experts have been telling us consistently for decades about the positive effects of exercise including controlling weight, managing blood pressure/blood sugars, increasing memory/judgment, reducing risks for cancer, falls, heart disease, and improving sleep and sexual health. Also, exercise releases the chemicals serotonin and dopamine into our bodies, increasing our mood and mental health (we will talk more about this in the **Cognitively** section).

• *Socially—Attend an AA meeting*. Attending an AA meeting can begin to reverse the isolation that was brought on by ongoing substance use. Connection is so important to each and every human being. Granted, as an introvert, this can be difficult and the last thing you feel like doing some days, but that does not make it any less important. People were created for community and relationships, but the use of drugs over time can make these things very difficult. When getting sober, it is important to share the struggle with others who can help you carry your burdens.

Many grandparents and parents warn youngsters about the friends they hang out with because they recognize that "you become who you hang out with" or "bad company corrupts good character" (*Holy Bible,* NIV, 1 Corinthians 15:33). Surround yourself with positive people, who uplift you and add quality to your life, and you will begin to notice a big difference. Be careful not to judge the whole AA program after attending one or two meetings. Meetings are made up of people who are also healing from their hurts and hang-ups, so you should not expect everyone there to be *fixed* or without their problems.

Take what you need and stick with it. Find an AA (or NA) meeting that works for you—a meeting that has people who have been through what you are going through and have found what you are looking for. Let them help you get there by following their recommendations and doing what they did. Remember, these are people who have been in your shoes and can help you if you let them.

I believe this area is important enough to take a side note. Something I have been telling clients for years is to create a *recovery support team*. Think about any sports team. If you had only one player or one position, it would be a fairly ineffective team. Well, that is what it would be like if you were trying to get sober on your own. So, you might think, "I'll get a sponsor." A sponsor is a great start, but I do not know of any teams who have won championships with just two players. So, build a full team. Finding different people with different strengths, personalities, and timeframes is important. Find someone who is a morning person, someone who is a night owl. Find someone who is sweet, compassionate, and full of empathy. Find someone who is straightforward, in your face, and will tell you how it is, to put you in your place. Find someone who is walking along the same path as you, someone a few steps ahead of you, and someone you feel has arrived at the destination you are heading toward. By doing this, you can put together a comprehensive support team and drastically increase your chances at success.

• *Cognitively—Read.* Read something positive. Many people can remember the PSAs about the negative effects of drugs on the brain, but how do we go about fixing the problem? The brain is an amazing organ and can heal just as your skin heals from a cut or your bone heals when it's in a cast. Creating new neural pathways is as easy (or as hard) as creating a new habit. The brain has to be trained to think differently. In combination with the new friends and new conversations, it is important to begin putting new ideas into the brain. This can be done through the aforementioned attendance at AA/NA meetings (or church gatherings). Additionally, this should also be accompanied by individual training through reading and studying positive literature. What I suggest is to read something daily. Read an article on the negative effects of addiction, read a few pages of the AA/NA book, read a chapter of the Bible, read *Chicken Soup for the Soul*, read a daily recovery blog, or read something positive and uplifting that will help you stay sober.

• *Emotionally—Laugh.* Laughter is the best medicine. This statement is a biblical truth from Proverbs 17:22, but is also based on the research done by social scientists that agree on the profound improvement in people's physical health based on their emotional health. We all know from experience that it feels good to laugh and that laughter can lighten some of the heaviest and darkest moods. When people get sober after a long period of using substances, they are almost surprised by this new ability to laugh and feel genuine happiness again. Find something to laugh at every day.
With the abundance of memes and YouTube videos, it should not be hard to find something that you can laugh at. Whether your style is old episodes of sitcoms or old movies, funny cat videos, comics, knock-knock jokes, whatever works. Going back to the idea of creating a support team, find someone who has a similar sense of humor and who you are always finding yourself laughing with so hard your side hurts or you are crying from laughter. Call them every day, hang out with them as often as you can, follow them on social media, or just use them when you need a little emotional *pick me up*.

• *Financially—Save.* As mentioned before, this is the most recent addition to my acronym, as the clients I worked with continued to report how bad their finances were affected by their substance abuse. To combat this deficit, save money daily. My disclaimer: I am not a financial planner and these are only a few suggestions that might be helpful in this area, certainly not an exhaustive list.

1.) If you don't have one already, open a bank account. This is something that many people may fear, but it can actually help them to save money.

2.) Turn down the debit card, which often provides access too easily for someone to act impulsively in early recovery.

3.) Have pay checks directly deposited into a savings account.

4.) Have two separate accounts—first, create a *rainy day* account, and second, start a *just for the fun of it* account. Not only will it feel great to be able to afford those unexpected costs that seem to come out of nowhere, but putting money aside for a big trip, experience, activity, or large purchase item will provide an added incentive to save money and reward yourself for having the freedom to achieve this saving. In recovery, all purchases, large or small, provide an opportunity to express gratitude to God for His provision and your freedom from substances.

5.) Find a deal or simply skip it. If you are able to buy a similar product for less money, do it. These small changes can add up in a big way. If you don't need it, think about just skipping it for today, knowing you are saving that money into one of your two funds (*rainy day* or *just for the fun of it*).

6.) If you like dealing in cash, you can get two envelopes and add money to them every day, week, month, or whatever works for you.

7.) Give generously. This financial principle seems counterintuitive, but it is tried and true. Find an organization/cause that you can support and give financially to support it. If you are going to a local church or organized AA/NA meetings, putting something in the baskets can be a great place to start.

The concept behind the acronym PEARLS is to develop daily practices to address each of the areas that were negatively affected by addiction. If the addictive behaviors occurred daily, do these things daily. If the behaviors are less frequent, think about how you can incorporate each of these practices into your weekly rhythms. These routines can help anyone, not just those struggling with substance use disorders. So, I invite you to join me as we continue to work on being better every day—pray, exercise, attend a meeting, read, laugh, and save.

Overall, I hope you have been able to gain some insight into who I am and some of the ways I have been able to help those suffering from substance use disorders. Remember, if you are trying to help someone who is struggling with addictive behaviors, they need to know you are with them. Reassure them that you have no judgment, and you will stick with them through the process. Encourage them to seek out an AA or NA meeting, to pick up the *Alcoholics Anonymous* book, and find others who have been able to achieve long-term sobriety. I often tell people to follow these three basis practices: "Go to meetings, get a sponsor, and work the steps." Pray for them. Pray with them. Seek out the wisdom found in the Holy Bible. Utilize the local church, mature Christians, and prayer warriors. God has always been in the business of rescuing people from their troubles. God can deliver people from the chains of addiction.

PSYCHOLOGISTS
&
PSYCHIATRISTS

Psychological and Spiritual Dynamics of Addiction

By Rev. Jared Pingleton, Psy.D.

Introduction to Addiction

Addiction is an ugly, unpleasant, and unsavory topic that no one likes to talk about. But addiction is unfortunately an extremely widespread reality in the United States of America. It is estimated that more than one in eight Americans over the age of twelve meet criteria for Alcohol Use Disorder, and that rate has been escalating for some time. More than 130 people die in America every day from an opioid overdose. Collectively, more than one in six Americans over the age of twelve struggle with a substance abuse problem, and untold more millions struggle with behavioral or process addictions.

Addiction is a complex and epidemic bio/psycho/spiritual/ social disorder, which creates a much higher cost to society than all heart conditions, cancers, and diabetes combined. Substance abuse alone costs the US economy over 1.25 trillion dollars each year in terms of workplace unproductivity, healthcare expenses, and crime-related costs (and this figure does not include the incalculable toll of behavioral addictions such as compulsive or excessive gambling, sex, pornography, shopping and spending, eating disorders, intense exercise, internet and technology including video games and social media, thrill seeking risks, and work). Chemical addictions cause or contribute to more than seventy other conditions, which require medical care—thus nearly one-third of all hospital costs are linked to substance use. Additionally, 85 percent of all inmates in American corrections systems are substance involved.

Obviously, not just the individual is negatively impacted. The truth is that addiction affects not only the addict but everyone around them. In this way addiction produces a nightmarishly insidious *trickle-down* effect from the individual to their family and even society as a whole.

Although addicts generally try to hide their addiction or be secretive about their addiction, all relationships in their family are affected. Communication is strained. Trust is eroded, and a myriad of other difficulties and dysfunctions are the consequence of addiction. Rates for divorce, emotional/physical/sexual abuse, domestic violence, scholastic underperformance and dropouts, criminal behavior, mental health disorders, teenage pregnancy, physical disease, juvenile delinquency, relational dysfunctions, secondary addictions (where family members themselves turn to addictive substances and/or behaviors to try to cope), and much more escalate dramatically in an addict's home. Furthermore, missed work, job loss, unpaid debts, missed payments, late fees, property foreclosures, bankruptcies, and a host of other problems created by addictions often plunge the addict, along with their family, into poverty, and even homelessness.

The multigenerational legacy of addiction is toxic—the Adult Children of Alcoholics (ACOA) organization verifies that all kinds of dysfunctionality, other addictions, mental and relational health problems, and spiritual struggles are a huge consequence of addiction in the family. Exodus 20:5 profoundly and poignantly observes that the sins of the parents exert destructive impact upon children to the third and fourth generations.

DEFINITIONS OF ADDICTION

So what constitutes an addiction? Functional, practical definitions of addiction include the following:
- *Anything that controls me instead of me controlling it*
- *Anything that comes in between me and God (operational idolatry)*
- *Anything I regurlarly turn to or depend upon to medicate or soothe my pain*

In general, there are two broad categories of addiction: chemical and behavioral. Chemical addictions include any mood-altering substance (alcohol, prescription medication, illegal or recreational drugs, caffeine, nicotine, sugar) which a person uses inappropriately and/or excessively. Behavioral addictions are any compulsive or excessive or habitual activities, which produce a rush or a high and become life-controlling (e.g., gambling, sex/pornography, work, binge eating, shopping/spending, over exercising, internet/electronics/video games, thrill-seeking/risky activities, etc.).

All addiction becomes a neurological disorder when a person, over time, engages in repetitive behavior, which causes the brain's reward system or pleasure center to progressively seek more of the same stimuli to obtain the same desired response—despite harmful consequences. This habitual ritual creates a self-reinforcing, destructive pattern, which is neuropsychologically reinforced and physiologically imbedded by means of the release of powerful neurochemicals in the brain. Thus, addiction can literally control—and destroy—one's life.

DIAGNOSTICS OF ADDICTION

There are several classic identifying signs and symptoms of addiction in an individual:

1. Denial: The hallmark of all addictive dynamics ["I really don't have a problem" "I can quit any time I want to" "I just had a couple of beers/joints/hits/pills" "It actually isn't that bad" "Everybody is doing it"]. These are typical efforts to minimize, justify, normalize, and rationalize the addiction.

2. Dysfunction: When the addict begins to display deterioration in their behavior [lying, stealing, spending large sums of money on their habit], appearance [often they will neglect routine hygiene due to being narrowly focused on their habit(s)], responsibilities [work productivity diminishes] and relationships [they will often neglect and/or abuse and exploit others in their life].

3. Dependence: The person's belief that they cannot be happy or even live without the addiction, leading to developing a psychological reliance on the addiction.

4. Destruction: The brain becomes habituated to the chemical or behavior progressively craving more and more of the same stimulus to derive the same result—creating adverse consequences and a self-reinforcing, self-perpetuating drive for more of the same indulgence resulting in devastated brains, bodies, relationships, and lives.

CONTRIBUTING FACTORS TO ADDICTION

1. Sin: Everyone suffers painful effects from three distinct yet interrelated areas. We are all negatively impacted by the reality of humans' universal fallen nature (see Genesis 3; Romans

3:23). Additionally, all humans suffer consequences of their own harmful choices (Romans 6:20-23; Galatians 6:7). And all people are wounded by being sinned against by others (as per the adage "hurt people hurt people").

2. Trauma: Many addictions are initiated in response to feeling overwhelmed with stress and being unable to cope with unforeseen and/or overwhelming traumatic and/or traumatizing events.

3. Grief and Loss: Feeling unable to cope with a new painful reality after a significant loss (including death, divorce, job loss, physical injury/disability/illness, assault, financial reversals, etc.) causes many people to turn to life-controlling substances and/or behaviors.

4. Faulty Learning : Dysfunctional families often de-monstrate addictiveness, which models and teaches children to emulate those decisions and activities as a maladaptive coping mechanism.

5. Genetics: Some people have inherited predispositions or proneness to addiction.

6. Co-occurring Disorders—often mental health issues or physical health issues create reliance on addictive ways to medicate the emotional and/or physical pain a person is suffering (including unintentional habit-forming reliance on prescribed medications), and vice versa.

7. Environmental and/or Situational Factors: Many addicts are introduced to addictive substances and/or behaviors through peers, military experiences, dependence on prescribed med-ication for pain, influences of friends, etc.

Frequently more than one of the above factors is involved in a person's struggles with life-controlling chemicals and behaviors. Regardless of the cause(s), every human being struggles with at least being tempted to inappropriately turn to potential addictions to medicate their pain, simply because that is the nature of the human condition. The truth about addiction is that it affects the entirety of our being: mentally, physically, relationally, emotionally, and spiritually.

Christians believe Romans 3:23 teaches us that all humans are inherently sinful and thus fail to glorify God in their own abilities, strength, or resources. It has been correctly said that the ground at the foot of the cross is level. We are all lost and utterly without hope in and of ourselves. But the good news—no, great news, of the gospel is redemption—that we have a hope, and not just a heavenly hope in eternity but real hope right now on earth because of Jesus Christ's life, death, and resurrection, which gives us victory. When an addict hits rock bottom, they often have nowhere to look but up. Any treatment regimen or program that fails to emphasize the spiritual transformation process involved in recovery will not achieve the kind of success that can be obtained by comprehensively treating the whole person as well as addressing the root causes of the addiction(s) rather than just treating the surface symptoms.

DYNAMICS OF ADDICTION

There are several classic dynamics of addictive-generating families, social systems, organizations, and churches. These characteristics are universally present in all addictive phenomena and can help us accurately identify and understand the nature and processes of addiction. They are also epigenetic, thereby helping to self-perpetuate addictiveness and addictive patterns. The following are typical dynamics of addiction and how they must be confronted and dealt with:

1. *Silence* –> we must *end the silence* of addictions.
2. *Secrecy* –> we must *expose the secrecy* of addictions.
3. *Shame* –> we must *eliminate the shame* of addictions.
4. *Stigma* –> we must *erase the stigma* of addictions.

In order to successfully deal with these core dynamics of the addictive process, we must first conduct a fearless and courageous inventory of ourselves and our intrinsic proneness to addiction. Developing this crucial sense of self-awareness is essential in order to understand one's vulnerability to life-controlling substances and/or behaviors. The acronym "HALT-B" is useful in explaining our universal human susceptibility and vulnerability to addictions. People are most apt to become addicts under the following conditions. When we are:

1. Hungry—we instinctively seek to fill our inner emptiness (physically, emotionally, and/or spiritually) with artificial and unhealthy but convenient and/or easily available things and actions when we are depleted and our resistances are down.

2. *Angry*—we are tempted to act out our pain and hurts with destructive substitutes when we are upset instead of talking and working them out (interestingly, rage-aholics can literally become physiologically addicted to their own brain chemistry, which is altered during experiences of extreme anger). One key distinction between unhealthy people, couples, families, and churches is that unhealthy people *act out their feelings*, whereas healthy people, couples, families, and churches *talk out their feelings*.

3. *Lonely*—we intuitively realize it is not good for humans to be alone (Genesis 2:18), thus we are often prone to reflexively but inappropriately soothe our pain when isolated.

4. *Tired*—we are most vulnerable to succumbing to temptation when our resistances are depleted, overtaxed, or exhausted and we are at a weak point.

5. *Bored*—we seek stimulation, excitement, and/or fulfillment in counterfeit, unhealthy but readily available (think *quick fix*) ways to avoid facing our pain when we are not occupied with meaningful and productive activity.

None of us are immune from the temptations to inappropriately medicate and/or act out our pain. Again, we are all human. We have all messed up. We are all sinners and thus have no right to judge anyone (including beating up ourselves!). We must foremost strive to honestly face ourselves without silence, secrecy, shame, or stigma and reach out for help as we support everyone in our family to do the same. Additionally, we need to be aware of when we are hungry, angry, lonely, tired, and/or bored since those normal human states of need may trigger addictive responses.

FAMILY SYSTEM ROLES IN CODEPENDENCY

Whereas the term *codependency* has perhaps been overused in the past several years, there nonetheless exist some fairly universal, typical dysfunctional roles of codependency within a typical addict's family system which can help us understand how to bring help, healing, and hope to addicts and their families. To be codependent means that family members unknowingly but automatically assume various roles in order to cope with the pain, problems, and pathos caused by addiction.

However, these roles all function to ironically exacerbate and even perpetuate the addictive dynamics in the family because they unintentionally enable the addictive process to continue. This is done by ignoring the seriousness and/or scope of the problem, not wanting to confront the addict by attempting to keep peace, buying the alcohol/drugs, and generally making excuses for their loved one's unhealthy habits and destructive behaviors. These are all subconsciously enacted in order to seek the addict's acceptance and approval, as well as to try and avoid confrontation and conflict.

Family therapists have identified the following unique, discrete roles (although there can be some overlap and/or combinations) in a typical addict's family:

1. Enabler/Caretaker/Rescuer: This individual insulates the addict by denying and/or excusing the addictive behaviors, is unwilling to hold them accountable, often motivated by fear and shame (is generally the spouse who tries to *protect* the rest of the family, but ironically perpetuates the addiction and problems by trying the same things but expecting different results).

2. Hero/Savior: The overachieving family *superstar* who looks good and is a hard-working perfectionist who tries to hold the family together in an effort to create a sense of normalcy and stability (is often the eldest child as they feel inordinate pressure to try and take on an overly responsible role. By *growing up too fast*, they usually sacrifice an innocent, carefree childhood and consequently hold on to deep resentment as adults).

3. Mascot: This person provides distraction from the family dysfunction by giving comic relief and uses humor to try and minimize or distract from the pain as well as attempts to gain approval (is often the youngest child and many times bottle up their own feelings and become addicts themselves as adults).

4. Scapegoat: This is the individual who receives the blame for the family dysfunction, thereby serving to shield the adults from responsibility and resentment, often creating other problems to deflect attention from the real issues (as they get older, males typically act out their pain violently and/or addictively where females often run away and/or become promiscuous).

5. Lost Child: This person tries to hide out physically and emotionally to avoid conflict and chaos by becoming *invisible*, suppressing or denying their own feelings so they do not *rock the boat* (is often the middle or youngest child, as adults they tend to drift and flounder, not becoming healthy, complete, fulfilled adults).

As you think through these roles, where do you see yourself? Which role or roles do you identify with? How do you see others in your family? Sometimes people relate with parts of several of the above roles in a combination of two or more. Regardless, we need to ask ourselves—what do these roles do to ourselves, and how does that affect the others in our family? In what ways are we helping? And in what ways are we unintentionally contributing to or perpetuating the problem?

It is both natural and understandable to become frustrated, angry, and even bitter toward a loved one when they habitually lie, deceive, manipulate, steal, exploit, and disappoint us with their addiction. Broken promises betray our trust, and repetitive relapse is deeply disappointing and can cause us to despair. But it is essential to understand that treatment and recovery is a multifaceted and complex process.

PHYSIOLOGICAL, PSYCHOLOGICAL, & SPIRITUAL ASPECTS OF ADDICTION

All potentially addictive chemical substances exert euphoric effects in the brain by activating its pleasure centers. The use of drugs or alcohol stimulates the brain by mimicking natural neurochemicals that it normally produces and releases into the blood stream. Because alcohol and drugs produce similar chemicals, the neurons responsible for normal brain functions become inhibited and no longer perform as they normally do.

Therefore, the artificial stimulation of the pleasure center of the brain induced by alcohol and drugs creates a distinct *high* or sense of euphoria. Persons who use alcohol and drugs for this purpose are often driven to seek that same feeling of euphoria again and again, thereby developing a self-perpetuating addictive cycle. Many neurological scientists believe that once these mesolimbic pathways have been established, they are permanent. Addictions literally alter and impair brain chemistry and functioning.

The physiological and psychological effects of prolonged addictive substances and behaviors are extensive and potentially cause serious harm or damage. The brain's regions and processes, which are impacted by chemical substances, govern extensive cognitive functions such as learning, reasoning, attention, memory, and impulse control. Many chemicals can also cause irreversible cellular neuronal damage resulting in seizures, strokes, ataxia (losses of muscular, visual, speech, and other sensory functionality), and even death.

Psychologically, most addicts are mentally preoccupied with their addictive substance(s)/behavior(s) and typically demonstrate an often-desperate fear of loss of control without the addiction. Unable to cope, an emotional dependency is thus created. This is exacerbated when the addict may try to quit, and then experiences the negative effects of withdrawal.

Once tolerance has been chemically established in the brain, the attempted cessation of the addictive substance often causes multiple other problems including nausea, headaches, disrupted sleep patterns, weight loss/gain, increased or decreased activity levels, pupillary dilation, fear, worry, anxiety, depression and many other physical and emotional difficulties, making it very difficult for an addict to stop.

Furthermore, some research suggests that certain individuals demonstrate a genetic predisposition to certain substances. Many persons have genetic, inherited DNA markers putting them at risk for addiction. Additionally, when brain chemistry and functionality are altered, one's unfettered choice is progressively more difficult to exercise. Consequently, for all these physiological reasons, many experts believe chemical addiction to be a disease.

However, others believe a strict disease conceptualization of addiction is overly simplistic and even dangerous to only define it as a disease. Among other things, this kind of black-and-white thinking can lead to inaccurately believing one's *disease* is untreatable and/or incurable or to dismiss it as exclusively physiological, thus avoid taking responsibility to enter treatment and work toward recovery.

The concurrent reality is that all addictions require initial decisions to activate and then to progressively continue indulging in the destructive addictive substance(s) and/or behavior(s). This behavioral choice functionally depicts the insidious and deteriorative dynamic of sin—all of which is both an artificial or counterfeit approximation of and substitute for the authentic gifts of God.

Yet it is likewise overly simplistic and even dangerous to only define addiction as strictly a choice. To not acknowledge the very real physiological components of the addiction process can in some cases be medically dangerous. Additionally, thinking that addiction is only a choice can lead to feelings of hopelessness, self-condemnation, and shame.

Contemporary research, as well as many scientists and scholars, agree that in many ways evidence suggests addiction possesses qualities of both disease and willful choice, and that each reinforces the other. Therefore, the question is more correctly understood as not one of *either/or* but of *both/and*. Initially, the person exercises free choices but once the brain chemistry is severely altered such that they lose control of their behavior(s), at this point, addiction is more clearly characterized by a disease model and as a degenerative process.

Regardless of confusion or controversy, God addresses both the personal choice and disease concepts. Fortunately, God heals all of our diseases, as well as forgives all our sins when we yield ourselves to Him (Psalms 103:3). Therefore, we have hope for immediate spiritual redemption as well as ongoing physical, mental, relational, and emotional healing and restoration as we reach out for help.

TREATMENT OF ADDICTION

Given that addictions are such complex, multifaceted phenomena, it stands to reason that effective treatment requires a comprehensive, multidisciplinary approach. To effectively treat addiction, one must address the intricate and interactive physiological, psychological, emotional, interpersonal, and spiritual elements involved. Addicts do not become hooked overnight, and they do not recover overnight. Nor can addictions be successfully addressed in isolation and aloneness. One needs to face themselves, reach out, admit they need help, and discover and experience healing connection and community.

In order to best facilitate recovery, it is imperative that all members of the family seek to become healthy. Individuals and families who exemplify the following characteristics create the healthiest atmosphere for recovery. Like effective treatment programs or centers, they must become:

1. Safe: They must strive to be safe physically, emotionally, and spiritually. They must seek to become a secure sanctuary of safety and a reliable resource of refuge.

2. Spiritual: They must learn about, internalize, and apply regular disciplines of prayer, devotional reading, church attendance, accountability, and other spiritual resources.

3. Supportive: They must develop trusted, mature, healthy relationships with others who will encourage, confront, comfort, and stabilize the addict by giving them acceptance, approval, and affirmation.

4. Strong: They must learn to become honest, vulnerable, resilient, and durable.

Additionally, addicts and their families must seek to heal and grow. While it is true that the family system is likely involved in the cause of addiction, it is also true that the family system can help be the conduit for the cure of addiction! Most people naturally experience their greatest satisfactions as well as sorrows, triumphs as well as tragedies, and pleasure as well as pain within the context of their family. Therefore, it stands to reason that God designed the family to be the primary unit of both relationship and of redemption. God simply delights in transforming blessings out of our brokenness! Specifically, families need to become messengers who communicate the love, grace, and mercy of God outlined in Titus 2:11-14:

For the grace of God has appeared that offers salvation to all people. It teaches us to say "No" to ungodliness and worldly passions, and to live self-controlled, upright and godly lives in this present age, while we wait for the blessed hope—the appearing of the glory of our great God and Savior, Jesus Christ, who gave Himself for us to redeem us from all wickedness and to purify for Himself a people that are his very own, eager to do what is good (NIV).

ADDICTION AND THE HOPE OF CHANGE: PROCESSES, STAGES, AND RESOURCES

BY DR. DAVID JENKINS

INTRODUCTION

Every contributor to this project is grateful you are reading it. If you put all of the authors and editors in one room, there would be much about addiction where there is overwhelming consensus and agreement. One of those areas would be the cost of addiction to persons, families, communities, and society at large. Recent economic costs of substance abuse exceed seven hundred billion dollars annually when you consider alcohol, tobacco, and other substances. And those costs occur every year. When you also add in the projected costs of behavioral (process) addictions, this figure rises to at least one trillion dollars.

Additionally, the opioid crisis alone has recently contributed over five hundred billion dollars to this economic devastation. Talk about a primary reason for chronic budget deficits and national debt! Yet, look at how relatively little attention is paid to this issue in our media, healthcare efforts, and social outreach. Based on accumulated evidence over the past decade or two, I believe substance abuse is the top societal problem in the United States. In large part this is because just considering economic costs is overwhelming, but when also considering *costs* that you cannot put a dollar amount on (e.g., family disruption, domestic violence, effects of deep chronic shame, etc.), it becomes increasingly apparent we have to confront the realities of addiction in order for us to be restored and flourish. Imagine a day, though, when we actually effectively, competently, and compassionately change this!

A second area of consensus among the contributors would be that addiction affects the total person—mind, body, spirit, and relationships. Certainly, some are more impacted than others and not every person who struggles with addiction is affected in the same way. This means that recovery from addiction will also not look the same for every individual—one size does not fit all!

So, recognizing our consensus that the total person is involved in addiction and recovery points us toward the need for encouraging a wide variety of ways people can recover. While this is an area of consensus, the varied pathways into and out of addiction unfortunately also lead to strongly held convictions about what addiction and recovery *should* look like; so much so, that those who struggle with substance use and addictive disorders are still too often forced to fit a particular mold rather than being treated with the dignity of being their own individual with the freedom and responsibility to make and live by their own decisions, for good or for bad.

Third, every contributor believes there is hope for those who struggle with addiction and those who love them! People who are not involved professionally with addiction and recovery in areas of practice, research, and social policy too often experience the differing opinions where there is not consensus in ways that can lead to confusion, frustration, resignation, and maybe even demoralization. If the *experts* don't agree on what to do, then what hope is there?

The goal of this chapter is to provide you with an overview of addiction and recovery based on broad areas of consensus. We do understand much about how people change in general and specifically regarding addiction. Also, much consensus suggests people go through a process of addiction even though that process might look different for each individual. And, importantly, increasing evidence about how recovery occurs can be utilized along with resources to enhance it. Think of these areas as providing key orientation points much like having a map and compass. Okay, to modernize, hopefully this chapter can provide some GPS coordinates and waypoints that not only provide direction but also the ability to *recalculate* when necessary or helpful. In doing so, our longing is that you experience renewed and increased hope on your journey through addiction and recovery and into a life of serenity and peace!

MODEL OF ADDICTION AND RECOVERY

Most people in the addiction field would agree that an integrated model for understanding addiction and recovery is one of the most effective ways to remain oriented when dealing with addiction and recovery. An integrated model should consider elements of dimensions, domains, and levels involved in addiction and recovery.

Perhaps the most common holistic understanding is the *bio-psycho-socio-spiritual* model. This model focuses on aspects of addiction that include the following **dimensions**: biological (e.g., elements of brain, heredity and genetics, etc.); psychological (e.g., elements of expectancies, thoughts and emotions, etc.); sociological (e.g., elements of primary relationships with significant others, community involvement, etc.); and spiritual (e.g., elements of belief in power greater that ourselves, purpose in living, etc.).

While these dimensions are important, it is also helpful to think in terms of various **domains** within and between the dimensions. These domains include thoughts, feelings, behaviors, relationships, and environments. Along with dimensions and domains, an integrated model will also consider **levels** including individual, familial, communal, and societal. These specific aspects of the model in each dimension, domain, and level can be thought of as **elements**. Taken together, an integrated model such as this one can help provide stability and direction when navigating through the various dimensions, domains, and levels involved in addiction and recovery. Each of these areas can involve resistance and resilience to addiction, as well as predisposition and vulnerability.

One of the greatest challenges in the area of addiction is the tendency to engage in reductionism. Often this is based upon personal experiences, biases, and traditions rather than trustworthy evidence across the field of addiction theory, research, and practice. For example, some tend to reduce addiction and its treatment to only or mainly the biological dimension, while others reduce addiction to only or mainly the spiritual dimension. Similarly, others believe addiction only or mainly involves the domain of thoughts or feelings, while others reduce addiction to only or mainly the relationship domain.

Consider the parable of the blind men and the elephant. Each one had an experience of only one aspect of the elephant based on which part they encountered and each forcefully argued that an elephant was definitively and only like the part they encountered. One said it is like a snake (the trunk), another a rope (the tail), and yet another a tree trunk (the leg), and so on. Each had a grasp on one aspect of what an elephant is like, but none had a holistic perspective. Imagine how the conversation would change if their blindness was suddenly healed and they were each able to see, understand, and experience the others' perspectives!

Try to remember the last time you did some cloud watching on a clear spring day. For some of you, it may not have been since you were a child!

Do you remember when you identified a figure in a cloud, and as you continued to watch, another cloud (or lobe of the same cloud) interacted with and maybe merged with the other? Remember how your interpretation of the original cloud formation changed? Often, the new shape was perceived and interpreted completely differently. There was distinctiveness, but yet also blending of shapes, textures, and colors—and that was part of the mystery of it all! In a similar way, the elements that make up dimensions, domains, and levels interact with each other in ways that morph and change the way addiction and recovery is perceived and experienced. There's a mystery to that process, even when it's a struggle. Hopefully, though, this brief discussion of how to think about addiction and recovery will help clarify rather than confuse, and motivate rather than overwhelm.

STAGES OF CHANGE

Over thirty years ago, on their own, Dr. Carlo DiClemente and Dr. James Prochaska began studying how people change addictive behavior. They began this area of study with people who wanted to make changes in smoking tobacco and developed the Stages of Change (SOC) model (see *Figure 1*), which often helps illustrate what is known as the Transtheoretical Model (TTM). Over the years, this has become one of the most widely accepted and used models for how people change generally, but specifically when changing addictive behavior.

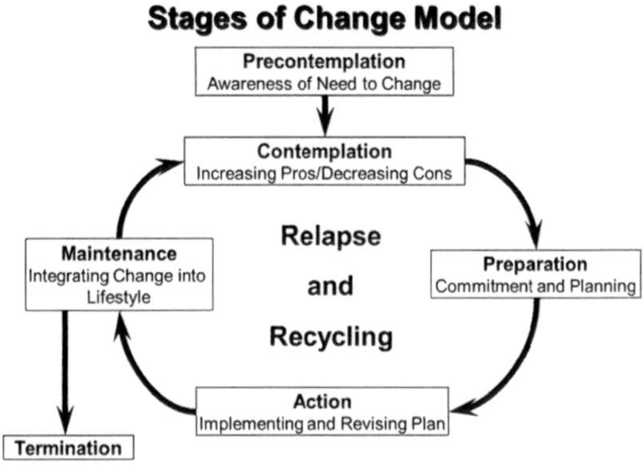

Figure 1.
Stages of Change
(DiClemente, 2018)

Stages of Change Model

Precontemplation
Awareness of Need to Change

Contemplation
Increasing Pros/Decreasing Cons

Maintenance
Integrating Change into Lifestyle

Relapse and Recycling

Preparation
Commitment and Planning

Action
Implementing and Revising Plan

Termination

Initially, the SOC was applied to changing from addiction to recovery. Nearly twenty years ago, though, Dr. DiClemente also applied the SOC model to people changing from not using (since people don't start off addicted) to becoming addicted. In other words, people changed *into* addiction and not just *out of* addiction. Although Dr. DiClemente has much more to say about the stages, processes, mechanisms, and indicators of change in the second edition of his book, this general model of change can be very helpful to those who are involved in a change process of some kind, particularly when it may involve addictive behavior.

The five stages of the SOC model, each with tasks and goals, are briefly described below.

The first stage is ***precontemplation***. This is the stage in which there is little or no consideration of change of the current pattern of behavior in the foreseeable future. Often, people in this stage may be described as being *in denial*, but this is really not an accurate view of precontemplation. They simply may have never considered (or had to) that something about their behavior needed changing in spite of how obvious it may be to others. Classic denial arises after, not before, a painful thought, feeling, or circumstance occurs. The primary tasks in the precontemplation stage are to increase awareness of the need for change, to increase concern about the current pattern of behavior, and to envision the possibility of change. The primary goal of the precontemplation stage is for the individual to give serious consideration of change for the behavior in view.

Contemplation is the stage of change where the current pattern of behavior and the potential for change is examined in a risk-reward analysis. Ambivalence about changing is a hallmark characteristic of this stage so it is important to help develop intrinsic motivation for change and a sense of self-efficacy that the person is capable of making the change. The primary tasks of the contemplation stage include analysis of the pros and cons of the current behavior pattern and of the costs and benefits of change. Reasons for and against both remaining the same and for changing need to be considered in a way so the person owns their freedom and responsibility for change without undue outside influence. A second task of the contemplation stage is decision-making. The primary goal of contemplation is to have an honest consideration that leads to a decision to change.

In the *preparation* stage, the individual makes a commitment to take action to change the behavior pattern and develops a plan and strategy for change. Here, the primary tasks are to increase commitment and to create a plan for change. There continues to be a need to resolve ambivalence and develop self-efficacy, but these are in light of a decision to change made during the contemplation stage. Before making change in the specific area(s) of concern, the individual may need to develop skills and put them in place before change occurs. The primary goal of the preparation stage, then, is to develop and commit to an action plan to be implemented in the near future.

The fourth stage, *action*, is the stage in which the individual implements the plan and takes steps to change the current behavior pattern, so they begin to create a new behavior pattern. The primary tasks of this stage include implementing strategies for change, revising the action plan as needed, and sustaining commitment in face of difficulties and challenges. It is important to keep in mind that *progress* and not *perfection* is expected. The primary goal of the action stage is successful action for changing the current pattern of behavior, so a new pattern of behavior becomes established for a significant period of time, typically at least three to six months.

Maintenance is the stage where the new behavior pattern is sustained for an extended period of time and becomes consolidated into the lifestyle of the individual. The primary tasks of the maintenance stage involve sustaining change over time and across a wide range of different situations, integrating the behavior into the person's life, and avoiding slips and relapse back to the old pattern of behavior. The primary goal of the maintenance stage is long-term sustained change of the old pattern and establishment of a new pattern of behavior.

Progression through the first four SOC can take about a year with the maintenance stage taking around six months to establish. Once the behavior change has become normalized in the person's life, *termination* of the change process for the specific behavior in view occurs. The individual has no desire to return to the previous pattern of behavior. Although it is not always considered a formal

---

8. DiClemente, C. (2018). *Addiction and change: How addictions develop and addicted people recover* (2nd ed.). New York, NY: Guilford Press.

stage of change, it is important to remember that termination of the change process is possible and a lifetime of remaining in the maintenance stage does not have to be the case.

The change process is not linear, but cyclical. It is important to remember that *recycling* and *relapse* are processes and are simply part of change. Recycling through stages of the SOC and slips or lapses can occur in a way that enhances learning, commitment, and successful change. Relapse, however, is a return to or re-engaging in the previous behavior pattern that reflects a type of *giving up* on the change process. When managed effectively, relapse is not cause for despair since the person can recycle through the stages of change, building upon what had been previously accomplished.

Remember that people change from non-addiction into addiction, as well as from addiction to recovery. Think of how important this is when considering prevention or early intervention efforts. Consider, too, how the SOC model depends upon how others who want to help relate to the person involved in the change process. At this point, it may be helpful to remember we are all in a change process in one or more areas of our lives at any given moment. Someone may have terminated the change process regarding healthy eating patterns, but they could still be in the contemplation stage when it comes to exercise. Keeping this in mind can help foster genuine humility when approaching those who may be struggling with addiction.

It is also helpful to think about the SOC in the context of the integrated model discussed earlier in the chapter. Change is possible at any given time in one or more elements of dimensions, domains, and levels! One of the greatest challenges of changing addiction is not that there are no options. What makes change so challenging is that there so many options. Which of these are selected and in what possible combinations?

STAGE MODEL OF THE ADDICTIVE PROCESS

One of the most encouraging aspects to keep in mind is that not everyone who uses substances or engages in certain behaviors becomes addicted. For example, we know that 30 percent of the adult population in the United States does not drink alcohol at all—ever. Of the 70 percent of adults who drink alcohol, 70 percent of those will not have any problems related to their use; and if they do, those problems are typically mild and very infrequent. For the 30 percent of those who do have some difficulties related to their use of alcohol, nearly two-thirds will have mild to moderate difficulties.

Many of these individuals will change on their own, with some deciding to not engage in the addictive behavior again and some deciding to continue to use in a nonproblematic way. Those who have the most excessive use and the most severe problems as a result are most likely to need some type of formal help as part of their change process. This general pattern applies to most addictive substances and behaviors.

Similar to the SOC, how someone progresses from nonaddictive use or behavior into addiction is not always a linear process. Throughout more than three decades of work in the addiction field, this author has periodically reviewed various models of the addictive process. A recent summary described one model that still seems to capture the essence of the addictive process, as well as others. The material below is based heavily on this recent summary.

People have tried in a number of ways to understand the process of addiction, how it develops, and the stages someone goes through along the way. A four-stage model (see *Figure 2*.) includes experimentation, social, medicinal, and addictive stages as someone progresses from use to misuse to abuse to dependence to addiction.

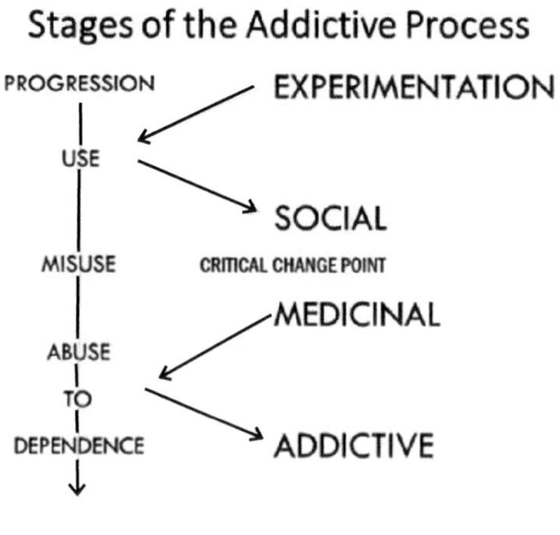

Stages of the Addictive Process

© 2007 David E. Jenkins, Psy.D
Figure 2. Stage Model of the Addictive Process.

The *experimentation* stage is characterized by infrequent use where a substance (or behavior) is tried a few times, generally not more than two to three occurrences. After all, how many times would you try something and still consider it an experiment? Curiosity is often the motive and, as with most experiments, learning is typically the outcome. Most of the time, other people are present in a supportive external environment. Think in terms of peer support versus peer pressure. During experimentation, there may be one-time consequences as part of *learning* that might include consequences such as nausea during use, a hangover after use, or a painfully tight budget after spending too much money. It is important to remember, though, that pain is an effective teacher, so, if someone doesn't learn from the consequences to change the behavior, there may already be indications that trouble is ahead. Based on the results of the *experiment*, someone will decide not to use again or to continue to use, but not repeat painful experiences if those occurred. If use continues, they typically progress to the social stage.

Social use is characterized by nonpatterned use on special occasions, such as parties and holidays. Regular use of small amounts, such as a glass or two of wine with a meal (or a Friday night nickel/dime poker game that doesn't hurt the budget), can also be social use. By definition, other people are typically present. After all, it is not *social* if you're only with *me, myself, and I!* Taste and enjoyment of the occasion for its own sake are acceptable reasons for use, and there are no, or very infrequent, consequences associated with the use. Using the substance or behavior as a regular means of mood management or social engagement is not true social use, even if use only occurs with others around. Most people who use do not progress beyond this stage. The experimentation and social stages are considered as use.

Medicinal. If use progresses beyond the truly social stage, a critical change point occurs. When *reasons* for the use begin to appear, no matter how minor or typical, the use becomes something other than social. Using alcohol, as an example, someone who has

9. Jenkins, D.E. (2019). *How to develop an effective opioid crisis ministry.* In T. Clinton & J. Pingleton (Eds.), *The struggle is real: How to care for mental and relational health needs in the church* (2nd ed.). Bloomington, IN: WestBow Press.

a drink or two a couple of nights a week to help them relax after work, has attached a reason to the use that does not normally need to be there. We can relax after work without consuming alcohol. This is not to say the use has become a problem or they are now addicted. It's simply recognizing that a reason has become attached to the use. Also, notice that this type of use tends to become more of an individual versus social activity. Another early reason for use is enjoyment of the using experience rather than enjoyment of the occasion for its own sake. As use continues, it is more likely to become a regular, customary way of dealing with or escaping from life and/ or relationship problems. Another indicator of the medicinal stage is when *consequences* of use, even minor, begin to appear. Examples could include periodic hangovers, concerns of significant others about use, or using credit cards to cover living expenses.

A third indicator of medicinal use is *constriction of lifestyle* where formerly non-using activities are deferred in favor of those that involve using. Life begins to narrow around the drug/behavior. Once this begins to occur, reasons for using become related to relieving consequences of using. At this point, a very serious but often deceptively subtle cycle begins to occur. This cycle often begins to increase in severity and speed, moving the person increasingly toward the addictive stage. This phase of progression involves substance misuse and abuse. When present, tolerance (needing more of the substance or behavior to achieve the same effect) and withdrawal (unpleasant effects experienced due to not using) characterize dependence and intensify if use progresses into addiction.

The ***addictive*** stage is characterized by tolerance and withdrawal, but also with additional aspects of *craving* and *loss of control.* The person now uses increasing amounts in an attempt to feel *normal* physically and/or mentally and, if deprived of use, withdrawal symptoms are present in the form of physical and/or psychological distress. Consequences of use continue to increase across several life spheres. Due to physiological changes in the body and brain as a result of chronic use, craving for the substance or behavior occurs and the person increasingly loses control of the frequency and amount of their use. Because of these changes, and due to recent advances in neurobiology, the person at this stage is considered by many to have the disease of addiction because of functional and even structural changes in the brain. While many of these changes can improve with recovery, some changes may be permanent leading to persistent challenges and vulnerabilities to recovery. The cycle of binge/intoxication (loss of control), withdrawal/negative affect (withdrawal), and preoccupation/anticipation (craving) now enslaves the person with the acquired disease of addiction.

As you can see, as someone progresses through the process of addiction, the elements of dimensions, domains, and levels are all involved and affected. The stages of change into addiction are apparent. It is important to let this sink in a bit even though it may be painful to do so. In large part, this is how empathy for those who struggle occurs in those who support them.

And for those who are struggling with addiction, perhaps this can help explain why and how your journey has been so difficult at times. Maybe this also a good point to consider vital aspects such as forgiveness of self and others, making amends where needed, and reaching out for help and support from those who genuinely care. As you consider these things, maybe just maybe, you will also experience the rise of hope!

RESOURCES FOR RECOVERY

The good news is that recovery from addiction is possible, and even likely, for many! And this is also true for those who may not struggle with addiction personally, but who love someone who does. Just as there is a range of expressions and experiences of the elements of dimensions, domains, and levels involved in change into addiction, each of these are also involved in change out of addiction and into recovery. Because of this, a continuum of care exists with a range of helpful options to consider. Along this continuum, think in terms of numbers of people, level of use and problem severity, as well as least restrictive alternatives (see *Figure 3*). **Settings** can range from self-help strategies, facilitation of twelve-step attendance, general outpatient counseling, intensive outpatient counseling, short-term residential treatment, long-term residential treatment, and medical detoxification in a hospital or specialized unit. **Modalities** where recovery efforts occur include individual, couple, family, group, and even multi-family group!

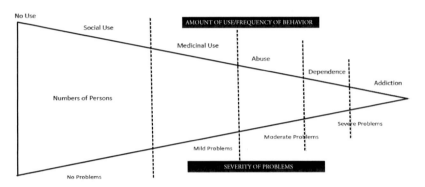

Treatment Settings: Medical Detox; Inpatient; Intensive Outpatient; Residential (e.g., halfway house); Outpatient; Mutual Help; Self
Treatment Modalities: Individual; Group; Family; Multi-family
Treatment Types: CBT; Contingency Management; Community Reinforcement; Motivational Enhancement; Matrix Model; 12-Step
Facilitation; Family Behavior Therapy; Multisystemic Therapy; Multidimensional Family Therapy; Brief Strategic Family Therapy;
Functional Family Therapy; Adolescent Community Reinforcement Approach and Assertive Continuing Care; Relapse Prevention

Figure 3. Continuum of Care and Resources for Recovery

It is important to remember, however, that most people who have addictive difficulties recover on their own without engaging formal treatment, including mutual help groups (MHG). This is sometimes referred to as *natural recovery.* Factors such as problem severity, degree of social support, unsuccessful quit attempts, and analyzing economic costs of the behavior are important considerations that could be effectively enhanced to support natural recovery. Triggers of natural recovery broadly involved stress resulting from loss related to problems with health, relationships, finances, employment, but also included lifestyle changes, changes in perspective regarding substance use, and religious reasons.

Unfortunately, relatively few (less than 25 percent) of those who need treatment access it at all, much less early in the development of addiction.

10 Koob, G.F., & Volkow, N.D. (2016). Neurobiology of addiction: A neurocircuitry analysis. Lancet Psychiatry, 3, 760-763. Retrieved from www.thelancet.com/psychiatry.

11. Bischof, G., Rumpf, H.J., & John, U. (2012). Natural recovery from addiction. In H.J. Shaffer (Ed.) APA Addiction syndrome handbook: Vol.2. Recovery, prevention, and other issues (pp. 133-155). Washington, DC: American Psychological Association. doi:10.1037/13750-006

12. Ibid.

For those who do want or need treatment for addiction, a continuum of options reflects severity of the disorder, intensity and duration of treatment, the degree to which counselors (lay, pastoral, and professional) are involved, and whether medical aspects need to be addressed. Tucker and Simpson described this recovery spectrum from self-change to seeking treatment. Screening and brief interventions, guided self-change, and internet resources have all demonstrated some effectiveness and are consistent with a public health approach.

Counselors must remain humble and keep in mind that nearly three-fourths of those with some difficulties related to their addictive behavior recover without formal treatment. And, although it is a very controversial subject, substantial evidence says a number of those who no longer have symptoms of addictive disorders and were untreated are able to use in moderation without further problems.

Those who seek treatment for addiction, though, tend to have more severe problems so abstinence is the more appropriate goal. This is especially important given that we really can't predict very well who will and who won't be successful in recovery. Often, treatment helps individuals consolidate changes that are already happening in their lives. Wise counselors, as well as clients, will tap into this naturally occurring change process, even when people decide to engage in formal treatment for addictive disorders.

A recent review identified nine evidence-based treatments for Alcohol Use Disorder (which also generally applys to other substances and behaviors) including: cognitive behavior therapy, contingency management, cue exposure therapy, community reinforcement approach, behavioral couples and family treatment, brief interventions, motivational interviewing and motivational enhancement therapy, twelve-step-based therapies, and case management.

Therapist and relationship qualities important in treatment outcome include therapeutic alliance, empathy, directiveness, and confrontation. It is important to note that while positive therapeutic alliance and greater empathy are associated with better outcomes, counselor directiveness and confrontation are associated with poorer outcomes including more client resistance, which is linked with greater frequency and higher quantities of alcohol consumption.

Think back to the SOC model and how the style of interaction between those who help and those who struggle have a lot to do with how the change process goes!

The National Institute on Drug Abuse recently released the third edition of *Principles of Drug Addiction Treatment: A Research-Based Guide*. NIDA regularly reviews and evaluates evidence for the effectiveness of treatments for substance-related and addictive disorders. It is beyond the scope of this chapter to describe each of those treatment options. However, even a brief search of the internet can locate a tremendous amount of helpful information on each of these treatment approaches. One of the most promising areas of treatment research and practice is the use of Medication for Addiction Treatment (MAT), especially for those struggling with addiction to opioids, tobacco, and/or alcohol. Once again, you will be able to recognize elements of dimensions, domains, and levels involved in addiction and recovery.

The internet can be one of the greatest sources of help for those who struggle with addiction and those who love them. While there is a clear risk of finding and using flawed information (sometimes severely flawed), there are several very trustworthy sources of information, much of it geared for the general public and not just addiction professionals. Primary resources include:

• Substance Abuse Mental Health Services Administration (SAMHSA, www.samhsa.gov)

• National Institute on Drug Abuse (NIDA, www.drugabuse.gov)

• National Institute on Alcohol Abuse and Alcoholism (NIAAA, www.niaaa.nih.gov)

• Nova Southeastern University (https://www.nova.edu/gsc/index.html). This website has helpful information about guided self-change.

HOPE

Hope involves expectation that something desired can happen or be obtained. There are also *valuing* and *optimism* aspects to hope. Reflect on the main topics that have been covered. We started by introducing an integrative model for understanding addiction and recovery, followed by looking at the change process generally and specifically applied to addiction and recovery. Then we reviewed the process of addiction with its several stages along with resources for recovery that have evidence to support their use. As this chapter concludes, our hope is that you are more oriented with a clearer sense of direction. We also hope how you perceive and experience addiction and recovery is different and more flexible than when you started the chapter. Most importantly, our hope is that you have more hope—hope based on the high value of your own life and the optimistic expectation that recovery is not only possible for you but likely. May God continue to bless you on your journey!

---

13. *Tucker, J.A., & Simpson, C.A. (2011). The recovery spectrum: From self-change to seeking treatment. Alcohol Research and Health, 33, 371-379. Retrieved from https://www.ncbi.nlm.nih.gov/pmc/articles/PMC3860536/pdf/arh-33-4-371.pdf.*
14. *Ibid.*
15. *Hallgren, K. A., Greenfield, B. L., Ladd, B., Glynn, L. H. and McCrady, B. S. (2012). Alcohol use disorders. In M. Hersen & P. Sturmey (Eds.) Handbook of evidence-based practice in clinical psychology: Adult disorders (pp. 133-165). Hoboken, NJ: John Wiley & Sons.*
16. *Ibid.*
17. *National Institute on Drug Abuse (2018). Principles of drug addiction treatment: A research-based guide (3rd ed.). Retrieved from https://www.drugabuse.gov/download/675/principles-drug-addiction-treatment-research-based-guide-third-edition.pdf?v=87ecd1341039d24b0fd616c5589c2095*

WORKS CITED – JENKINS

Bischof, G., Rumpf, H.J., & John, U. (2012). Natural recovery from addiction. In H.J. Shaffer (Ed.) *APA Addiction syndrome handbook: Vol.2. Recovery, prevention, and other issues* (pp. 133-155). Washington, DC: American Psychological Association. doi:10.1037/13750-006

DiClemente, C. (2018). *Addiction and change*: How addictions develop and addicted people recover (2nd ed.). New York, NY: Guilford Press.

Hallgren, K. A., Greenfield, B. L., Ladd, B., Glynn, L. H. and McCrady, B. S. (2012). Alcohol use disorders. In M. Hersen

& P. Sturmey (Eds.) *Handbook of evidence-based practice in clinical psychology: Adult disorders* (pp. 133-165). Hoboken, NJ: John Wiley & Sons.

Jenkins, D.E. (2019). How to develop an effective opioid crisis ministry. In T. Clinton & J. Pingleton (Eds.), *The struggle is real: How to care for mental and relational health needs in the church* (2nd ed.). Bloomington, IN: WestBow Press.

Koob, G.F., & Volkow, N.D. (2016). Neurobiology of addiction: A neurocircuitry analysis. *Lancet Psychiatry, 3*, 760-763. Retrieved from www.thelancet.com/psychiatry.

National Institute on Drug Abuse (2018). *Principles of drug addiction treatment: A research-based guide* (3rd ed.). Retrieved from https://www.drugabuse.gov/download/675/principles-drug-addiction-treatment-research-based-guide-third-edition.pdf?v=87ecd1341039d24b0fd616c5589c2095

Tucker, J.A., & Simpson, C.A. (2011). The recovery spectrum: From self-change to seeking treatment. *Alcohol Research and Health, 33*, 371-379. Retrieved from https://www.ncbi.nlm.nih.gov/pmc/articles/PMC3860536/pdf/arh-33-4-371.pdf.

Understanding Dual Diagnosis

By Dr. Karl Benzio

In order to define Dual Diagnosis, let me step back and clarify some vocabulary. *Psychology* is the study of why we do what we do—decisions leading to behaviors—and using that information to help us become better, more godly decision-makers so we can achieve our God-given potential. *Psychiatry* is the medical specialty devoted to the study, diagnosis, prevention, and treatment, of our faulty decision-making process. The modern term, *behavioral health*, is more politically acceptable and less stigmatizing than what we've traditionally used—the term psychiatry. Behavioral health/psychiatry is divided into two main categories, mental health/illness is one, and addiction is the other. *Dual diagnosis*, sometimes called co-occurring disorders, is the term behavioral health clinicians use to refer to patients with a diagnosis from both a mental health diagnosis and an addiction diagnosis.

So first let's examine the mental health part of the *dual* in dual diagnosis.

Do I Have a Mental Health Issue?

I look at this a bit differently than most, so hold on. Insecurity, inadequacy, inferiority, shame, guilt, sadness, depression, anxiety, fear, jealousy, anger, bitterness, hopelessness, concentration issues, relationship issues, struggles with self-esteem or identity, peer pressure, people-pleasing, conflict avoidance, or impulsive behaviors—that is just the tip of the iceberg of underlying psychological struggles or symptoms that lead to mental health disorders. And these are just the mild ones. When I was in medical school and I started reading the list of symptoms and disorders for our *Foundations in Psychiatry* class, I panicked as so many video clips of my past experiences flashed through my mind. My overwhelming conclusion was, "I've had many of these symptoms. I'm doomed." If you are normal, and honest, you periodically have similar video clips and thoughts running through your head when you read some of the symptoms I listed, or around New Year's Eve when you want to purge some of your defects and bad habits.

Remember, this book is about pulling back the curtain to understand your mind better so you can be better equipped to understand, persevere, and conquer any struggle intended to steal, kill, and destroy God's plan and blessings for you and your life. So, as I wade into this discussion, relax. Even if you do have a psych diagnosis, like in my life, a diagnosis doesn't have to impair or derail what God desires and where He will take you in your life's journey. This book is intended to not only help you get back on track but also use any past psychiatric struggle to actually strengthen you and powerfully impact others.

So, here's the bottom line regarding whether we have a mental health issue or psychological defect. Like all our bodily organs, we all have corrupted and imperfect brain chemistry/circuits. We all make wrong decisions, both because of our faulty brain chemistry, as well as our wrong decisions, which further damage our brain circuits. We all have distortions, baggage, hurts, wounds, losses, and emotional blinders. We also have limited spiritual awareness and connection with God and thus sin a lot more than we'd like to think or admit. As a result, we *all*, 100 percent of human beings, have psychiatric struggles. Sometimes we have enough symptoms to rise up to the level of meeting criteria for a DSM-5 (*Diagnostic and Statistical Manual*) official psychiatric diagnosis. Sixty-one percent of us will have a major psychiatric diagnosis at some point in our life and 100 percent will have at least a minor diagnosis at some point in their lifetime. But for those fortunate enough to not have a present DSM psychiatric diagnosis, many struggles exist that don't have a DSM official diagnosis yet, such as insecurity, inadequacy, anxieties, misplaced dependencies, vulnerability, integrity, confidence, people pleaser, conflict avoider, workaholic, martyr syndrome, codependent, enabler, self-sabotager, and many other personality or temperament *quirks* that interfere with functioning or cause episodic distress. These defects happen so often that we just call them a variant of normalcy—quirk, choice, stupidity, immaturity, work-in-progress, or some other label kind instead of a disorder or defect.

Don't despair, you're not alone. Everyone who has ever lived has a psychiatric problem—yes, except Jesus. For that reason alone, we should want to study and know Jesus better and have Him as a close friend. But please have hope as well because treating these struggles isn't as difficult as you think. Overcoming, being a conqueror, running a good race, being victorious, and living in freedom using good science and biblical principles is easier than you think when taught the correct way.

DON'T BE AFRAID TO DIG IN!

Okay, I hope you've gotten over the shock of realizing you, all of us, have psychological defects and psychiatric problems. Take a deep breath and let's dive into the other side of behavioral health, the addiction issue.

Now we have to ask, "Do I have an addiction?" *Wow*, the term addiction carries such baggage, doom, gloom, stigma, fear, shame and judgment. For these reasons and many more, discussing addictions openly, with honest self-reflection and assessment, is difficult for all of us. But trust me. Part of my goal in writing this is to pull back the curtain and educate us about our mind so we can powerfully use it to move forward because our mind is our biggest asset... or hindrance. But I really want to reduce the fear and isolation that's so common when we're concerned we might have a mental health or addiction issue, and struggle to do something about it.

Because of the fear cancer induces, most people don't even perform self-examinations or get the recommended screening tests. We often ignore symptoms or warning signs, don't tell anyone, overreact thinking we're going to die while suffering in silence, being paralyzed by the fear. All psychiatric issues, mental health and addiction, are very treatable at any stage. Many people with psychiatric struggles are afraid of their symptoms, feel they are the only one who is defective, and won't tell a soul. Don't be paralyzed and let words like cancer, tumor, addiction, depression, anxiety, psychoses, narcissism, borderline, bipolar, PTSD, or any other symptom or diagnoses overwhelm you and interfere with accessing healing services that are available.

WHAT IS ADDICTION?

Now that we've pulled the curtain back to reveal some of the basics about mental health struggles, let's pause for a moment to dive deeper into one specific issue—addictions.

Addictions through the ages

Throughout human history, mankind has held various different perspectives on just what addictions really are and what causes them. From the dawn of man, beginning with Adam and Eve, all the way up through the 1600s, the main view of addictions held that they were the result of moral failure and a sign of poor character, immaturity, and sin, as they involved giving into the lusts of the flesh. When the 1700s rolled around, the birth of modern science and medicine brought with it the discovery of the brain and body's complexity.

During this time, various disease models were proposed to explain addictions as it seemed clear that something physical must be the cause of why some who drink become alcoholics while others who drink don't. But in the mid-1800s, a religious revival caused the view to flip-flop again, refocusing the conversation around addiction back to sin, moral failure, and lack of will power. Then, during the late-1800s, a new theory challenged both the religious and disease models of addiction. Through his research, Sigmund Freud theorized that addictions were a psychological defect—a coping strategy or a faulty defense mechanism to protect a person from their own psychological issues.

With the introduction of this theory, the battle was on. Addiction—is it sin, disease, or a psychological defect? In 1935, Alcoholics Anonymous was born, a seemingly miraculous program that powerfully helped many alcoholics overcome their addiction through twelve, Bible-based steps. The program encouraged people to focus on God and realign their lives with Him at the center instead of allowing alcohol or their own faulty mind to rule. At the same time, many followers of Freud's theory continued to push the importance of understanding why we do what we do, with addictions being one of many dysfunctional psychological outlets. In the 1950s, medical science exploded, with many research discoveries about the brain, alcohol, and disease birthing a variety of adduction theories touting the importance of receptors, genetic predisposition, early stress and trauma, and other theories.

Flash forward to the present day. Turn on the news at any given time, and we see many issues directly related to addiction: drunk driving tragedies, overdoses, the opioid crisis, the legalization of marijuana. The list goes on. We hear about gangs, domestic violence, the high school dropout rate, increased crime, suicide, human trafficking, and child abuse. And even now, the debate rages on. I speak to many different audiences about addiction, and the people I speak to are almost always an even split, with one-third believing addiction is a disease, one-third believing it's a sin, and one-third calling it a psychological defect.

A number of years ago, I was asked to evaluate Mark, the twenty-seven-year-old son of a pastor. Mark was athletic, played the piano, and was very outgoing and friendly. He grew up in a large church, as the pastor's oldest child. Unfortunately, Mark always felt the need to be perfect, not only for his father, but also for all the eyes in the church that were scrutinizing him as the pastor's son. He felt pressure to be a good student in his private Christian school, which was run by the church, and to excel in all his many areas of gifting. The pressure grew each year, and by the time he had to decide on a college, the weight on his shoulders was immense. Should he stay close to home or go away? Should he major in engineering like he wanted or in ministry like the rest of the church wanted? Should he continue dating his high school sweetheart, whose father was on the church's staff, or break it off in order to have the space to learn more about himself?

Ultimately, Mark decided to stay close to home, continue to date his high school girlfriend, and major in ministry at a small Christian college. But before long, he grew more dissatisfied as he was rapidly losing his identity and always being who others wanted him to be. To figure himself out, he explored and fell in with the wrong crowd, began using alcohol and then marijuana to relieve the anger and anxiety he felt at not being able to live the life he wanted without the expectations or hurting of all those around him. The weight of his guilt, shame, and poor decisions began to grow, but he kept them all pent up inside so he could remain the smiley, friendly, Christian boy everyone knew and expected him to be. His mind was crumbling and so confused, and his addiction was spiraling. He felt like a failure, like he had no hope, and that his family and friends would be better off without him. His suicidal thoughts finally grew so strong, he crashed his car in an attempt to end his life. A broken leg and more feelings of failure were the result, but with the secret of his struggles finally out, he was willing to take action to turn his life around.

Over the next several years, Mark made several attempts to cure his addictions and suicidal thoughts through spiritual means by recommitting his life to Christ and reading the Bible religiously. Several other times, he worked with a therapist to discuss some of the pressure, the anxiety, and the shame. Still at some points, he tested out a couple of different antidepressants, each for only a short stint. Exasperated and at the end of his rope, he was referred to me for an evaluation and vented: "I've prayed, I took my meds, I love my parents—but I'm still so screwed up. I'm dying and I don't know what's wrong with me? I've tried to change but I can't. Can you help me?"

Mark tried to address the spiritual component. He tried to address the psychological component. He tried to address the physical component. But sadly, the answer to addiction isn't just one of these, but all three of them together. Mark finally realized this and was willing to address all three spheres.

Rat Park

In the 1950s, a number of groundbreaking studies were performed to try to understand the true root cause of addictions. In these studies, lab rats were kept in separate cages, each containing two different bottles to drink from. One bottle contained plain water, while the other contained water laced with an addictive substance. It didn't matter what drug they added—alcohol, cocaine, heroin. In a relatively short amount of time, the rat would die of an overdose. Then the researchers would slice up the rat's brain to figure out why it would choose to drink from the dangerous bottle instead of just drinking the plain water.

In the late 1970s, psychologist Dr. Bruce Alexander began to look at these studies with a more critical eye. He theorized that if he was living all alone in a steel cage with nothing to play with, no one to talk to, and no hope of getting out, he would most likely drink from the drug-laced bottle as well. This brought a novel idea to Dr. Alexander's mind. What if we give the rats some different surroundings and see how it plays out? So, Alexander designed Rat Park, a highly stimulating rat enclosure, which included other rats to socialize and mate with, balls to play with, structures to climb, tubes to run through, and lots of cheese and other foods to eat. And into Rat Park, he also put two bottles to drink from—one with plain water, and one with drug-laced water.

Unlike those initial rat studies, in Rat Park the rats had fun. Not only did they thrive socially, but they preferred the plain water over the drug-laced water. Occasionally they might try the drug-laced water, but only intermittently, and they never overdosed. They always went back to the plain water before long. Through Dr. Alexander's Rat Park, we learned addiction isn't just a biological issue. The way you think and the things going on in your life carry more weight than your biology. The psychological and spiritual spheres are strong influencers on our behaviors. Belonging is the key and the opposite of the isolation that comes when the relationship with an addiction crowds out everything else.

Several Definitions of Addiction

Almost all other medical fields diagnose disorders by first getting some information from the patient and then performing a physical exam, before finally running some tests. In these other fields, clear diagnoses can only be made through examining, testing and imaging a person's biology. Infections are diagnosed by observing the infected area and acquiring a culture. Diabetes is diagnosed by measuring the sugar levels in the blood. Heart attacks are diagnosed using electrocardiograms and blood tests.

But psychiatry is the one area of medicine that doesn't diagnose based on chemistry or biology. We diagnose based mainly on the patient's self-reported feelings, thoughts, and behaviors, and then the impact these have on their life. Because the psychological and spiritual aspects are hard to quantify with a test, and trying to measure the brain is so difficult, addiction's definitions are still a work in progress. So, to pull the addiction curtain back a little further, it's important for us to look at each sphere's contribution to the ways addiction is defined or diagnosed.

A simple lay person definition for addiction is continuing to use, pursue, or do something even though it is unhealthy or causes negative consequences. But to provide a more all-encompassing definition, addiction is typically broken into two different categories based on what specifically the individual is addicted to:

Substance Addiction: Continuing to pursue or use a substance despite continued consequences. The object you're after is a chemical you are taking into your body. Some of the more common ones include alcohol, nicotine, heroin, marijuana, cocaine, amphetamines, Ritalin, hallucinogens, food, and the most common addiction—caffeine.

Process Addiction: Also known as behavioral addictions, this is when a person continues to engage or pursue a thought, feeling, or pattern of behavior despite continued consequences. These thoughts can be: I'm not smart enough, I'm not pretty enough, I'm not lovable, I'm lonely, I'm not important, this is too hard for me, I'm never going to make it, They expect too much from me, I need control or power—the list goes on. The feelings might be hurt, sadness, worry, jealousy, anger, loneliness, insecurity, shame, guilt, fear, or victimization.

A person can also pursue certain behaviors, like gambling, stealing, pornography, self-harm, perfectionism, codependency, eating rituals, physical fighting, bullying, gossiping, or intimidation. They can also sometimes be seemingly positive behaviors, like obsession with one's children or spouse, exercising, work, or studying. In some cases, these behaviors can also be spiritual in nature, like excessive confessing, praying, going to church, or performing other religious rituals. These may of course be done for biblical reasons—to increase connection with God—but they may also be ritual actions used to decrease fear, and as such, can become a destructive addiction. Some, like me, pursued certain elements to minimize hurt, so I was addicted to power and controlling situations and others, thinking if I had those, no one could hurt me anymore. When you are driven by something in your life, can't stay away from it and it interrupts your other life activities or decision-making or is consistently disruptive, it's highly likely to be an addiction.

Now to get a bit more technical, let's look at some scientific definitions of addiction, courtesy of the _Diagnostic and Statistical Manual_ (DSM-5). In this modern edition, the DSM tried to get away from the judgmental term _addiction_ but didn't know how to describe process addictions like gambling. So, it named this category _Substance-Related and Addictive Disorders._ Substance use disorder is defined as a problematic pattern of substance use leading to significant functional impairment or psychological and emotional distress, as manifested by at least two of the following criteria occurring within a twelve-month period:

- Using the substance in larger amounts or over a longer period than intended
- Desiring to or unsuccessful efforts to cut down or control the substance use
- Spending lots of time on activities necessary to obtain, use, or recover from the substance
- Craving, a strong desire for, or urges to use the substance
- Recurrent use resulting in a failure to fulfill major role obligations at work, school, or home
- Continued use of the substance despite having persistent or recurrent social or interpersonal problems caused or worsened by substance
- Giving up or reduction of once important social, occupational, or recreational activities because of substance use
- Recurrent substance use in situations in which it is physically hazardous
- Continued use despite persistent or recurrent physical or psychological problems caused or worsened by the substance.
- Increased tolerance, need of increased amounts of the substance in order to achieve the same effect, or getting lesser effect from the same amount as you used to use
- Experiencing withdrawal, or a physically or psychologically uncomfortable feeling when having to go without the substance for several days, or using the substance to avoid this physical and psychological discomfort

In addition to needing to manifest at least two of these within a twelve-month period, substance use is also classified through the use of a severity scale based on exactly how many criteria are met. Zero to one of them shows no addiction, two to three is a mild addiction, four to five is a moderate addiction, and six or more is a severe addiction.

In 2011, the American Society of Addiction Medicine (ASAM)—a national group of doctors, psychiatrists, clinicians, and researchers—defined addiction as "a primary, chronic disease of brain reward, motivation, memory and related circuitry. Dysfunction in these circuits leads to characteristic biological, psychological, social, and spiritual manifestations. This circuitry and resultant manifestations lead to the individual pursuing reward and/or relief by substance use and other behaviors."

With this definition, ASAM was the first scientific organization to include a spiritual component. They also accurately identified that these biological, psychological, social, and spiritual manifestations cause distress and the addiction is a person's attempt to reward or find relief from the distress. But their definition also made two errors. First, they called it a primary disorder, meaning that the brain's physiology is the first step. And second, they called it chronic, meaning lifelong, but it doesn't have to be, because healing is available for all.

Thus, in 2019 ASAM revised their definition to state: "Addiction is a treatable, chronic medical disease involving complex interactions among brain circuits, genetics, the environment, and an individual's life experiences. People with addiction use substances or engage in behaviors that become compulsive and often continue despite harmful consequences."

Brain Chemistry and Addiction

As described by ASAM, the physiological component of addiction has to do with disrupted brain circuitry. Substances are toxic to all of our body's cells but especially our brain cells. On top of these substances' toxic effects, the decisions we make as a result of using them, the process addictions, and the pleasure we get from these activities also have a disruptive effect on the nerve cells, impacting the electrical and chemical activity necessary for optimal and integrated brain circuits. One of the brain areas most affected is the prefrontal cortex, where a lot of our decision-making and executive functioning take place. The other primary victim is the limbic system.

The brain's reward circuits and emotional control center are part of an intricate cluster of brain structures that connect in the limbic system. They regulate our ability to experience pleasure and try to help us get more of it. When we do something that causes us to feel pleasure, we are automatically motivated to repeat those behaviors. The limbic system doesn't discriminate based on whether they happen to be harmful to us or not. Those circuits are simply activated whenever an activity causes us to feel pleasure. When it comes to pleasure, dopamine and serotonin are the main neurotransmitters involved, but other transmitters are involved in this intricate circuit that addictions hijack, as well.

THE HOLY BIBLE AND ADDICTION

The Bible clearly addresses addictions in several places, though it uses some different terms than science does. For starters, the first two commandments are all about addiction. The first commandment says: "You shall have no other Gods before me." (Exodus 20:3 & Deuteronomy 5:7) And the second says: "You shall not make for yourself a carved image, or any likeness of anything that is in heaven above, or that is in the earth beneath, or that is in the water under the earth. You shall not bow down to them or serve them, for I the Lord your God am a jealous God, visiting the iniquity of the fathers on the children to the third and the fourth generation of those who hate me." (Exodus 20:4-5 & Deuteronomy 5:8-9)

If you've ever met anyone who struggles with addictions, you've seen that when someone becomes addicted to something, it basically becomes their master, their god, controlling and dictating everything about their lives. But nothing of this world, or even above it or below it, should replace God as our Master. When it comes to addictions, the issue is misplaced worship, exalting something more than we exalt God. We were designed to worship God, but we belong to Him, as well. Satan and the world systems twist our thinking and we start worshipping the created, instead of the Creator. Thus, we end up having a pretty poor master, belonging to it, and being disconnected from all that is life-giving.

When Jesus was asked which commandment was the most important of all, he answered, "And you shall love the Lord your God with all your heart and with all your soul and with all your mind and with all your strength." (Mark 12:30)

But when we're addicted to something, we end up loving it more than God and are willing to sacrifice anything for that addiction, even our relationship with God Himself. But God calls us to do the opposite—to die to both the self and to the things of this world. To always put Him first.

In Ezekiel 14, we hear the term "idols of the heart," referring to people, objects, or goals that a person exalts and holds at the center of their mind and heart. Their decision-making revolves around protecting the idol and keeping the idol in a supreme position in their life. Ezekiel warns us that idols of the heart are highly displeasing to God and bring only destruction. Why? Because putting all our eggs in the basket of something limited, powerless, and finite is not what God has in mind for our lives He designed us for.

As you can see, the Bible is pretty clear that anything we exalt as more important than God, or that gives more power to direct our lives, is an idol. We're worshipping something other than our Creator and Savior. Jesus paid our price. He paid our ransom, so our life should be His. But instead we turn our lives over to other powerless and ineffective impostors. First, we let it run our lives. Then it ruins it.

THE STAGES OF ADDICTION

Addictions are incredibly complex, progressing differently for everyone. For some, the addiction crops up in just a few months while for some it takes several years. And for a small group, developing a full-blown addiction can take decades. But when we really dig in and analyze the general progression of addictions, we see that the vast majority tend to pass through the following six stages. Each person will spend a different amount of time in each or go back and forth. It's important to remember that a single person can experience multiple addictions at the same time but be in different stages of each. Many young men experience addictions to porn, conflict avoidance, video games, and marijuana or alcohol—that's four simultaneous addictions. But they will often be in different stages of each. Likewise, many young women experience addictions to social media, a need for approval/love, restricting food or excessive exercise, and alcohol. But each of these can be in different stages.

Despite what kind of addiction someone is experiencing, the six stages tend to look similar though they are usually easier to identify in substance addictions than they are in process/behavioral addictions:

1. **Experimental Use**: Trying the addictive substance or experience once or twice to see what will happen. No agenda.
2. **Recreational Use**: Trying the addictive substance or experi-

ence socially, such as with friends or at a party. Done only as something to do with no real drive or intention to engage in it unless others initiate or are involved. Can take it or leave it and the quality of their functioning isn't affected.

3. *Circumstantial Use*: Using the addictive substance or experience to avoid personal problems or circumstances, or to get through a challenging situation. For example, taking caffeine to study for exams, drinking alcohol to fall sleep, taking opioid pain medication to feel happy, using marijuana (THC) to escape, eating to de-stress from a tough day, working relentlessly to prove you're worthy, or viewing porn to feel connected, loved, stimulated.

4. *Regular Use*: Expanding the circumstantial criteria for when to engage the addiction, leading to faster and more frequent use of the addictive substance or process addiction.

5. *Intensified/Risky Use*: Increasing use of the addictive substance or experience over a period of time. This describes the regular user who experiences ongoing symptoms or consequences (physical, psychological, emotional, spiritual, relational, material, financial, legal) because of their use, but still engages in their addiction.

6. *Compulsive Use*: The individual feels that giving up their addiction on their own would be impossible. The person feels out of control, the addiction essentially runs their life, and they need outside intervention to stop. They seemingly lost the ability to choose not to use and suffer significant disruption in multiple life arenas because of their addiction.

The most dangerous and important of these stages is circumstantial use. This is when random, purposeless use turns into purposeful self-medicating. The individual thinks they've found a solution for their problem, and the addiction actually benefits them. And once the person is tricked into thinking this substance or process addiction can help them achieve something they otherwise could not have, the slippery slope is greased, and the downward spiral starts to escalate. Though they might find some immediate, short-term relief, their addiction actually worsens everything in their life—in both the short term and the long term.

For some, when the consequences start to mount, they may lose a significant relationship. They may lose their job. They may flunk out of school, ruin their finances, or even wind up in jail like I did. In some cases, hitting rock bottom can be enough for the person to realize their addiction is doing more harm than good. But for others, the decline into the final stage—compulsive use—often leaves the person with no option other than seeking help. For these people, strong external forces are nearly always needed to turn the destructive momentum around.

THE COMPONENTS OF ADDICTION

With these different addiction definitions giving us a better handle on addictions, let me give you some terms to flesh addictions out a little more.

Addiction Trigger: A stimulus, stressor, or situation that prompts the urge to engage the substance or process addiction. Some examples include: job stress, an argument, family issue, loneliness, financial loss, rejection or hurt, loss, reading a news story that reminds you of something upsetting from your past.

Addiction Role: Addiction's role is to be a coping skill meant to reduce discomfort, reduce or relieve stress, escape the present, avoid dealing with something, distract us from the distress, slip into a different reality, or reward us with a high or temporary buzz.

Addiction Goal: The desired outcome of using or engaging in the substance or process addiction. For the most part, the goal of every addiction is comfort. Our desire to avoid, escape, or distract ourselves from pain or discomfort is the primary pursuit of our flesh that leads us down the path of addiction. We are all addicted to comfort!

Addiction Object: The "it" we turn to, thinking it will deliver the comfort we desire. It could be a substance, object, behavior, thought pattern, feeling, person, role, or activity. Anything under the sun has the potential to grab our attention, tricking us into thinking it will make our life better.

To help make this clearer, I'll use myself as an example. Usually, my trigger was being faced with a situation I didn't feel I had complete control over or a situation that wasn't going according to my agenda. The role of my addiction was to help me cope with feelings of inadequacy and insecurity, as well as the fear that if others had control over me, I was going to suffer in some way. My goal was comfort and to avoid the hurt. And for a long time, the objects of my addiction were control for power or alcohol for relaxing. I was also addicted to having temper tantrums, manipulating others, arrogance, lying, excessive working, productivity, pornography, and being the best at things. All of these objects allowed me to exert control over situations and people, or in the case of alcohol, quickly soothe the pain of not being in control, while helping me escape into an alternative reality when I was under the influence.

DR. KARL'S DEFINITION OF ADDICTION

As we see, the problem of addictions goes a lot deeper than just our external behaviors, our brain chemistry, or even our deepest thought patterns. That's why, taking into account what the Bible says about addictions, as well as everything else we've learned and discussed, I'd like to put forth my own, comprehensive but simple definition of addiction.

Addiction is choosing or pursuing something—other than God and the healthy solution He provides—in a habitual, patterned, or repetitive way to get particular needs met. Or, to put it more succinctly: a coping mechanism, repetitively used, that isn't focused on or given to us by God. These objects we pursue to help us cope are the idols of the heart, or false gods, that the Bible urges us not to pursue as they will bring destruction to our doorstep.

Once an addiction starts to pick up momentum, it doesn't matter how it started. Its impacts and consequences are felt in three spheres—spirit, mind, and body. Let's look at this example.

Say a person grows up in what looks like a relatively normal household, at least from the outside. But on the inside, they aren't receiving much love or encouragement and very little attention. Being a child, they don't know how to make sense of this treatment, so like anyone would, they take it personally. God doesn't know or love me. I'm alone. They try to come up with reasons for their struggles and their own answers on how to improve their life. I must be defective, a screw up, unlovable. I don't fit in. Over time, these spiritual and then psychological struggles lead to low self-esteem before developing into anxiety and depression. The person starts to eat more to help feel better. They feel inferior at school and then later at work. A marriage might have its rewards, but the person continues to struggle, as they become a people-pleaser or conflict avoider.

As their adult life goes on, the problems grow, and they start to struggle spiritually. They're unsure of their identity in Christ and how to access God's peace. They feel distant from God and see no purpose or uniqueness. These spiritual struggles only increase their psychological issues, deepening their anxiety and depression. Their mild eating issues become more pronounced as the only coping skill that brings any relief or control. Their weight begins to increase, and after twelve years, rising blood pressure, cholesterol, and heart disease rear their ugly heads. Instead of going to God to deal with their stress and using healthy coping skills from psychology and the Bible, they go with their own plan—food, their go-to addiction object. Sure enough, these physical issues pile up, and though they sometimes try to eat healthy, they finally get the news from the doctor that they've developed diabetes.

As you can see, spiritual, psychological, and physiological elements were all at play, all sophisticatedly intertwined. Though the problem started in the spiritual sphere, it went to the psychological and then pinballed between physiological, spiritual, and psychological until all three spheres were significantly damaged. At this point, the problem can't just be prayed away or solved through therapy, because the person needs insulin for their diabetes. Because all three spheres are involved in the damage, all three spheres must be involved in the treatment, as well. But most importantly, the person has to get to the root of the food addiction—the psychological hurt from the perceived early rejection and isolation. They self-medicated with something other than God—food—for relief, escape, soothing or comfort that resulted in more poor decisions.

Addictions are used by Satan to isolate us, so he can devour us. Addictions separate us from God. We start worshipping and following something else, allowing it to be our master. Addictions separate us from others, as the addiction object is jealous and will help us push loved ones away. Addictions separate us from ourselves, as we diverge from our purpose and ability to run our own lives, becoming a puppet with our addiction object being our master. The longer and deeper our addiction gets, the more isolated we become.

But the opposite of addiction is belonging. Instead of isolation, God wants us to belong to Him, to know that we are loved and accepted by Him. He has made us in His likeness as relational beings. We need to be connected to God and others. If we aren't, our own Rat Park promised land of psychological and spiritual abundance will be nothing more than a fantasy, dooming us to a life of despair in a steel cage of suffering.

AM I AN ADDICT?

Let's summarize. When we struggle, God should be our first step in any problem-solving game plan. Addiction objects are other items we pursue instead of God to solve a problem or get our needs met. If we aren't diligent, addictions progress through stages from initial experimental and random use to intensified compulsive use, where we can't stop on our own without some major help. The critical point in the progression is when we are tricked into thinking the addiction object is useful to help us deal with some underlying psychological issue—either minor or major—fueling the addiction to escalate from there. So, our addiction object is something we continue to pursue even though it's unhealthy, brings consequences, or sets our growth process further back. Anything can be used as an addiction object, not just a substance. Both the substance and our faulty decisions bring a myriad of damage. As our thinking, emotional, memory, and reward circuits in our pre-frontal cortex and limbic system are hijacked and short circuited, our psychological growth is stunted and often frozen developmentally. Spiritually we are turning away from God for help and worshipping something else instead. These consequences in all three spheres sadly just fuel more psychological struggle, which is self-medicated with more addictive behavior.

So, given these explanations and definitions, we have to ask, "Do I have an addiction?"

Let me propose a quick screening scenario to help you determine if you have an addiction. Remember the last time you experienced an addiction trigger. You know, you didn't get your way, life threw you a curveball, or you experienced some hurt, discomfort, adversity, setback, or challenge. It doesn't have to be major, but it could be. What is the first thing you turn to or enters your mind? Do you turn to God in prayer or think about what He is planning, doing, or wanting for you in this situation? Or do you go to some other coping mechanism you think will ease the discomfort, be a good distraction, or escape? Try to see how long it takes you to loop back around to bringing God into the situation. How many other addiction objects did you turn to before God popped into your strategy? Write those objects down and see if they pop up again when the next triggers hit. If you do this exercise for a week or two, you'll be able to catch that addiction object hopefully before it gets into the regular, intensified or compulsive addiction stages we discussed above. If it is already at those stages, you now have arrived at a very important realization.

One of my life verses that helped me dig out of my anxiety, depression, alcoholism, and control addiction is Isaiah 26:3, "He gives him perfect peace whose mind is fixed on Thee, because he trusts You." This verse clearly points out what our first response to stress, adversity, success, discomfort, pain, or any addiction trigger should be. Turn our eyes, thoughts, focus, total mind to God and fixate to stay on Him first and always. Anything else is Satan's impostor option and our addiction object. Satan is really good at tricking us into believing our me-centered coping skills benefit us while he hides their consequences from us. Or we blame the consequences on overwhelmed parents, ignorant teachers, greedy bosses, peers blinded by their clique affiliation, never getting a break, or God punishing us because He's judgmental, busy, or doesn't care. So, another way of sorting out whether we have an addiction is looking at the consequences, not just those listed in DSM-5, but relational disruptions, sin areas of our life, material glitches, not feeling peace, emotional instability, frequently coming up short, or what's missing from our life and assess what dominoes preceded these struggles to identify some addiction patterns.

BAD NEWS FLASH

So, as we take in all this addiction info, let's get down to the nitty gritty of your heart.

I haven't met a person yet who turns to God in prayer, thought, attitude, and guidance for every situation, especially the adversities that bring discomfort. What I did, and most people do, in my early adulthood was go to God only after all my attempts at solving the problem or soothing myself were exhausted. I still needed urgent help, so I prayed to God. We all go to something else instead of God when we don't get our way, experience adversity or loss, get rejected in some way, or just aren't feeling like we want to. Some of these go-to addiction objects are pretty concrete and clear—food, substances, porn, work, approval, kids, shopping, screens/gaming/social media. But most are a more subtle and complex set of thoughts, emotions, and behaviors. Like power, control, manipulation, temper tantrums, status, materialism, productivity, workaholism. Then, if you look closely enough, you will see some consequences from those *coping skills*. We often think these are self-protective, but they are actually self-destructive. However, the more we use them, the more that circuitry in our brain gets fertilized, cutting a deep rut that is easy for us to fall into the next time we are faced with a similar situation.

So yes, we all have an addiction, idol of the heart, something we turn to other than God in a repetitive, habitual, or patterned way. Those idols reap consequences in all three spheres, drifting us farther from God, others, and ourselves than we would be without these addictions. Sadly, most of us have several process addictions that usually have some overlap to achieve some level of comfort, while allowing us to temporarily escape the discomfort we desperately fear and try to avoid. That was the reason for the first two commandments. God knew we would quickly and frequently be star struck by or tricked into thinking something else could deliver the desires of our hearts and we would follow and then worship it. So, He warned us not once in Commandment 1, but a second warning in Commandment 2. Paul encapsulates it beautifully in his Romans 7:15 self-assessment and confession. "For I do not understand my own actions. For I do not do what I want, but I do the very thing I hate." We all think or say this same thing in one way or another.

AM I DUAL DIAGNOSIS?

Listen up. Jesus is the Wonderful Counselor and Great Physician. Put those two professionals together and you get the Perfect Psychiatrist. Yes, Jesus is the Perfect Psychiatrist whose counter-culture teaching and actions started a Behavioral Health Revolution as He made clear a unique prescription for psychospiritual healing. If we're really ready to be honest with ourselves and God, which is a necessity to navigating life well, when we look through the lenses of the Perfect Psychiatrist, we're all dual diagnosis patients.

In case you are still having trouble believing me, the Bible communicates this truth using the commutative property of math. Let me refresh you on this elementary school principle (and hope no one has a flashback) which states: if a=b and b=c, then a=c.

"Jesus came to die for all of us." John 3:16

"Jesus said it is not the well that need a doctor, but the sick." Luke 5:31.

So, a = all of us, and b = Jesus, and c = all the sick.

Jesus only heals the sick, Jesus came for all. Therefore, every person is sick and it manifests as psychological issues and addictive patterns.

Mainstream Psychiatry has different views that affect the dual diagnosis group and treatment in several ways. First, it views addiction as a primary disorder, which can exist on its own. Second, even though a 2011 study by Steven Sussman out of University of Southern California found 47 percent of adults over the last twelve months, had an addiction to tobacco, alcohol, illicit drugs, eating, gambling, internet, love, sex, exercise, work, and shopping—they didn't even include caffeine, the most prevalent substance addiction or pornography, the most common process addiction—they believe the lifetime prevalence of addictions is around 10–15 percent. Third, they believe the lifetime prevalence of having a mental health disorder is about 30–40 percent.

Of those 15 percent with addictions, mainstream psychiatry estimates 45 percent are dual diagnosis. The most common are depression, PTSD, Borderline Personality Disorder, ADHD, Social Anxiety Disorder, Generalized Anxiety Disorder, Bipolar Disorder, Schizophrenia, Eating Disorders (these really are categorized as mental health disorders, but are actually process disorders), OCD, and Antisocial Personality Disorder.

Putting these numbers together, even giving the benefit of the doubt saying the high end of having an addiction is 20 percent, 45 percent of those would be 9 percent of the population would fall into the dual diagnosis category.

In order to properly treat, we need to properly diagnose. As you see with the preceding numbers, mainstream psychiatry views only 9 percent of our population being dual diagnosis, when in fact, 100 percent are. I believe this is one of the major roadblocks that put a low ceiling for success in behavioral health treatment. The other limitations we will get to shortly are the lack or real spirituality and lack of depth psychologically in most treatments.

ADDICTION TREATMENT

Even though process (sex, power, gluttony, greed, and gambling to name a few) and chemical addictions have been plaguing society for thousands of years (as we see in the pre-flood days of Noah), treatment has always and continues to be disjointed, inadequate, and simplistic leading to poor success rates. One of the main reasons poor outcomes continue has been the lack of understanding of what an addiction really is. Remember, addictions aren't just a sin… or just a psychological or personality defect…or just a biological disease you are genetically susceptible to. God designed us to worship Him, but we are self-centered and have short attention spans, so we easily worship other objects because of defects in all three spheres. Since all three spheres are compromised, addressing all three spheres in depth is going to be an essential part of the addiction treatment plan.

Addictions and addiction treatment have a convoluted history with many special nuances and a myriad of controversial opinions and ramifications in our society. My conceptualization of addictions and treatment often markedly differs from both secular clinicians and the Christian community (including many in the addiction recovery field), so in order to clearly give you what is important for you to understand, let me unpack addiction treatment a little first.

Since the 1950s, when medical and addictions research revealed significant medical aspects for cocaine, heroin, and alcohol addiction, yet no medical cure, addiction progressively migrated into its own special and isolated category of psychiatric disorders. Subsequently, addiction *specialists* developed a very unique strategy for treating addictions that was quite different and significantly separate from other psychiatric care and disorders. This separation of addictions from all the other psychiatric disorders even occurred at the governmental level, so research, development of public services, prevention and education campaigns, treatment programs, and funding streams for treatment were also dysfunctionally separated. Minimal collaboration between addiction and mental health (mainstream psychological) providers occurred and the poor patient was stuck in the middle of these two systems similar to that of a child stuck with two parents after a hostile divorce.

1. Even though we knew addictions could co-occur with another mental health illness, like depression, PTSD, Bipolar, ADHD, Panic Disorder, Schizophrenia, or any other psychiatric disorder, in order to treat addiction, the addiction was isolated and compartmentalized into its own treatment bubble while the psychiatric issues were confined to a different treatment bubble. The addiction bubble might contain more than one addiction, as is usually the case, and the psychiatric diagnosis bubble might also have more than one psychiatric diagnosis. As addictions cause many profound problems, including psychiatric disorders, while also distorting a person's functioning, so oftentimes, getting an accurate history to diagnose the addiction or the underlying psychiatric issue is impossible. Separating the two bubbles seemed to make some sense. After separating the diagnoses, the prevailing wisdom dictated treating the addiction first. Treating the addiction first seemed to make good clinical sense and provide immediate life-saving advantages for the following reasons:

1. Substance abuse is dangerous and the next substance use can result in the patient's death or that of a bystander. People can die from an addiction in a number of ways including: overdosing, having impaired judgment or coordination leading to accidental deaths from a motor vehicle accident or falling down the steps, exacerbating a medical condition (heart, liver, or kidney disease, esophageal varices and diabetes), or having a deadly interaction with another medication or supplement they are taking.

2. Sadly, some addicts actually die when they try to abruptly stop the substance. Alcohol or benzodiazepine withdrawal killed (and still kills) many from the late 1800s into the 1960s and helped push the mindset that treating the acute addiction needs to take precedence over treating psychiatric disorders. On the other hand, although most psychiatric disorders cause much

pain and suffering, they are rarely acutely dangerous except when psychoses impairs judgment or intense suicidal impulses require acute psychiatric hospitalizations to ensure safety.

3. Both acute and chronic substance abuse cause many acute psychiatric symptoms with psychoses and anxiety being the most common. A patient using marijuana, LSD, or other hallucinogens will often hallucinate or become delusional/paranoid. In order to determine whether this patient has schizophrenia, mania, postpartum psychoses, or a substance induced psychosis, the patient needs a significant period of sobriety for their brain to heal and function appropriately to see if the hallucinations only occur because of the substance use. Sometimes thirty to sixty days of sobriety and proper nutrition is enough, but in extreme cases, depending on the frequency and quantity of use, brain circuitry healing can take up to one whole year to reverse the toxic damages that substances inflict on the brain.

4. Substance detoxification (detox) and withdrawal symptoms often mimic various psychiatric disorders. Withdrawing from most addictive substances leads to severe anxiety. Withdrawing from alcohol or benzodiazepines, for some, mimics panic attacks. Some substance withdrawals have hallucinations or paranoia as a symptom. So again, taking time to get through the detoxification period allows the clinician to see what is only from the substance issue versus the psychiatric issues.

5. When a person is struggling with an active addiction, their limited self-awareness of symptoms and inability to piece together a reliable history makes accurately diagnosing underlying medical and psychiatric issues very difficult. Many struggles are overlooked or misdiagnosed.

6. Ongoing substance use often causes chronic symptoms that are more difficult to detect. Also, because the patient has *adjusted* or acclimated to their addiction so much, they don't even remember what normal thinking, mood, anxiety level, energy, or functioning was. They either have no radar to detect those symptoms or, if they do detect them, they have no idea the symptoms are in large part or totally caused by the substance itself. Connecting the symptom cause to the substances is very difficult for the addicted patient. Examples would be depression

from ongoing heroin or other opioid use, anxiety and depression from regular alcohol overuse, OCD from ongoing stimulant abuse, or intermittent explosive disorder (anger) from steroid abuse.

But the trap that ensnared the treatment community was believing the addiction bubble needed to be addressed, treated, and then significant sobriety of three to six months *before* addressing the psychiatric bubble. *Then*, with the addiction gone, the person thinking more clearly, and the brain healed from the toxic substance, we could reasonably assess and start to treat whatever is now left in the psychiatric disorder bubble.

But contrary to mainstream addiction and psychiatric community wisdom, I view addictions using a biblically-informed foundation while integrating sound science, which reveals that every addiction develops as a result of trying to cope with a psychospiritual struggle. Sadly, during this modern era of treatment from the 1950s until around 2015, addictions was viewed as a separate illness and addiction specialists with very little training in psychological understanding or treatment were providing the treatment. Only in the last several years has the addiction community realized that in order to achieve the best possible treatment outcomes, they needed to move away from sequentially treating addictions first and then the mental psychiatric issue second to a new strategy of *simultaneously* treating the addiction *and* the underlying psychiatric issue together.

So, with that background, let's look at treating the patient who is struggling with an addiction and their underlying psychiatric issues.

The substance-related disorders family is divided into two categories. First are the substance-induced disorders and the other are the substance use disorders. This is a good place to start as it helps us conceptualize a timeline for addiction treatment.

TREATING SUBSTANCE-INDUCED DISORDERS

As the name implies, the three substance-induced disorders— intoxication, detoxification/withdrawal, and other substance-induced disorders—are the direct result of the substance. Because of their quick onset, acute danger, and judgment cognitive impairment, these need to be addressed immediately and were some of the reasons I listed earlier that tricked the treatment community into treating the whole addiction before the psych bubble.

Intoxication

We've all seen someone in this condition, if not even ourselves, and it isn't pretty or safe. Depending on the substance, quantity used, strength of substance, tolerance, and health of the individual, intoxication can last a couple hours up to twenty-four hours and in extreme cases a couple days. Intoxication can be dangerous in three specific ways:

1.   Overdose is using more than your body can safely handle. Alcohol, sedatives (barbiturates and benzodiazepines, like Ativan and Xanax), and opioids slow our breathing, leading to coma and death, while stimulants (cocaine, methamphetamines, and even caffeine in high concentrations for workouts or dieting) increase blood pressure and heart rate, leading to heart attack, arrhythmia, or stroke, and can overstimulate the brain leading to seizures. Choking as the result of inhaling their own vomitus kills many intoxicated people. Keeping the patient away from the substance and providing oxygen for breathing or meds for the heart might be needed in extreme intoxication. Narcan is frequently used by first responders and ER personnel to reverse an opioid overdose. Intoxication is especially dangerous to new users of a substance and to those with a significant time of abstinence, who then relapse and think their body can handle as much as they used to use.

2.   Having our thinking controlled by a substance leads to impairments in reality-testing, judgment, decision-making, impulse control, reaction time, and emotion management. Some common dangerous circumstances can be driving under the influence, falls resulting in death or traumatic brain injury, getting into fights (my MO), intentional self-harm, such as cutting or suicidal thoughts as intoxication amplifies many uncomfortable feelings, irrational behavior like jumping off a balcony or out of a car because of paranoia. Pretty much all illicit substances as well as alcohol, marijuana (sadly legal in some states), caffeine, and steroids can impair judgment even with just a small amount of the substance. This is one of the reasons they are, or once were, illegal or highly controlled by the DEA.

3.   Acute intoxication also can cause certain underlying medical issues to acutely worsen, causing acute or lasting damage and

even death. Again, the biggest culprits are alcohol, sedatives, opioids, stimulants, and steroids. Disorders for the heart, respiratory, kidney, liver, nervous, and digestive systems are the most susceptible to this danger.

Treatment during the intoxication stage involves keeping the patient away from taking in anymore substances, supervision, and monitoring vital signs. If the patient has any significant medical issues, is losing consciousness, or their alertness level seems odd, calling 911 or going to a local ER is a reasonably cautious move. If they are passed out, make sure they are still breathing, and keep them on their side so if they do vomit, they do not inhale it.

Detoxification and Withdrawal

Once the intoxication phase is over, other than hallucinogens and inhalants, all the other addictive substances (including marijuana) have a detoxification and withdrawal phase. Some addicts are binge users and go intervals without using, so their body never becomes physically dependent on the addiction object nor do they go through withdrawal. On the other hand, most addicts are pretty consistent users. For these regular users, the body's systems become hijacked by the addiction object because the object often produces some shortcuts to euphoria or altered states. The body then changes to accommodate the addiction object being incorporated as a needed part of the body's circuits. When the patient decides to stop using the object, *detoxification* is the process of ridding the addiction object from the system. For many substances (and even for process addictions), *withdrawal* is the collection of symptoms that occurs as a result of the disruption to your brain and body when the ongoing addiction object is no longer available. Basically, the addict's system is revolting, or throwing a loud physiological temper tantrum, because it was tricked into believing the addiction was the best way to function and now has to abruptly switch gears and live without it. This means having to deal with the acute changes in brain dopamine, serotonin, endorphins, norepinephrine, and other important chemicals, as well as the resulting ripples in all those circuits. This time of disruption, from the onset of symptoms until your body transitions to the pre-addiction way of functioning, is called withdrawal.

If you've known a regular smoker or caffeine drinker, you've probably witnessed the withdrawal phase when they tried to quit. And those are two of the easiest ones to withdraw from. Withdrawal symptoms can be physiological, cognitive, emotional, or behavioral (pacing, picking skin). Cravings, nausea, vomiting, diarrhea, chills, headaches, tremors, disrupted vital signs, cloudy thinking, psychoses, insomnia, moodiness, irritability, agitation, pacing, distractible, low energy, and skin-picking are just some of the many withdrawal symptoms depending on the addiction object. As it sounds, withdrawal is pretty uncomfortable, and the severity is worse when the patient uses higher quantity, more frequently, is older, or has medical issues.

I once treated a man in his fifties with liver disease from his longtime alcohol use. His body went into withdrawal while he still had alcohol in his system, but his blood alcohol dropped below 0.1. In most states, 0.08 is the legal limit in for DUI. Sadly, he drank almost nonstop, so his body was so accustomed to always having alcohol in his system that dropping below 0.1 put him into withdrawal. It was a rare and sad case.

Depending on the substance, frequency, and quantity, most withdrawal periods start within two and twenty-four hours after last use, peak around day three to five, and then taper over the next one to two weeks. Many still have some psychological effects for one to three months after the bulk of the physiological withdrawal is over. A less common syndrome is Post-Acute Withdrawal Syndrome or PAWS, which can last several months and even up to two years. PAWS can occur with any substance, and the symptoms are less physical and more cognitive, emotional, and behavioral, often intermittent, and arising usually when a person is stressed.

Although most withdrawals, even from process addictions, are very uncomfortable, they are rarely dangerous unless the person has significant medical issues or psychoses is a withdrawal symptom. Sadly, though, withdrawal from alcohol or sedatives/tranquilizers in the barbiturate (phenobarbital) or benzodiazepine (Ativan, Xanax, Valium) families can be fatal. The *DTs, or delirium tremens,* is a rapid onset of confusion, shaking, irregular heartbeat, increased temperature or seizures that can be deadly. This is how many people died of alcoholism up until the 1950s when detox protocols were implemented. Sadly, people still die of alcohol withdrawal, and, to a lesser extent, sedative withdrawal. For this reason, detox from alcohol and tranquilizers should be performed under medical supervision and management. Because opioid detox is so painful and complicated, it should also be with medical supervision and management.

One other at-risk group is newborn babies. If the mother was using regularly, while in the uterus, the baby had substances flowing through its system same as mom. But upon delivery, the baby now is cut off cold turkey. So, these poor little babies go through a withdrawal as part of their introduction to a fallen world.

These very painful and often debilitating withdrawal symptoms are a major reason why those who want to quit their addiction have so much difficulty. You see, the quickest way to relieve the pain of the withdrawal symptoms is to use the addiction object again. And the vicious cycle continues as they know when they stop using, withdrawal is the *punishment* they try to avoid, but knowing the addiction is painful as well presents the ongoing dilemma.

Treatment for withdrawal symptoms has come a long way over the last decades. In the past, the suffering from withdrawal was viewed as the punishment for bad/addictive behavior. So, the prevailing treatment strategy was to give almost no treatment so the addict would reap in full force what they sowed. As with any severe punishment, the hope was to deter any future misconduct. Sadly, this mentality still persists in many places today. My philosophy is to extend grace and mercy to the addict who wants to stop their addiction. Appropriate treatment avoids death or serious medical complications that can occur, allows the patient more comfort and peace, shortens the length of the withdrawal timeline, and also communicates God's love, grace, and mercy to someone who is full of shame and guilt. Appropriate treatment also builds a therapeutic relationship as compassion and trust start to build a foundation for deeper psychological and spiritual treatment that is to come next.

Withdrawal treatment falls into two categories. The first is targeting the various symptoms and providing relief for them. Some are OTC meds for diarrhea, fever, runny nose, nausea, or insomnia, while some are prescription meds for leg cramps, increased blood pressure or heart rate, anxiety, psychoses and more significant withdrawal symptoms. These symptomatic medications, nurturing support, and addressing sleep, nutrition, and even some safe, light exercise are key to comfortably navigating the withdrawal phase for almost all the withdrawals except opioid or alcohol/sedative/hypnotic withdrawal.

The second category of treatment, Medication Assisted Therapy (MAT), is primarily used when a patient is withdrawing from opioids, any one of the central nervous system depressants (alcohol, sedatives, hypnotics, anxiety medications), and nicotine. Instead of taking a person off a substance cold turkey, MAT prescribes a chemically similar but safer substance to more slowly taper the patient off the more harmful addictive substance. Depending on how slow the taper, the body can be tricked into thinking they are getting enough substance so minimal withdrawal symptoms occur. In the olden days (into the early eighties), doctors would actually prescribe alcohol in small doses to lessen the disruption to the body. Buprenorphine and methadone are used for opioids, a safer benzodiazepine like lorazepam (Ativan) or chlordiazepoxide (Librium) is used for alcohol/sedative/hypnotic/anxiety med withdrawal, and nicotine patch/gum/lozenge is used for nicotine withdrawal. Although these options use a safer addicting substance to taper off the more harmful addiction substance, the goal is to prescribe Buprenorphine (I've never prescribed methadone for long-term opioid abuse) for one to two weeks, and Ativan for three to ten days for alcohol and up to three to four weeks for sedative withdrawal. But these treatments should have an endpoint when physiological withdrawal is over. Sadly, many are kept on these MAT medications for withdrawal for years and years. These can cause many psychiatric and physical issues similar to the substance they were replacing and often lead to old addictive behaviors resurfacing as well.

Also, we never forget to teach and implement psychological and spiritual treatment interventions for soothing, encouragement, and infusing hope that this withdrawal period of suffering has a light at the end of the tunnel. Reducing the stress, helping them get through one day at a time, and keeping them focused on the overall long game of healthier living through incremental healing lessens the severity of the withdrawal symptoms. Most important is submission to the well-planned multi-modal treatment plan because left to their own urges and impulses, they want to go out and use to immediately stop the withdrawal symptoms.

OTHER SUBSTANCE/MEDICATION-INDUCED
MENTAL DISORDERS

Sometimes, either during the acute intoxication or shortly after, substances can induce other psychiatric symptoms such as psychoses, delirium, depression, anxiety, cognitive impairment, mania, OCD, sleep disorders, and sexual dysfunction. These usually last only several days to weeks during the intoxication or withdrawal phases. Occasionally they can last up to a month. Exceptions are certain neurocognitive deficits (memory or attention usually) from long-term use, as well as visual hallucinations from hallucinogen use that could last years and even for the remainder of their earthly life.

Treatment involves keeping them away from the substance, managing the withdrawal phase well, supportive care, psychological and spiritual help with coping skills, nutrition, sleep, and any specific medications targeting the issue that is induced.

TREATING THE UNDERLYING PSYCHOLOGICAL AND ANY
CO-OCCURRING DISORDERS

Once the acute intoxication, withdrawal, and any induced disorders phases are addressed, the next phase is preventing relapse and maintaining sobriety. This is called the recovery phase. But we want more than just recovery to the pre-addiction state, the goal should actually be transformation. God actually wants to use the experiences and lessons learned during the acute addiction struggles to not only transform our lives but also be a catalyst in transforming other lives as well. This amazing and humbling phenomenon occurred and continues to occur in my life, and we see it daily in the lives of our staff and patients at Honey Lake Clinic.

Even though the psychological and spiritual treatments are softly implemented in a supportive and encouraging fashion during the intoxication, withdrawal, and induced-disorder stages, once those phases subside and as the patient's cognitive and emotional skills improve, the psychological and spiritual interventions become more intense and dig deeper. Remember, addictions are generated in each of us due to struggles in our spiritual, psychological, and then biological spheres. All addictions are our feeble attempt to soothe or self-medicate an underlying psychological hurt or loss, or to compensate or fill in for some psychological deficit. Instead of using spiritual truths and principles to address these struggles, we all turn to something created, and not the Creator, to get us through the circumstance.

So, addiction treatment will hinge largely on implementing heavy doses from the buffet of spiritual and psychological interventions with two main areas of focus. The first is unpacking and understanding the underlying hurts, losses, wounds, traumas, misinterpretations, or psychological issues the addiction has been self-medicating. Then infusing the lasting psychospiritual healing Jesus brings and psychiatry helps us apply specifically to the individual's issues. This treatment would be similar to the treatments for any psychological issues we've discussed while we eliminate the patient's primary go-to *coping mechanisms.*

Some basic biological interventions are essential during the treatment phase. Staying away from the substance, sleep, proper nutrition, and exercise play significant roles for the brain to heal, properly rest, and get the valuable nutrients to repair damaged brain cells and circuits, replenish neurotransmitter production, and provide the juice for the electrical activity our brain produces and uses to communicate.

Sometimes a patient is on medications for the co-occurring mental health disorder, so they safely continue those during intoxication and detox/withdrawal stages. But as those stages subside, more accurately diagnosing and then intensifying the treatment for these co-occurring disorders can really get going. Definitely full-force spiritual and psychological interventions are paramount, but when possible, the biological treatments are also very helpful.

Psychiatric medications for the underlying and co-occurring illnesses, but also Transcranial Magnetic Stimulation (TMS), Neurofeedback (NF), and Complementary and Alternative Medicines (CAM) reduce psychiatric symptoms, so relapse is less likely and the psychospiritual healing speeds up. Again, these treatments for the psychiatric issues commence right after the withdrawal period is over and as soon as a clear diagnosis is evident. In looking for the right psychiatric medications, we always want to avoid potentially addicting medications such as stimulants for ADHD and depression, benzodiazepines like Ativan, Xanax, and Valium for anxiety, and some of the addicting sleep medications for insomnia. Using these medications in someone with a substance addiction can easily trigger a relapse so should be avoided almost entirely.

A common treatment obstacle is believing a patient is an adult when they have the look, job, and vocabulary of an adult. But when a person frequently uses an addiction to cope with adversity and stress, they haven't been using or growing the other life skills needed for psychological growth and maturity. So often a person's psychological and emotional growth is stunted and has the level of maturity of when their addiction progressed from recreational to circumstantial use. As a therapist, I might expect a thirty-year-old to have thirty-year-old skills and ability to implement them, but the patient could have the skills and maturity of a sixteen-year-old. This is why, even sober, they still make a lot of mistakes and relapse easily. So, healing from past, forgiving self and others, and growing skills, especially decision-making skills, are the major focus.

But healing and growing skills requires digging into the past, and that's painful. Remember the addict's urge is to avoid immediate pain regardless of the long-term consequences. Avoiding pain plays out as either dragging their feet in therapy and not engaging as they should or using their addiction object to self-medicate, soothe, escape, or distract them from the pain of therapy. So, the second focus of addiction treatment is trying to keep the patient away from their addiction object to keep them from *relapsing* while they wrestle with past baggage, consequences of their addiction, or guilt/shame as they re-hash any of their past that they always tried to bury with their addiction.

Helping them avoid relapse is vital to building momentum, as well as just keeping their body, mind, and spirit healthy while avoiding more significant damage that sets the process back a bunch of steps. Remember, like a sentimental teddy bear or toy from childhood, a patient views their addiction object as that sentimental soother that was always there for them. Even when loved ones scattered, left, rejected them, or were confused, the addiction object was always available and willing to help. Just like it is hard to give up on your favorite sentimental toy of childhood, it's very difficult for addicts to give up and reject, cast aside, their go-to *security blanket* for good in favor of a new untested replacement. So, treatment helps them realize the addiction object was there but also very harmful and no longer needed. They are grown and can use better, more robust security blankets spiritually and psychologically to avoid the relapse of snuggling up with their old faithful go-to.

Avoiding relapse comes in many ways, and again, psychological and spiritual elements are foundational. So now let me share with you some of those I've helped patients employ for successful recovery and then transformation.

1. Basic healing routines. Remember, intentionality and consistency builds habits and achieves goals while random and sporadic leads to destruction. Sleeping seven to nine hours during usual times. Eating three balanced meals per day. Physical activity every day for thirty to sixty minutes, even if it is just walking outside. Building school or work routines and flow to the day builds structure, engages the mind, and allows a person to start to trust themselves and their ability to follow through with a strategy. An idle mind is the devil's playground and nothing good is achieved randomly.

2. Acute relaxation and stress management skills. These help with anxiety and minimizing the escalation of their discomfort while allowing thinking to be clearer and better options to surface.

3. Increasing awareness and understanding of all the spiritual, psychological, relational, physiological, including brain chemistry, financial, legal, and occupational consequences, and practice bringing them to mind when tempted to use.

4. Identifying common triggers that quickly lead to urges or addiction activity. Triggers can be internal, like negative thinking, fear of failure, or loneliness. Or they can be external like a financial bill, argument with spouse, or any stressful event.

5. Developing a better behavioral plan to avoid addiction traps and options. Don't go by that bar, get internet screening tools so no porn, give your money to someone you love to hold so you have none in your pocket to buy drugs, walk away from conflict, change past people, places, and things to lessen the chances of falling back into the old addiction habits, go to twelve-step or Celebrate Recovery meetings instead of a drug-using activity.

6. Finding four to five healthier options to cope with the

underlying issues and going through that list regularly, even when life is good, to practice them but especially when starting to feel stressed so alternatives to the addiction object become instilled. Options like calling a loved one, listening to a favorite worship song, favorite physical activity, deep breathing, meditating on a favorite verse or Bible passage, remembering some positive and healthy personal experiences, journaling, distracting with a work or yard task, or working on a puzzle.

7.   Community is vital. We are built for relationships and we need to engage with others. Addictions heap a lot of shame, which can be a barrier limiting our engagement with others. But we need to help the patient fight that fear so they can develop a community to practice their new skills with, get encouragement and learn from, and feel accepted and loved. Remember, the opposite of addiction is belonging. If we don't feel we belong, we build a relationship with an addiction object as our go-to buddy when life is tough.

8.   Accountability is an essential part of a healthy community. While the addiction was growing, the patient was accountable only to himself. Having a trusted person who the patient can honestly and transparently be vulnerable with to report what is happening is so important. It allows light into a dark place. It also forces the patient to articulate what's going on inside, making it more tangible and less overwhelming. They get to hear another perspective and get some guidance and feedback to move them forward. Obviously, their treatment clinicians can fill this role to some extent, but it is essential for them to find several others in their lives they trust and have the sensibility to guide and hold them accountable in this journey. Recovery meeting sponsors, church mentors, or disciplers, healthy spouse or sibling, parent, peer, or coach can serve these roles, as well. Ideally the accountability partner gets to see the patient function in real life as well to make sure what the patient states they are doing is actually what they are doing. Periodic urine drug screens can be administered by clinicians or from various accountability partners to enhance patient accountability. Random screening is the best frequency, so the patient doesn't cheat the system.

9.   Supervision during various times of the recovery period is

essential. No addict is able to manage every temptation on their own as soon as they stop using. Supervision means someone is in close physical proximity and overseeing the patient to make sure no addiction activity happens, as well as being engaged in the treatment interventions above. Supervision takes many forms from a residential treatment facility, like Honey Lake Clinic, Sober or Halfway House Living with a house *leader*, living with an accountability partner or parent, or taking someone with them to a wedding reception to help resist the alcohol that's available. The supervision can last two hours or two years. It could be intermittent and needed only when the individual is experiencing a stormy time and is uncertain they can navigate it on their own. Better to err on the side of having unneeded supervision rather than trying to do it alone but really needing supervision. Humility to ask and submit to the supervision is key.

10. Recovery meetings like Celebrate Recovery (a spiritual growth program to overcome many struggles), Alcoholics Anonymous (AA), Narcotics Anonymous (NA), or ideally the many similar Christian versions for addiction recovery meetings (like Addictions Victorious, Overcomers in Christ, Reformers Unanimous) are specific ways to accomplish some of the elements above. They do not substitute for therapy nor provide it, but many positive elements are available such as being part of a community where the playing field is equal as all are struggling or have struggled with a life altering addiction of some sort. Supervision and accountability are available, as well. These meetings have a time of sharing, fellowship, and education to equip the participant to move forward. The secular versions are led by peers in recovery. The Christian versions are often led by a pastor or a lay leader in the church.

    a.   Twelve Steps of AA—AA was founded in 1930s and used twelve steps as a set of guidelines for spiritual and character development. The goal was not to just maintain sobriety, but to use absolute honesty, purity, unselfishness and love, with public confession and vulnerability in the meeting to get at and heal the underlying issues. Initially, the Twelve Steps were very Christian, but this has gotten diluted over the years. Also, since no professional clinician is at the meetings, most twelve step meetings have become more behavioral and sobriety focused and less attentive to the spiritual and psychological healing and growth.

b.   A large majority of the residential rehabs are twelve-step programs, using the twelve steps as the main curriculum. The founders of AA, Bill W. and Dr. Bob, never intended the Twelve Steps to be an intensive treatment center curriculum, and it isn't. The Twelve Steps were meant to be a set of principles for lay people to use to facilitate a growth experience. Because of the reliance on the Twelve Steps as their curriculum and lack of psychiatric and therapists, most rehabs have a low success rate.

11.   A plan for relapse is necessary as most will have some slip as they try to live life without their addiction object. Obviously, we would rather not see a relapse, but after a number of years of a certain habit, immediately and permanently stopping is very difficult. For this reason, residential treatment, as mentioned above, allows for supervision and a safe supportive environment to build good habits. But if relapse happens, use the tips above to confess, repent, seek out the accountability partner to determine the next steps of supervision, treatment, and learn from the relapse to start building more clean time again and get back positive momentum. Many times, though, when the addict relapses, shame and guilt lead to lying, hiding, and isolation. All the progress and skills they worked on go out the window because they've let themselves down and feel others will be upset at them or just sad. So, they often hide their relapse and the negative spiral starts spinning downward.

12.   Medications to help maintain sobriety can be helpful in the early stages and provide a safety net in ongoing recovery. Medications help avoid a relapse or minimize the damage and extent of a relapse. These ongoing medications aren't prescribed until after the withdrawal period is safely navigated and are used for opioids and alcohol recovery or maintenance.

a. For alcohol recovery maintenance, a number of medications exist, and they are all *non-addictive*:

i. Disulfiram (Antabuse)—taken every morning and

the patient will get violently ill and vomit if alcohol is consumed while it is in their system. This is good for the person who is regimented to take it each day and the knowledge of the consequences stops them from drinking. Others can choose not to take it on the days they want to drink.

ii. Acamprosate (Campral)—taken three times per day (difficult for many to remember each day) and works on the brain to decrease alcohol cravings.

iii. Oral Naltrexone (Revia)—is taken daily and reduces cravings while especially reducing the euphoria when drinking so the person has less incentive to use alcohol.

iv. Injectable Naltrexone (Vivitrol)—a shot lasting four weeks to accomplish the same as oral naltrexone.

v. Topiramate (Topamax)—taken daily and helps reduce cravings and impulsive behaviors. Not as much research behind it, but one of my favorites to prescribe for alcohol addiction.

b. For opioid recovery maintenance, the following medications are used:

i. Methadone—very long-lasting opioid with less euphoria. Still addicting and overdose is possible. Less abused than heroin and other prescription opioids. Methadone clinics are highly regulated and ideally are the last resort when all other recovery attempts have failed. I do not recommend or refer to methadone clinics.

ii. Buprenorphine/Naltrexone (Suboxone)—as a partial opioid agonist, buprenorphine can be addicting but is far less potent than the street version of other prescription pain killer opioids. I use it to help a patient get through withdrawal and maybe a couple days after. Many in our society are using it for long-term maintenance, which I do not view as a good strategy.

iii. Injectable Naltrexone (Vivitrol)—a long-lasting opioid blocking (non-addictive) shot lasting four weeks that blocks the effects of opioids. Because of increased sensitivity as the shot wears off, an increase risk of overdose exists if relapse occurs.

c. For the maintenance phase of substance abuse treatment, I never prescribe any addictive medications, like buprenorphine or methadone. When an addict has an addictive chemical in their system, relapse is easier and ongoing sobriety and growth is harder as these opioids lead to depression, anxiety, cognitive issues and impulsivity, which all compromise the treatment and skill acquisition goals.

13.   Assessment and diagnosis tweaking is an ongoing activity. As the brain heals and the trust in the therapist grows, more information emerges and they articulate their past timeline better. The dynamic psychiatric assessment continues to became more accurate and refined. New information might lead to new or refined diagnoses. Common are Major Depression, Bipolar Type 1, or Schizophrenia, but other subtler diagnoses such as ADHD, PTSD, Social Anxiety, OCD, cyclothymia or Bipolar Type 2 eating disorder, somatization disorder, dissociative disorders, or sleep disorders are also often discovered.

14.   Medical treatment of any medical issues that either pred-ated the addiction, but were then made worse by the addiction, or new medical issues as a result of the addiction. Increase stress from un- or under-treated medical conditions will increase the probability of relapse as well as worsen the underlying psychological issue that needs healing.

Managing and treating someone with a significant addiction is a challenging and very dynamic process as the recipe of which treatment interventions and how much of each is always changing, sometimes very quickly. The patient and those close to the patient must keep on their toes, especially if they are helping in some of the roles I listed. They must be diligent and engaged to help the patient move forward while anticipating any stressors that can influence a relapse. If a relapse occurs, obviously significant reshuffling of the treatments above needs to be considered.

,

PROCESS ADDICTIONS

Process addictions are more subtle than substance addictions. Certainly, no toxic chemical is a positive, but intoxication and withdrawal can happen. Sex, porn, gambling, work, hoarding, shopping, video games, social media, stealing, exercise, eating, and other process addictions although gambling, stealing, hoarding, and eating disorders are the only process addictions the DSM-5 recognizes.

Treatment for process addictions uses the same principles as for substance addiction and sometimes are even more difficult to treat because the *use* can be a lot more subtle or hidden more easily. Sadly, even though process addictions damage people's lives and contribute to so much suffering, other than eating disorders, insurances will not cover intensive treatments for these issues because of minimal medical danger during intoxication or detox/withdrawal stages.

Treating the underlying psychiatric issue biologically again is same as substance addictions, but some particular medications I've found beneficial for process addictions are the following:

• Antidepressants, especially the serotonin-focused ones, to reduce some of the obsessing about the addiction object and the compulsive activity of using or other addiction-related behaviors associated with the addiction object. Also, these meds can decrease libido to decrease sex and porn addiction. Lexapro, Viibryd, and Trintellix are my favorites.

• Mood stabilizers/anticonvulsants help decrease impulsive behavior, and since addictions are wrought with impulsivity, this class of medications resources the patient some in this area. Added benefits are some anxiety reduction and mood improvements. My favorites are Topamax, Trileptal, and Gabapentin.

• Naltrexone, as we discussed in the substance addictions, negates the high from substances, but it can also reduce the high some receive from cutting, burning, or other intentional self-harming behaviors. I use naltrexone (Revia) to negate that buzz and over time (along with lots of other psychological and spiritual interventions) it helps reduce self-harming addiction.

BIGGEST ADDICTION OBSTACLE

The biggest struggle in my recovery and in the recovery of every addict I have treated is making the mistake in thinking intellectual knowledge is the same as skill acquisition. Let me explain. A person can go to a lecture and watch a video on playing and hitting a baseball. The instructor could be phenomenal and humorous, allowing the viewer to really understand the various elements of the game. They might be full of confidence as they go out onto the field, ready to play conquer this sport everyone says is so difficult. But they are easily crushed by their opponent as they have absolutely zero skills. You can switch out baseball and insert piano playing, baking, crocheting, football, or anything that requires a large and complicated set of skills that need to be finely integrated together.

When a person is in treatment, residential or outpatient, they hear a lot of information and education about addiction, triggers, consequences of use, better options, decision-making skills, spiritual truths and principles. None if it is really complicated like rocket science or brain surgery. Since it is easily taken in and makes sense, the patient assumes they also have the skills to leave their addiction behind. So often they prematurely leave treatment or put themselves back into the game without having any real skills, and they get bludgeoned again. Their treatment team is usually telling them stay in treatment to learn and practice the psychological and spiritual skills, so they become part of your *muscle memory* and almost automatic for use in situations because of regular practice.

But most of us think we know better. We write our own instruction manual and think with some significant knowledge, we are the expert in also implementing it. Nothing can be further from the truth. By definition, an addict's track record is poor. So, willingness to submit to the timeline of the authorities in their life is so important. Due to the dangers of intoxication, overdose, and withdrawal, erring on the side of safety and less risk is always the best strategy. Better slow and steady than too fast, relapse, and go backward.

People struggling with chemical addictions have had lives that were hijacked and so many bad habits developed while all their gifts, strengths, and skills atrophied and died away because of lack of use. It takes some time of living life differently, implementing and

experiencing life in positive ways without the addiction object for
the bad habits to die away and good habits and skills to start, take
root, grow strong, and bear lasting fruit. Instead of having patience
and self-control, the person in recovery feels a sense of urgency to
make up for all the lost time and atone for all the mistakes they've
made. Reassuring them and helping them think with spiritual lenses
of God's forgiveness and grace while enjoying the blessings of each
day can help them slow the pace and feel God's love and peace
moment by moment.

Recap

1. Dual diagnosis means a person has a psychological issue and an
   addiction issue at the same time.
2. Everyone has a psychological defect, as Jesus is the only
   person with perfect brain chemistry and perfect psychological
   functioning.
3. Everyone has an addiction—something they pursue other than
   God to get their needs met and have trouble stopping even
   though consequences occur. Addiction is a person's effort to cope
   with their underlying psychological defects and stressors.
4. So, we are all dual-diagnosis patients.
5. Addictions are the most difficult category of psychiatric disorders to treat as they are deep-seated issues of the heart and took
   many years to practice and perfect, so don't leave over-night.
   They take time, intentionality, and very consistent and regular
   training and practice.
6. The four phases of addiction treatment are intoxication,
   detoxification/withdrawal, recovery/maintenance, and life
   transformation.
7. Once the intoxication and detox/withdrawal periods are over,
   aggressive simultaneous treatment of both the addiction and
   the underlying psychological struggle significantly increases the
   chance of recovery and transformation. Aggressively treating
   any mental health diagnosis plays a critical role in lessening the
   chance of relapse as well.
8. Spiritual and psychological treatment interventions are vital in
   the recovery and transformation but also helpful to navigate the
   intoxication and detox/withdrawal phase, as well.

9. Biological treatments, such as basic life activities—sleep, nutrition, and exercise—as well as psychiatric medications, supplements, and other brain stimulation techniques also play a major role in the psychiatric healing process.

10. Once the withdrawal phase is over, the psychiatric evaluation is regularly updated as more history, signs and symptoms, both present and past, periodically emerge and thus the three-sphere treatment strategy adjusts to address the updated findings.

11. It takes a long time for the severe addict to really be an informed director of their life. Even though they want to be the decision maker and believe they now know all there is to know about addiction to stay sober the rest of their life, it takes years for them to really be a clear and objective thinker. Until then, supervision, safety, accountability, and humbly submitting to the recommendations of others is the safest course of action.

Thank you for your attention, and I pray this has been helpful to your healing as well as those God has brought into your path to help.

SPIRITUALITY

A Non-Addict, Treatment Executive's View

By Trinity Phillips

I never thought I'd be sitting here writing my very own contribution to a book having anything to do with addiction in any way. I'm not a person in recovery and none of my immediate family suffers from addiction. My original thoughts on addiction and recovery were very negatively slanted. Based upon my very own experiences, those of others, and even the media I was exposed to, I believed addiction to be a moral failing of weak people who couldn't just deal with life and just stop using. Now, as I'm sitting here as the president of The N.O.W. Matters More Foundation and someone with many friends in recovery, as well as many years in this industry, I can admit that my assessment was way off. My journey isn't the craziest, but it's relatable to many. Let's talk about fear, ignorance, judgment, and how that turns into acceptance and advocacy.

I grew up in the eighties and during that time drug/alcohol issues weren't talked about in an open and educational way. They were instead talked about as people with emotional and behavioral issues who failed to overcome them and were hurting everyone around them. Emotional and behavioral issues? What does that mean? I had those growing up. Does that mean I'm going to abuse drugs or alcohol and become an addict? In my childhood years I experienced a wide array of painful things and trauma—everything from abuse, abandonment, violence, inappropriate sexual conduct, and a few more. Those events contributed to an angst and rage many can't understand, but addiction? I never turned to drugs or alcohol as a coping mechanism, but I had many risk factors, so that means I'm better than them, right? No, I was just lucky enough to be surrounded by a bunch of people who weren't good at drug use.

See, part of my angst was to defy anyone telling me what I was *supposed* to do. Consequently, being raised by a single mother from my background meant you were supposed to be stupid, in jail, and addicted. I set out to prove everyone wrong. I maintained a 4.0 GPA throughout my scholastic career and many friends who were failing so happened to also be abusing drugs. This correlation to me meant that drugs equaled stupid and I was terrified to be stupid. I did, however, commit numerous crimes and befriended several addicts, but I always chose to abstain and was most likely guilty of some severe judgment as I watched them fall into the pitfalls of drug addiction.

As I went into my adolescent and teenage years, I enjoyed the occasional disgusting beer or sugary mixed drink at a crappy high school house party, but I was always able to stop before getting drunk and never shied away from saying no. My aversion to losing control ensured that I avoided drunkenness like the plague. I would be that guy helping drunk kids get home safely and even made drinks for tips at a few parties as a way to make some cash. Watching everyone participate in this while I was able to enjoy one or two and then call it quits only added to my belief that anyone strong enough could just stop whenever they truly wanted. Add to those experiences a media world that portrayed addicts as horrible bottom dwellers that broke into houses, hung out in alleys, and robbed anyone dumb enough to venture into the wrong area, you have a perfect storm of judgment. It was so easy to look down on addicts and even easier to find others to join in on the judgment and make it an us versus them mentality.

Enter my early adult years and I still hadn't met anyone who could alter my perspective of what an addict was. That was until Dan. Dan was a co-worker I knew and interacted with a lot for several years. He worked on my bikes and we spent many an hour chatting about nonsense. One day he mentioned he wouldn't ride with me because I wasn't sober. Wasn't sober? What the hell does that mean? I'm not drunk and I don't drink and ride either. What I didn't understand until he elaborated was that he was in recovery and only rode with his group that was sober (never drank). Welcome to my very first addiction *aha* moment. You mean this guy I've known for a few years and respected enough to hang out with and even allowed to work on my motorcycle was one of *those* guys? He never went into too much detail about his past or recovery, but he openly admitted to issues, and that was enough to shock my system and open the door to what was to come.

Fast forward to my invitation to a now close friend and business partner. I invited this guy Lui to come to a weekend event for my fitness company to run a mental health group. He came and knocked it out of the park, but as our friendship began to blossom, I started to be exposed more and more to the addiction world. What I didn't know about Lui at the onset was that he not only was a certified addiction professional, but was in long-term recovery, too. He was more open than anyone I had ever met or even seen. He began to slowly shatter any perceptions I had of what it meant to be addicted. He was very well respected and achieved quite a lot of success in the business world.

I didn't know people like this existed and thankfully he was more than willing to answer questions about his life, his journey, and his addiction. The next step was insane. He had me come to his treatment center to discuss fitness and teach spirituality. Wait, what? I'm supposed to go and help a bunch of addicts? Yeah, and it was amazing! I spent the next few years within treatment centers helping addicts learn about spirituality and how to make healthier decisions in their lives. Mind blown. These people were some of the coolest individuals I had ever met. After hearing their stories and getting to know them, they were just like me and everyone else. They were people who made an unskillful decision at some point in life (using a substance to cope) and now were trying to come back from that. Their stories weren't that different from everyone I'd ever met, but they were unlucky enough to have the disease of addiction.

I am now an advocate for those struggling with the disease of addiction and I'm proud of it. Some of the most rewarding moments I have ever experienced are when someone comes to me and tells their story of how I played a role in their sobriety and getting their life back. I am so proud of the work I am involved with these days, and I couldn't imagine doing anything else. That guy Lui started a foundation to help those with addiction, but without the means to get the help they require, and asked me to be a part of it. I, of course, joined and began fighting the fight as a soldier on the front lines.

Over the years, I have become more heavily involved and now I even claim the title of president of that very foundation. I have learned so much about this industry, this disease, and the people who it impacts. Let's start with this industry, and by that I mean the treatment world. There are so many good and so many not-so-good places to send a loved one to get help. When I say good, I really mean places that offer a wide variety of techniques and protocols that have been proven to successfully treat addiction. These typically include medically assisted treatment (MAT), different treatment modalities for dealing with trauma, great aftercare, and alumni organizations just to name a few.

However, there is a dirty side to this industry and that usually involves some shady practices like body brokering among other nefarious practices. Sadly, though, even when you do find a worthy facility, insurance doesn't seem to enjoy paying for addiction services in the same way they pay for other life-threatening diseases. Because society and many shot callers don't fully accept or understand the disease of addiction, it can be difficult to get the proper funding for help like you do for cancer, as an example. Everyone hates cancer and *good* people can get it, so we all expect insurance to pay whatever it takes to heal them. In addition, there's a very clear and universal way to figure out if the cancer treatment has worked. Whereas addiction can be much trickier to decipher.

Now, the disease of addiction. Whew boy, this thing really sucks. What so many addicts, family members, and common people don't understand is this thing invades and takes over like the body snatchers of old. That loved one you knew is still in there, but their entire decision-making and logic processes have been infected with this disease. This shows up as erratic behavior, stealing, lying, hurting loved ones, crimes, etc. What we as nonaddicts have a hard time wrapping our heads around is how someone could do these things. Well, someone wouldn't, but the addict would. They're not themselves, and that's precisely why this disease is so destructive. Cancer lets its host remain them, but ruins the body. Addiction hijacks the mind while letting the person most often *look* the same physically. It's not the disease that makes them look like the typical news interview of the *poor* addict. That's the particular drug of choice that takes care of that, while the disease makes them ignore what's looking back at them in the mirror. This leads me to the people who are impacted by this disease. The people come from all walks of life. I've seen rich people, poor people, beautiful people, not so beautiful people, Black, white, Hispanic, mother, father, brother, sister, son, daughter, young, old, smart, not so smart, introvert, extrovert, American, non-American, good parent, bad parent, etc. It literally impacts *everyone*. They all have something in common, though, and that is *nobody* wants to be an addict. Nobody chooses to be an addict.

So, what works? What do you do? I've learned a few things that have seemed to be universal in a successful long-term recovery plan. For starters, no *one* way works. Some people absolutely love AA or NA while others can't make it through the doors. Some treatment facilities seem to be perfect for one and horrible for another. Some people absolutely need faith-based while others require more subtlety. Bottom line to understand is recovery is possible for anyone who wants it, but it doesn't come easily. It won't always be the first path chosen. However, you never give up on it.

The second thing I'll say is the recovery community is vast and strong. When you surrender and join the community as a whole, you will never be alone. Someone will always understand your challenges and be willing to help, and I think that's friggin' awesome. The next thing is *trust the process*. I know that sounds cliché, but it's totally true. So many have walked this path prior to you and they deserve to be listened to. While driving at night, your headlights don't show your destination, but you keep going with the trust that the next few feet will be there. Recovery is like that. You might not understand the whys at first, but trust that the people there to help you truly have your best interest in mind and are leading you to the life you want and deserve.

For the family, seek your own counseling and never give up. Your loved one is still there. However, understand that you must have boundaries to keep the disease from pulling you down, too. A good counselor or program will assist in understanding what those boundaries should look like and how they should be enforced. Just remember that you can only control *your* responses in any given situation. You can't do any of these things if you don't talk about it or reach out for help. Don't be scared and don't be embarrassed. Many more people suffer than you know, but not reaching out only hurts you and/or your loved one.

What I've seen that doesn't work in any addiction scenario is to ignore it and hope is goes away. This thing is progressive in nature and will eventually win by killing its host. Don't try and beat it on your own unless you're the type to try and set a broken bone on your own. There are people in this world whose sole purpose is to help you recover, so let them help you. Anyone reading this, know you're loved and you deserve happiness. Whether my personal story of enlightenment mimics yours or you have your very own journey, I sincerely hope I was able to offer up some value for your time. I hope as you read the chapters offered up by the numerous authors from numerous perspectives, you're able to gain whatever insight and wisdom you seek. Use this as the catalyst to start your own journey. If you're struggling with addiction, start by asking for help and accepting it.

If your loved one is struggling, start by talking about it and reaching out to see what resources best fit your needs and use them. If you're not an addict and have an unpleasant view, start by getting involved in your local community and getting to know someone different than you. If you've ever been hurt by an addict and are having trouble forgiving, start by hating the disease and forgiving the sick person who hurt you. If you're already involved in helping, start by sharing the message and encouraging others to get involved in some way. Thank you for checking out my story and I hope you read it with the compassion that was intended. I wish you good luck and much happiness, whatever your journey.

SPIRITUALITY IS A PERSONAL JOURNEY

By Keith Everett Brooks

It is a great honor to have the opportunity to contribute this chapter on spirituality and to be in the company of such awesome co-authors. I humbly share these words for the purpose of assisting those who are recovering from addictions and for anyone who simply wants to explore the great mystery within each of us that is beckoning us to step into our true greatness. In this chapter, I will provide a general definition of the term spirituality. I will discuss how I have come to know spirituality in my life and some of the key learnings I have attained. I will discuss how these key learnings are transferable skill sets for those who are in drug recovery.

WHAT IS SPIRITUALITY?

Spirituality is a very ambiguous term that has many meanings to many people. The concepts I will present about spirituality in general, and as it relates to drug rehabilitation, are derived from my own studies and experiences. Though the concepts I will present may challenge the readers' current understandings, they are in no way intended to negate or insult the reader. My intention is to share ideas and information that, if perused with an open mind, may lead the reader to a more in-depth exploration of their own spiritual journey.

Let's look at how the dictionary defines spirituality:

The quality of being concerned with the human spirit or soul as opposed to material or physical things.

In essence, spirituality is the study of the human spirit or the soul.

What is the difference between spirituality and religion?

The dictionary defines religion as:

A set of beliefs concerning the cause, nature and purpose of the universe, especially when considered as the creation of a superhuman agency or agencies, usually involving devotional and ritual observances and often containing a moral code governing the conduct of human affairs.

In my experience, I have found religions to be narratives born out of stories of how incredible men, women, and supernatural beings embarked upon spiritual journeys that ultimately lead them to define a path and a set of guidelines, which helped them and their followers to know God and to achieve heroic accomplishments that continue to shape our world today.

"You must be the change you want to see in this world." ~Mahatma Gandhi

Spirituality, as it concerns the individual, is one's personal story about how they have come to know themselves as a spiritual being having a human experience or not. One's spirituality is an interpersonal pursuit with societal ramifications. Your beliefs about yourself dictate how you show up in society. Conversely, society often has a strong influence on how you feel about yourself. There is a symbiotic relationship between the self and society. We live in a world where hurt people hurt others. Many of us have no clue what our soul is or how to connect with it. We are bundles of source energy/love bound by chains of fear, anger, and pain. In short, the spiritual journey is about how you free yourself of the chains/beliefs that bind you so you may one day know you are truly a unique, divine reflection of God.

Religions, pastors, and gurus can lead you to the doorway of your soul, but to explore the depths of your own spirit you must enter a space that only you can traverse, your inner universe. Others can assist and give guidance as you describe your inner experience to them, but they can only go so far when it comes to true personal transformation. Deep within us, beyond the reach of our empirical mind, is an omnipotent place of knowing we all have access to. It is our spiritual connection to that which created all that is. This sacred place within each of us is constantly calling to us. It reaches out to us through gentle nudges or soft whispers. It is never intrusive and always respectful of our free will. Its advice is always sage, if we are able to perceive it. The goal is that at some point, as you explore your inner universe you will become conscious of the guidance that comes from within… *intuition.* Experience has shown that when I am able to decipher this innate guidance and adhere to its direction, my life is much more fulfilling than when I go at it by my own empirical devices.

Decipher and adhere to the spiritual guidance that comes from within is a personal mantra I have used with varying success over the last thirty-plus years. It can be very difficult to tune out the tempest of distractions that seek our attention from sun up to sun down, and even as we sleep. It is my hope that as you review this chapter, if you are sincerely ready, something within will shift. I pray this shift will act to liberate the reader from a thought, a belief, or a personal narrative that is no longer serving them well. As we learn to let go, we open ourselves to our best.

THE DAY MY LIFE CHANGED AND MY SPIRITUAL JOURNEY BEGAN

My personal spiritual journey was initiated through the indoctrinations of organized religion. Most of my knowledge about God was fed to me through block buster movie series, like *The Bible*, and through my Catholic school experience, which I attended throughout my primary school years, though I am not Catholic. In the inner-city, academically, a Catholic school education often proves to be far superior to that of a public-school education. My real spiritual evolution began after I started my freshman year in college.

During my first days at the University of California at Berkeley, my whole concept of God and religion imploded. During the eighties, history and religion were primarily taught from a Eurocentric perspective. All the heroes were white males. As a young African-American man raised in America in the eighties, I was fully indoctrinated by the teachings of that time. I envisioned God and all of his angels as white males. Besides Martin Luther King and Caesar Chavez, my high school texts were largely devoid of heroic people of color.

Well, all of that changed during my first days in college when African American upperclassmen began introducing me to the teachings of African American thought leaders—Aswa Kwesi, Jawanza Kunjufu, Angela Davis, Lerone Bennett... These thought leaders provided me with information that drastically shifted my understanding of self, history, and religion.

I was raised in a Christian family with a father, mother, and younger sister. My parents sought to protect my sister and me from the trials and tribulations they had experienced in their lives, with little to no discussions about their experiences growing up as African Americans in the sixties or their experiences in the South. I would not learn of the collective struggles of African Americans until I entered college.

One of the greatest shifts in my understanding of religion and spirituality came after learning that many of the important characters in the Bible were people of color, some even being Africans. My young mind was blown wide open. I could not believe that God would allow revisionist historians to put forth such blatant lies about the teachings of God. I felt heartbroken and betrayed by God. How could the Almighty allow Himself to be lied about? I became an Atheist. I held the belief that all religions were manipulations of man and that God did not exist.

I held this belief for about a year. Then, the day came that changed my life forever. It was 2 a.m. and I was asleep in my dorm room when I was awakened from a deep sleep by *a presence*. I felt the presence of my best friend, Pookie, very distinctly. I remember thinking how odd that was and then falling back to sleep. The next morning my sister called me from Los Angeles and told me that Pookie had died at 2 a.m. that morning. I was devastated. He was the first person who was very close to me to die. I had never felt what I was feeling before. This was the guy who made sure that he was in town and came to my house on my birthday every year. We had a longstanding tradition of playing table tennis in my garage on my birthday. My heart was broken.

I was also mind blown by the fact that I had definitely felt his presence in my room near the time of his death. The realization that his spiritual presence made direct contact with me changed my life forever. Now, I was confident there was spirit, and if there is spirit, God must be real. I had experiential evidence. I was now on a mission to know the truth about God. My true spiritual journey had begun.

I made a commitment to myself that before I pledged allegiance to any religion, I was going to research every religion I could find information on. I wanted to know how other cultures described and experienced God. I wanted to determine for myself which one felt right for me. I studied Buddhism, Hinduism, the Metu Neter (Egyptian), Islam, Judaism, Hari Krishnas, as well as various Native

American and West African cosmologies. I researched the Bible and its stories as written by other historians around the world. I studied the Dead Sea Scrolls.

I found myself swimming in an array of dogma. The most interesting thing I discovered was that most of the religions I studied had more in common than different. I discovered the difference between Eastern and Western religions. I found that Eastern religions and indigenous faiths focused more on the inward experience, nature, and spiritual development while Western religions seemed to focus more on outward manifestations of faith and productivity.

After several years of exploring, I found my match. I chose to study and become initiated as a priest in an Afro-Cuban indigenous/nature-based faith that originated out of the Congo. During my study with this faith I learned to connect with Spirit. I spoke with my ancestors and spirit guides every day. I learned to commune and communicate with nature. I was introduced to both the benevolent and malevolent sides of the spirit realms. My concept of God was no longer that of a white man. God no longer took on the shape of a human. God was/is beyond material. I learned energy healing techniques. I had amazing spiritual experiences that were evidence of that which is beyond the conceivable. During this episode of my life I learned to engage with Spirit directly. But I had not learned how to explore the nature of my own spirit effectively.

After twenty years of study within the Afro-Cuban faith, I had decided that it was time for me to discover the nature of my own spirit. I wanted to discover my direct connection with God. I began studying the inward path. I researched and studied those who had achieved the highest levels of spiritual evolution. I studied the masters… Jesus, Buddha, Mohammed, Osiris, Isis, Solemn, Imhotep, Krishna, Yogananda, and many more. I wanted to learn how each of them had uniquely achieved their spiritual evolution. I started meditating. I practiced Qi Qong. I obtained my certification in Reiki and as a Yoga Instructor. I had become a spiritualist. I define a spiritualist as one concerned with illuminating the inward path to understanding what it means to be a spiritual being having a human experience and to walk this earth one day in total unison with the Source of All things. I no longer sought a religion. I sought knowledge of my spiritual self.

SPIRITUALITY AS IT RELATES TO RECOVERY

In 2015, I began leading therapy groups at drug recovery centers. I created a curriculum called the University of Life. It is a three-part curriculum: 1) "I Am/Know Thyself," 2) "Your Life Perspective," and 3) "The Power of Choices." It is a synthesis of much of what I have learned along my own journey inward. I have been blessed to have had great teachers both in the flesh and in spirit. This curriculum is full of borrowed knowledge.

When working in recovery and discussing spirituality, I found it necessary to develop a common baseline understanding of what it means to be a spiritual being having a human experience. So, I synthesized the following imaginary creation story from the various cosmologies I have studied.

In the beginning there emerges this malleable ball of energy that is an extension of or an outgrowth from the Source of All that Is— God. This ball of energy has freewill, it is innocent, and it does not yet know itself as being separate from God. When this individualized energy enters the womb of its human mother, it starts to form its own unique identity, first through the DNA of the parents and then through the external inputs of the parents and social environment of the parents while developing in the womb. As it is developing in the womb, this ball of energy begins to transform itself into internal organs, skeletal structure and finally its outwardly distinguishing parts—limbs, sexual organs, face, skin, etc. We can think of this ball of energy as one's spirit/soul.

While developing in the womb, this spirit is clear about its nature as spirit and must become acclimated to its new life in the flesh. So, imagine this initial ball of energy being your center, where your soul rests. This center is said to reside in the heart, which is the first organ to form in the embryo. This part of you knows you are and will always be a unique expression of God/Source.

Even before leaving the womb, this ball of energy, this soul in the flesh, begins its official training. It will be educated/indoctrinated into the ways and beliefs of the human family line it was born into. The first phase of this socialization is an orientation of sorts about what it means to be a human being on earth. As a human, this spirit must regulate itself to being limited to all the bindings associated with being human. We are subject to gravity. We have a very analytical mind that often works contrary to the guidance of the soul. We live on earth, a planet that revolves around the sun every twenty-four hours, etc. Little by little we are introduced to the intricacies of being human. The more we begin to know ourselves as human, the more we tend to forget our innate connection with God.

Next, once out of the womb, we begin our socialization into our particular family line. You will be informed consciously and unconsciously about the meanings of the biological markers that you exhibit such as: ethnicity, gender, sexual orientation, personality traits, physical capabilities, concepts of time and age, and thought narratives. This forms a layer of held beliefs that act to build the foundation of one's personal identity. Typically, these learnings occur through the age of seven.

The next level of socialization is cultural. This is when this developing personality begins to anchor itself to a persona. From the age of seven through adolescents and young adults, we are consciously and subconsciously trying to figure out who we are and why we are here. At this level, one's relationship with their ego is firmly developed. In this level our persona is shaped by: education, personal habits, income, nationality, religion, hobbies, socio-economic background, political affiliation, geographic location, work background, appearance, language, parental and marital status, military experience, etc.

The final level of socialization is largely organizational—our groups, our clans, our entitlements, our rank in society. We tend to gravitate toward these identifiers as we mature into our adulthood. During this phase, we qualify ourselves by our successes and or our failures. In this layer you are defined by your titles, employment status, functional level/classification, management status, field of work, etc.

If you imagine these layers as the concentric circles of an onion, you will see that as you move further away from the center, you move further away from the true knowledge of who you are. By the time you get to the outer layers, you are usually fully enrolled in the personality and internal narratives you have accepted about yourself. You truly believe you are the person you have created with all of these associated traits. This is where most of our problems are born. We do not know who we really are. We forget the fact that we are this amazing ball of malleable energy in the flesh that can do anything it imagines.

When I finish sharing this story with my groups, I admit to them that this is a very linear way of describing the dynamic way in which we form our personalities. It does not take into account the grand theater of every moment in which these lessons are being ingrained into our consciousness. This journey toward the development of our personality is peppered with an array of feelings and emotions, from high to low.

Everyone likes a good story. Without fail, by the time I finished painting this picture, the whole group was engaged. Often, they began to share memories from their childhood.

One or two individuals always shared how they sincerely tried to be their authentic selves, but were forced to abandon their truth because the lie was safer. I encountered numerous individuals who shared that as a child they had unusual spiritual encounters. Some spoke of having invisible friends or speaking with grandparents who were no longer alive. Others spoke of unusual encounters or having dreams or premonitions that came true. Far too often these children were ridiculed and/or punished by their parents and forced into silence, regarding their spiritual encounters. As a result, many of these children shut down their abilities to communicate with the spiritual realm because as a child it was safer to simply fit in. They abandoned their truth because it was safer and easier to exist with the lie. This is a detrimental sacrifice that will influence these children for the rest of their lives or until they discover a way to reclaim their talents and their spiritual acuity. In my opinion, this is truly what spirituality is about—one's own personal journey toward rediscovering who they truly are as a spiritual being having a human experience.

Every person who is in recovery from an addiction is in some way trying to reconnect with their soul, or the most grounded and untainted part of their being. In truth, all humans face this challenge. Most souls in the flesh get lost in the maze of manmade circumstances/the matrix. It is as if we are actors in a play and we volunteer to play a role, like a police officer or a nurse, a mom or a dad. You become so committed to these roles that you forget who you really are at the level of the soul. You never take off your uniform.

It becomes your identity and you view life through the narratives created in that particular theater of your life. You become entrained to search for identity, love, happiness and self-worth externally. If I get a new lover or a new car, I will be happy... Most of these external accomplishments are short lived and leave you thirsty for more, never really satisfied.

Imagine being lost in character and not being able to remember who you are. It would be like spiritual dementia. You would be stuck in the never-ending soap opera of that role. Most of us are experiencing spiritual dementia. We don't remember who we truly are, and we become ignorant to the fact that true self-transformation is an internal journey.

Most who have become addicted to drugs, habits, or behaviors had and may continue to have internal narratives that ultimately lead them to their first experience with the addictive substance or behavior of choice. This internal narrative is the outgrowth of a belief or a set of beliefs that were adopted in response to experiences and circumstances that were incurred at some point in their lives. Oftentimes, the experiences are traumatic and life-altering, such as childhood and/or spousal abuse, the loss of a job or a loved one, the inability to self-manage emotional or psychological imbalances, etc. In each of these scenarios the subject adopts a role in the theater of that moment. Often this adopted role entices the actor to view themselves as a victim, powerless, unworthy, and stuck. Every form of addiction is accompanied with some sense of powerlessness that acts to keep the subject entangled.

With addictions, most tend to view the addiction as the culprit. Drugs, gambling, sex, etc. have all been identified as the villains. While these may not be viewed as the most noble of pursuits, they are not inherently *bad*. Within limits, all of the aforementioned endeavors can be a form of healthy fun, entertainment, and education. The true villain in addictions is the internal narrative, the concept of self that enables one to be enslaved by drugs, gambling, or sex without limits. The true villain is what we have come to believe about ourselves.

I have found that in order to help a client overcome a major life obstacle, I must listen intently to their story. Active listening is an invaluable skill when it comes to helping others. When I focus on actively listening to a client, I clear my mind and listen with my heart. I literally imagine I am watching a movie. I allow myself to feel the emotions and the energy that accompanies the story. Often, it is as if I am in the movie with them as a silent observer. In this way, I gain access to their internal narrative, the set of beliefs and feelings that ran their lives in that moment.

Like a computer or a cell phone, all humans have a prevalent internal operating system (IOS). This IOS fuels our internal narrative. Actually, our minds operate very much like a computer. Our minds synthesize a collection of historical inputs to compute a logical output based on the available data within the internal operating system of the individual. Essentially, our mind uses inputs to compute outputs. The qualities of the outputs are inherently dictated by the qualities of the inputs. If your inputs are tainted with dysfunctional viruses, your outputs will also be impacted by these same viruses. While actively listening to one's story, you can detect the viruses or the programming errors within their internal narrative that impact the quality of choices the individual can derive. Examples of some of these narratives are:

- I am unlovable.
- I am inferior or stupid.
- I am a major screwup.
- As a woman I am devalued,
- I am unworthy.

Mental viruses are opportunistic. They can invade and contaminate our concept of self at any given point in time, but most often they become an insidious part of our IOS during our childhood years. Just like with a computer, these viruses/self-limiting beliefs hide in our blind spots. Most often, they have been embedded within our concept of self for so long we don't even realize they are there.

In Joyce Meyer's *Battlefield of the Mind*, she states, "You cannot have a positive life with a negative mind." When our concept of self is negative, our mind becomes our worst enemy.

The path to successful recovery from addictions and the path to reconnecting to one's soul are one and the same. Both require that you address the faulty programming running in our minds. How do we do this? Joyce Meyer gives us a clue when she states, "Don't reason in the mind, just obey the Spirit."

"The Chatter of the Mind Drowns the Wisdom of the Heart."
~Egyptian Proverb

"Just obey the Spirit." How do we shift our focus from the chattering mind to the spiritual wisdom of the heart? This is a difficult question. Most have very few tools and little training in this area. Many have established some type of prayer, meditation or mantra practice, but few truly engage in a true conversation with the Divine within.

In Western cultures we tend to submit prayers of supplication in times of need. We have been programmed to operate in the victim/ savior construct. We want some benevolent force to materialize miracles that will save us from our current obstacles. In Western cultures we have been trained to envision God as some external omnipotent force that has the power to liberate or condemn us.

This victim/savior construct is a prevalent internal narrative that keeps us locked in the most primitive part of our minds, the amygdala. This mindset keeps us stuck in survival mode ready to fight or flee when faced with difficult circumstances. The amygdala is the prison in which most addicts find themselves stuck.

In Bruce Lipton's newsletter, "Think Beyond Your Genes—May 2018," he states: "The amygdala, deep within the brain, controls the behavioral response to stimuli or events that produce strong emotions. Fear, an especially powerful emotion, automatically engages the *Imperative's* life-sustaining survival programs. Protecting ourselves and keeping our loved ones safe from harm is possibly the strongest human motivation in the face of fear. The fear of death keeps the subconscious mind 'on guard' twenty-four-seven in sensing and responding to anything perceived as a life threat."

There are basically two polarized pathways one may follow in responding to perceived threats to survival: a) Engage a positive belief system that will enable individuals to overcome, manage, or adapt to the stressors, *or* b) Engage a protection response by walling-off, defending against, the perceived stressor. The behavioral pathway an individual will choose is based upon their developmental experiences. If childhood is filled with self-confidence-enhancing programs and a belief in an immortal soul's existence, that individual will likely respond to threatening stressors by engaging in social behaviors that support the survival and welfare of the community (i.e., species). In contrast, children who grow up in the shadows of fear and feel they are vulnerable to life's stressors will adopt defensive or aggressive behaviors to protect their personal survival.

While Joyce Meyer simply says don't follow the mind, follow the Spirit, Bruce Lipton takes us into the neuro-pathways of the mind to explain this process. Bruce points out that one's choices are largely influenced by their early childhood experiences. The quality of our early childhood experiences impacts our ability to "calm the chatter of the mind" so we can follow the guidance of spirit. If we were raised in a nurturing and empowering environment that introduced us to the concept that we are a spiritual being having a human experience, we are more likely to listen to the guidance of our heart/soul and make choices that serve the greater good, for ourselves and society at large. But when our internal narrative is tainted by trauma, early in life or later, our concept of self is likely to be confounded by doubt, fear, anger, self-hate and selfishness. Our view of life and the scope of its possibilities are limited by the viruses that contaminate our internal narrative.

The mind is a powerful tool that is meant to help us survive and navigate our life journey. It is not inherently bad or dysfunctional. Simply put, it is a database that stores memories or data points. It uses these data points to formulate our choices and interpret our experiences. If the mind is like a computer, then who or what truly determines which programs are allowed to run in this computer?

This is a paramount question. Who or what is responsible for the internal programs that run my life? Am I solely the product of a bunch of external inputs? Or is there an internal source that is ultimately responsible for programming or reprogramming my mindset?

When I ask my clients (all adults), "Who is responsible for the programming that determines your internal narratives?" most point to an external source such as family, friends, society, or circumstances. This answer aligns them with the victim/savior construct. Many sincerely believe they are a victim of their circumstances. The victim/savior construct is a belief system that is based in powerlessness and hopelessness. The victim's only hope is that some external being or force will rescue them from their current misery. The victim/savior construct does not require that the subject take responsibility for their life's outcomes. Their prevalent IOS does not allow them to see an internal source of salvation.

Some of my clients are aware that they are responsible for their current situation. They readily admit they knew better and are capable of making better choices. But they are not quite sure of why they have a tendency of not listening to their better judgment. They are not aware of the internal narratives that act to sabotage their good intentions.

In both scenarios the clients are not aware that thought viruses or self-limiting beliefs were operating in blind spots within their own minds. This lack of self-awareness is a central theme for most who are unable to resolve their current life dilemmas. When your mind is the only tool you use to navigate your life, you are subject to the limits of the programming that guides your thinking.

"We cannot solve our problems with the same thinking we used when we created them." ~Albert Einstein

Self-awareness is a key that unlocks the door to self-discovery. Through self-awareness or compassionate self-observation we can gain access to the intuitive guidance of our own souls.

We all have an innate connection to an intuitive knowing that rests in the center of our being. This inner knowing is our personal connection to the supernatural, to God. It is not limited to the constraints of the human mind. It does not adhere to the laws of human logic. It is our personal relationship with that which cannot be defined or quantified with words. It is our connection to our true essence as a spiritual being having a human experience. It is a conscious reunion with that malleable ball of energy that emerged as a unique reflection of the All Mighty/Source/God, in the flesh. This is the omnipotent part of our being that intuitively knows our next best step in any given now moment.

The soul's guidance is not dependent upon the computing of the mind. But its sage advice can be confounded by self-limiting internal narratives of the mind as we mentally try to interpret what is being shared with us from the divine source within. For this reason, it is imperative that we utilize compassionate self-awareness to help us systematically review, redefine and reconstruct our fundamental beliefs/internal narratives about who we are and what we are capable of achieving in our lifetimes. As we discover the viruses that are the source of our self-limiting beliefs, we clear the way to perceive the gentle guidance of our own souls. Some call this "facing your shadow self." This is the essence of the spiritual journey, unfolding all that we believe about ourselves that confounds our ability to receive and correctly interpret the divine guidance that comes from within.

Facing your shadow can be very difficult. It requires that we face what we fear, we address topics or memories that haunt us, and we become honest about how we truly feel about ourselves. Our conscious spiritual journey often begins when we find the courage to look honestly and compassionately within. We learn so much about ourselves when we observe how certain thoughts, memories or circumstances trigger us. We can discover the origin of our pains, our fears, and our feelings of unworthiness. We can observe how these stories play out in our minds and how they stir up emotions and feelings. We can observe how these emotions and feelings impact our choices.

When we observe ourselves, we can actually detach from being the actor in the drama of our stories and observe ourselves from the director's chair. When we are able to face our shadows in this way, we create the mental and emotional space that we need to objectively and compassionately observe ourselves without judgment. Compassionate self-awareness eliminates the need to judge and replaces it with a sincere desire to understand the inner workings of the self. The sincere desire to understand why we are and who we are gives birth to the courage that one must have in order to face the shadow self.

We learn so much about ourselves when we face what we fear. This is the beginning of every heroic story. The main character has to harness their fears or their doubts. They have to review and transform self-limiting internal narratives. They have to incorporate more productive mindsets, disciplines and practices. They then begin to have experiences that affirm the positive impact of their new way of being. The most difficult life circumstances often harbor the most beneficial rewards for those who are able to turn their poop into fertilizer.

In drug rehabilitation centers, clients are guided by therapists, sponsors, mentors, and peers to follow the teachings of *Alcoholics*

Anonymous aka the "Big Book." This is Alcoholics Anonymous' bible. Its main teachings or guidelines are found in the Twelve Steps. The twelve-step program is a thorough process that helps clients to achieve and maintain sobriety. The principal teachings of this program are anchored in spirituality. Early on, in Step Two, it guides a client to the understanding that a power greater than themselves can help them to restore their sanity. The presence of God is honored throughout the entire twelve-step process. As a matter of fact, the twelfth step states, "Having had a spiritual awakening as the result of these steps, we tried to carry this message to alcoholics, and to practice these principles in all our affairs." As mentioned before, the path to spirituality and the path to sobriety are very similar if not the same.

When leading groups at drug rehabilitation centers, it is my goal to inspire introspection as often as I can. Introspection is an invaluable skill in both sobriety and spirituality. One of my favorite icebreakers is asking, "How do you turn your poop into fertilizer?" After the laughter dies down, I often see bewilderment as the participants consider the question.

While they were pondering this question, I began telling the story of the seed that was complaining because it was stuck in a pile of poop. This seed was miserable. It tossed and turned in the poop and could not find a way out. It became hopeless and resigned to being stuck. Until one day it noticed another seed not too far from it in the same pile of poop began to change. It began to open up and a root began to emerge. He noticed that this rooting seed began to thrive. The miserable seed asked the rooting seed what was going on. The rooting seed said, "I don't know. All I knew was I got tired of complaining. I got tired of being miserable. I got tired of being stuck in poop, so I surrendered. I just kind of relaxed from the inside-out and next thing I knew, I realized that I was exactly where I needed to be. When I accepted this, I stopped feeling miserable. Something in me began to open up and I became aware that if I change my perspective I could grow. I can pull nutrients from my current circumstances that will help me grow and eventually flower if I keep it up." The complaining seed was definitely tired of being in his current situation, so he asked, "How can I begin to grow like you?" The rooting seed looked over at him and smiled and said, "You already have begun to grow."

Even before the end of this story I can see the group participants looking inward to see if they can turn some of their poop into fertilizer. Some quickly come up with tangible examples of how some of their worst experiences taught them valuable lessons while others struggle with this exercise.

Another question I ask that illuminates that same point is, "Does life happen for you or to you?" Usually, there is a pretty even split in the room. Some believe they have little to no control over the outcomes in their life. This half of the class believes life is happening to them—victim/savior construct. Others express they believe that if they shift their perspective, they can discover the lessons that are embedded in every now moment. They believe life is happening for them.

To summarize this lesson, I ask one final question, "Are you a puppet getting manipulated by your circumstances or are you an alchemist, who can transform their poop into fertilizer?"

The goal of this question is to get the participant to seriously think about what it takes to transform their current situation into a positive outcome—to be an alchemist.

This is when I introduce simple, easy-to-repeat exercises that will help them to become an alchemist with their life.

Most of the exercises I share are about incorporating compassionate self-awareness techniques into their daily lives so they can gradually begin to detect and transform the negative internal narratives that act as viruses in their mental programming. Also, the act of self-awareness requires the observer to detach themselves from the drama of the scene the actor is participating in, as previously discussed. When we are able to energetically detach from an experience, we give ourselves space to make a different set of decisions that are outside of the scope of our standard set of reactions.

Here are three helpful exercises that can be practiced daily to develop the habit of compassionate self-awareness.

1. Every morning do the following three things:

    a.   Wake up and give thanks before you do anything else. Say gratitude prayers for every little thing you can think of. I ask my coaching clients to create a list of one hundred things that they have gratitude for. I invite you to do the same. Remember to be thankful for the little things. Also, gratitude prayers are useless if you really don't mean them when you say them. Make sure you feel gratitude when you say these prayers.

b.   Set the intention to maintain a positive attitude all day, no matter what happens. I know that this sounds unreasonable, but this is the most impactful intention you can set for your day. This means you will not let anything negatively trigger you. Remember, this is a practice. The goal is to build this ability gradually over time. Failure is an important part of success, especially with this exercise. When you fail, how will you handle this? Do you engage in negative self-talk? The fact that you are able to notice that you allowed yourself to be negatively triggered is a success. Compassionate self-awareness is key. Love yourself through this process. Keep trying until you are able to maintain a positive attitude all day.

c.   Pay attention to your intentions. Make sure you are checking in several times a day to measure your success. Recognize and celebrate when you notice that you did not allow yourself to be triggered as you normally would. Recognize and love yourself when you find yourself negatively triggered. Take a deep breath and get back to being positive.

2. During your day, meditate, sit in nature, exercise and/or pray several times.

a.   Find three five-to-ten-minute meditations that you like on YouTube. At least twice a day, practice one of these short meditations and journal.

b.   Nature heals. Put your phone down, go sit under a tree, and listen to the birds.

c.   Exercise three times a week.

d.   Upgrade your diet. Consciously choose to eat more healthy veggies and drink more clean water.

3. Nightly review:

a.   Every evening before you go to bed, mentally go over your day. I invite you to go backward from your most recent experience prior to bed all the way to your morning activities. Mentally walk backward in time. As you do this, journal on anything that stands out; successes, failures, lessons learned, emotions felt, great ideas, or missed opportunities. This one exercise will drastically improve your ability to compassionately observe yourself.

b.   Write your to-do list for the next day.

c.   Consciously relax your body, clear your mind, and sincerely repeat your gratitude prayers before or as you fall asleep.

The hardest part about these exercises is practicing them consistently. It is said that if you practice something daily for twenty-one days, it will become a habit. Personal growth and evolution require dedicated commitment. There is no way around this fact. Over 80 percent of all those in a drug recovery program will relapse. An even greater percentage of those who are on the spiritual path fail to achieve the ultimate reunion with the soul while in the flesh. I believe that is a tragedy. This is because, as Joyce Meyer points out, the mind is a battlefield. Our self-limiting beliefs do not surrender without a fight. Are you a puppet or an alchemist?

In conclusion, the path to recovery and the path to spiritual evolution both require that we learn to build a bridge from our heads to our hearts through compassionate self-awareness. This introspective journey will help us to become more aware of the profound lessons that are embedded within every moment while on this roller coaster called life. Through the practice of compassionate self-awareness, we can reshape our concept of self and reconnect to the divine within.

The spiritual journey requires that we face our fears and look into the dark shadows within our internal operating system. When we learn to embrace and persevere through the most challenging times of our lives, we give ourselves a chance to eventually access unknown talents and abilities. We give ourselves a chance to reunite with the malleable ball of energy that is an outgrowth of God, that is our soul.

Einstein said that the imagination is infinitely more powerful than the mind. In closing, I ask you to imagine this one last image. Imagine that you are a single cell in the body of God. You are unique and one of a kind. You have freewill and you came to perform a specific purpose in the body of God (like a liver cell or a heart cell).

You are both significant and insignificant in the collective of an infinite number of cells that make up the body of God. Because of freewill you can choose to perform your specific purpose or you can choose to go your own way. You can work with the collective body of God or against the collective as you pursue your selfish desires. When you perform your role in support of the collective you are acting in service to others. When you ignore the call of the body of God and choose to pursue your own desires, you are in service to self. Whether you are in service to self or in service to others, you are and will always be a part of the divine body of God.

Spirituality is about liberating ourselves of all that separates us from knowing who we truly are. It is about each of us being able to live a life full of happiness and joy in spite of the circumstance. It is about knowing that we are a cell in the body of God, and we are God incarnate.

We are the seeds to the flowers of tomorrow. Awaken from within, liberate your soul from shackles of the mind so that you may know the heavenly fragrance of your own flower. Every morning when you awaken remember that you are a cell in the body of God and ask yourself, "What incredible experiences shall I create today?" Imagine...

Love and light to you all.

ADOLESCENTS

ADDICTION AND ADOLESCENTS

BY GRAHAM BARRETT

My own personal experiences brought me into the field of
adolescent recovery. I was a senior in high school and I was detonating.
I ended up getting thrown out of high school in New Jersey and was
intervened upon. I didn't know what was actually happening at the
time, and I ended up in adolescent treatment in Minnesota for about
a year. Fast forward to today, some 20 years later... Everything I have
in my life now is a result of God and the intervention that got me
into adolescent treatment. My experience drove me into this field
and gave me the drive to help people struggling in the same way that
I had.

Many challenges are unique to adolescents in recovery, and I
experienced some of these challenges personally in varying degrees.
My intervention took place when I was seventeen, a senior in high
school. They told me my life was a mess and that I needed to look
back at things to try and understand what was going on. They told
me I was not going back to school. Instead they were sending me to a
substance use disorder program because they believed that was what
was wrong with me. I didn't fight the process. I had my white flag.
I didn't need to hear anything more. I knew I had a major problem
(progressive substance use disorder). I was drinking differently than
others. I was using cocaine differently than others. I was using all
sorts of other substances differently than others. Millions of high
school kids end up using substances, and I'm not encouraging that,
but a large majority of them use them, enjoy them, and can safely
go on with their lives. They will become a Phi Beta Kappa, or a
graduate from an institution—whether it's community college or ivy
leagues—and have no issues with it whatsoever. However, I knew
something was different with me. At the time I entered treatment, I
knew I had a substance use problem.

I grew up as an altar boy in the Catholic church and had always
struggled with God a little bit, but when I got into treatment I
looked up at the Twelve Steps as traditions. Step number one—I was

powerless over alcohol, and my life had become unmanageable. Step number two gets into God. I think most adults, most individuals, let alone adolescents, look at the Twelve Steps, and look at the second step ("We came to be aware that a power greater than ourselves could restore us to sanity") and ask, "Are the Twelve Steps leading to the fact that God is going to get me out of this?" A lot of people question that.

I'm only speaking of my own experience and my own observations of others when I say this, but I believe the bulk of adolescents who are using alcohol and drugs, in particular weed and Xanax, whether they end up in residential treatment or not, do not have a progressive substance use disorder like I did. I believe that use of drugs and alcohol is a manifestation of something that's underlying, some type of adverse childhood experience or developmental trauma, or some type of anxiety or depression.

They may have been adopted, they may have been bullied, or they may just have really bad ego strength and low self-esteem and thought that because they got a C on their science project, they were worthless. Subsequently they wanted to use pot to make themselves feel better. This is the way kids think, and this is why kids do all sorts of crazy things like cut themselves and attempt suicide. There's not a lot of rational thought, but no matter how large or small that fear or that anxiety is, it's real to them. The biggest struggle people have is to realize the weed itself is not the issue. Kids can stop smoking weed, doing other drugs, or using alcohol, but the driving factor behind this behavior is the bigger underlying issue. Most kids and adults don't want to get uncomfortable and start to expose that.

YOU DON'T TREAT ADOLESCENTS AND ADULTS THE SAME WAY

Adolescent treatment is different than the treatment of adults, mainly because kids are more adaptable, easier to change and still moldable. If you get your claws into a thirteen or fourteen-year-old kid as a clinician, you can change that kid for the better pretty quickly, especially if you get them into a good therapeutic setting with some other kids. A thirty-five or even a fifty-year-old guy who's been using substances or has struggled with mental health for many years has their heels more dug in. I'm not going to say it's like teaching an old dog new tricks, but similar to DNA, a pattern has been laid down in terms of years of depression, anxiety, or substance use. The adult is so much further down the road than a fifteen-year-old, who has maybe been doing a lot of stupid things for six months, a year, or maybe even two or three years, and it is easier to change things. A lot of times with adolescents, you know the plane is headed toward the mountain. It's self-evident. When kids come into treatment, they may be angry that they are there, but they know why they are there. Kids are really smart. Broadly speaking, kids are more malleable than adults, and that is a key differentiator.

A lot of the time with adolescents they understand they are going to go back to their home environment. Their home environment may be a really good home environment, or it may be a really bad one, but they don't have a choice. They're adolescents, so they legally have very few rights. For an adult, if they have to go back to a really bad family situation or situation with a spouse, they can ultimately walk away. If they get supportive services around them, they can choose not to go back there and do what's best for them. For a kid, if he's been in an abusive home, an abusive relationship, or a really dysfunctional family, he still has to go back to that family. That makes it all the more challenging.

Another thing is, while kids are more easily changed and more malleable, it is all the more complex in the sense that a lot of families will drop a kid off in treatment like dirty laundry and say, "Clean my clothes. Fix my kid." The kid that ends up in adolescent treatment has a huge role to play in why they are there, but they are not always the underlying reason why they're there. Generally, a family system is massively dysfunctional. Again, that kid plays a very large role in it, but, with almost full certainty, I can guarantee many times the kid is there because of Mom, Dad, or some other situations.

We can look at another real differentiator between the treatment of adolescents and adults. When an adult comes into treatment, if they have some traumatic experiences throughout their life and the therapist in the first, second, or third week is having a monumental therapy session with that adult, where he or she opens themselves up and explains what went on, all of a sudden it's the first time he or she has shared that in his or her life in an open setting. It is a breakthrough when that happens because that adult has been hardened.

The older you are, the more difficult it is. If I try to get my father to open up about his adverse childhood experiences, he's seventy-five, he would never tell me. If all of a sudden you get an adult to open up, the heavens open, and you can start to pick away at that.

With an adolescent, it's totally different. An adolescent has no self-control, no idea how to regulate, and no idea what to share and what not to share. You can put an adolescent in front of a ton of people and he or she will open up. They will just gut themselves internally and talk about how they are worthless and what they went through, just throwing everything out there. If you just let them sit there and ride it out for a couple of days until their next therapy session, that kid is going to have to be hospitalized. They'll have some type of psychotic break because they have all of a sudden gutted themselves, and there's nothing left. What's successful about our program is a kid will gut themselves and then we do what's called a five and seven, which is five individual therapy sessions in seven days. In an adult program, we only get one individual session a week. In that adult program, the therapist can follow up and say, "Last week we talked about your childhood and what happened with your neighbor," and continue from there, but with a kid, if you wait until next week, all bets are off. You have to hit that kid with another therapy session the following day and then hit him again and again, and that keeps that kid stable and regulated. This creates a safe environment for them. With adolescents you have to have a much heavier clinical program than you would in an adult program.

ADOLESCENT TREATMENT OPTIONS

The biggest problem you see today in the treatment of adolescents is when treatment centers take a cookie-cutter model of treating adults and think if they plug in and play it on kids it will work. Meaning, taking an adult program, using the model of how adults are treated, and putting that in place with kids… It doesn't work. That is not how you should treat kids. Kids require so much more attention, so much more empathy and love.

To put it in perspective, we have twenty kids in our program today. We have forty-six staff. That's how much staff it takes to properly address kids. No adult program in the country has that more or less two-to-one staff to patient ratio. If an adult goes into treatment, less is required than what would be required for a fifteen-year-old kid. You need to have eyes and ears on a fifteen-year-old at all times. Adults don't need to be watched at all times when they go into treatment. There is more of an educational focus, as well, as these kids are in junior high or high school and go to school with us every day; so that's unique.

Certain tools that apply to adults—such as linguistic programming, AA, NA, and EMDR (Eye Movement Desensitization and Reprocessing)—can be good for kids. Are they good for everybody? Probably not. If you go on any behavioral health website today you will see the word trauma everywhere. I think it's great that we're looking at that. We know more about the body today than we've ever known. I believe certain tools that apply to adults can be just as effective for kids. They're effective for kids as long as they're used properly.

EMDR is a wonderful modality for someone who suffers from a singular shock trauma event. That could be a soldier whose tank exploded, a woman who was sexually assaulted, a man who was in a car accident, or a school shooting victim. We had one of those recently. With single events where the body neurologically is completely dysregulated, you can use EMDR to tease that out and regulate the body. That is, bottoms up from body up to mind, we've gotten very good at that. There are limitations in top down, mind into body, troubles that kids have—which is, for me, my parents' divorce. EMDR is not going to do anything for that. I need to come to terms with the fact that all of my anger and frustration stem from resentments to my dad and my mom. All of those tools are really good as long as they are properly applied and people understand the limitations of them.

The transition for an adolescent from a treatment center to the environment they came from is critical. That adolescent cannot get a fresh start in a new town or city. Families are going to try to put together a bunch of pieces to mitigate the chances for recidivism as best as possible. A kid with a progressive substance use disorder is going to have a very different discharge plan than a kid who has anxiety and depression. The kid with a substance use disorder needs longer-term treatment. He might need to go to a halfway house or get connected with a twelve-step program. If his progressive substance use disorder problem is from opiates, the family might want to look at medication-assisted treatment, or they might not. In most cases, that kid should be in treatment longer than an anxiety and depressive kid. Their discharge should look more along the lines of going home and making sure that Mom and Dad are doing work, maybe getting counseling, maybe marriage counseling.

It might be important for the kid to see Mom and Dad work on their marriage. It could be that Dad and son have had an abusive relationship in the past, and they need to do group counseling or family counseling together. Some highly educated, highly intelligent kids need to be pulled out of their advanced school programs. That can be too much for them. The kid may need a step back from that. The transition is about realizing what these triggers and issues are and addressing them—from the family and the psychiatrists to the school. The family should take a comprehensive look at everything.

Sadly, we are in an age of school shootings, suicides etc. The good news is towns, municipalities, and counties are coming together as more communities are being affected. There are support groups for families and individuals needing help, not just for substance use for adolescence, but also mental health related stuff. There are also private groups. In a private group, you pay twenty dollars to go there on a Tuesday night at six o'clock and they serve pizza. A couple hundred people are in the room together, all families looking for help. They can always reach out to Family First Adolescent Services, but another thing families can do is call their county Health and Human Services. Every county has an office. Reach out to them and find out what's available in your area.

I would also reach out to your local church. Even if you're not a Christian, even if you're Jewish or Muslim, call your local places of worship and find out. A lot of churches host nondenominational meetings in their congregations. Oftentimes they are not only welcoming of that, but they are also free. Call around to congregations and find out because I guarantee temples and churches, even if they're not hosting meetings in their church, know other congregational members they can direct you to. They are just a phone call or a Google search away.

The kids who come out of the treatment center and suffer from anxiety and depression are going to be on medication. Many times they ultimately end up staying on them. For depression, they're called SSRIs (Selective Serotonin Reuptake Inhibitors). SSRIs include any class of drugs that are used for any sort of major depressive disorders. That can be any drug from Lexapro to Prozac or Zoloft. There are lots of drugs for those kids with major depressive disorders. The way these kids are wired, neurologically, is going to cause them to need to take these medicines for the rest of their lives, which is fine if properly managed. They will get back to having some normalized brain activity and then these kids are good.

Many of these kids sustain on these for quite a while, and they are very effective. Families may have an issue with the long-term use of medication, but they need to talk to their providers about that. If anyone, a family member or a loved one, or you as an individual are uncomfortable with a therapist, don't keep going back to that therapist. Not every therapist is right for every person. If you don't like a twelve-step meeting, find another one. I certainly don't like every meeting I go to.

Different treatment options are available for adolescents struggling with recovery. I'm a huge believer in trying to make things work at home. So often we're in this thinking of *what is it going to take to fix my kid?* We'll do whatever it takes. So the kid is sent off, then Mom and Dad get a break, a little vacation from worrying about the kid. With adolescents, the families are looking for help. They believe it's a substance use issue and/or a mental health issue. They're probably already finding out what services are available at home. Sometimes that can be through school resources, as public schools are exceptional at providing services. In private schools, it depends. Some private schools don't allow that to happen.

In the last couple of years, sadly, many private and public schools both might have had a major incident—God forbid, a real suicide attempt that was successful. They lost a kid, or some tragic incident happened that called attention to this. A lot of schools don't want to believe that there might be a bit of a problem in their school. The same thing goes with the families. They do not think their home situation, or family setting, is the problem. The reality is, it's not always the kid.

Often the families think no adult or relative at home is struggling. It's cowardly to think that. It's rather naive and it's very dangerous.

Regardless, a lot of schools, families, and places still think that today. Even some churches don't believe that maybe they have a problem, and it runs the gamut. The problem is absolutely everywhere.

Families should try to make it work at a local level with a therapist or school psychologist. They should use school resources combined with a twelve-step AA or NA program, or they can look into an alternative to twelve-step programs, like Celebrate Recovery. Many different options are available.

Oftentimes when I talk to families, they have tried to make it work. They usually call me and say, "I don't know what happened to my kid. He did great his freshman year and did awesome his sophomore year, and then all of a sudden, he started hanging out with a bunch of different kids. Now, in the last, ninety days or six months, I don't even know my kid." The reality is that it didn't just happen in the last six months or ninety days. It may appear to them that all of a sudden, it just happened, but that happened over a course of time.

Ultimately, residential treatment becomes a viable option when families have exhausted all the local options, and they realize they are losing their kid and don't know what to do. Those are the most beautiful phone calls I get because the family has capitulated and realized that they need outside help beyond what they're getting locally. I look at it as a beautiful thing because the family and the kid can put the shovel down and stop digging. In the midst of that tragedy, even for the kids in facilities for suicide attempts, I look at that point in time as the most beautiful time in the world. It's the time we can think about things and things can change.

Prior to the kid leaving the residential treatment, there should be a contract put into place, whereby the kid hears the rules and hears what's expected of them when they go home. Kids are really smart. They may hate the fact that they are in residential treatment, but they know exactly why they're there. They may try to play dumb and say, "My mom's horrible," or, "My dad's a jerk." They say things like that all the time, but they know that being in treatment didn't just come out of left field all of a sudden. They know they don't just end up in residential treatment because they got drunk on a Friday night and punched something. They know there is more to why they are there. There is history.

If a contract is written out, they can see behaviors laid out and know what to expect. They can see what repercussions will occur if they don't follow the rules, and that can be emotional for them. I trust the providers who are treating those kids to lay down those repercussions. Oftentimes, a spoken contract may include going back into a residential treatment program if their behavior necessitates it, or sometimes into a longer program. It could mean going to Teen Challenge, a longer Christian-based program that is going to be a little more strict and a little more stringent, for good reason. Sometimes that helps kids toe the line. But I think for any family, and I struggle with this with my four-year-old and my two-year-old, if you draw a line in the sand, it is so important to hold that line. If you move that line those kids will run over you. If you start to move that line, the kids are always going to win. It's best to stick to it because kids are defiant, and they will remain defiant. Kids will do whatever they are going to do. They are just so stubborn. Holding that line is the best thing you can do for a kid.

I was that kid, defiant to the core to move that line. I ran over that line. My recovery was not linear. I slipped up and there were repercussions for that. I believe kids don't always get it the first time. Adults don't always get it the first time either. You will never know when that light is going to go on, when they will get it.

WHAT'S THE PROBLEM?

Recovery and treatment of adolescents can become more and more effective as they achieve a deeper understanding that they are not the *entire* problem. In addiction recovery, in the treatment center, these kids feel they are the problem, and the problem is isolated within themselves. Whether right or wrong, there is constant finger pointing at the kid.

Good parents and bad parents often feel as though the kid is the problem. They blame the kid and tell them they caused the issue. There is this constant judgment of the kid. I think largely unless the parents are just really bad people, and there are those out there, families are trying to do the best job they can. I don't jump to thinking that the parents are out in a malicious fashion to affect the kids, although that certainly does happen. Commonly, that is not the case, but they have affected these kids. Looking at things from the kid's perspective, they are used to that finger being pointed at them saying they are the problem. They are used to being told they're the reason for this. When and if you get into a treatment center or a therapeutic setting, and the kid realizes they are not the sole reason for the problem. That realization is a highly effective treatment method.

We turn to these kids and tell them they do play a large role in terms of why they are there, but they are not the sole reason they are there. Most likely, this is the first time in their life they've heard that. When we do family systems work at our Family First treatment center, for instance, and a therapist can turn to a mom and dad with the kid in the room, and tell the parents some of what they did was not good, the kid's jaw inherently drops because it's the first time anyone has ever confronted their mom or dad on something. Now, that kid is about to get slammed himself in a second right there for his part in this. His life may come back because someone is shoulder to shoulder with him and knows where he is coming from.

It's a matter of relatability, showing a kid you are shoulder to shoulder with him and not punishing him. This is not retribution. You are not a behavior modification program where there are three hundred rules. We are not saying, "I need you to follow all three hundred rules. Don't look out the window. Look straight this way. You can't do this, and you can't do that." A lot of military schools and highly disciplined schools are like that.

With our program, and with a lot of really good programs out there, when the kids feel as though the therapists are walking shoulder to shoulder, wanting them to get better, and advocating for them, they thrive. When you put a kid in a situation where they need to change, they're either going to comply or they're going to defy. You don't really want either one because if they defy, all hell breaks loose, and if they comply, all of a sudden they're just toeing the line. You don't want them to comply because they are just waiting for the next opportunity to raise hell. You don't want either of those. You want a therapist to dig in, in terms of asking why these behaviors are happening. I think that's the most effective way to talk to kids.

Parents

I think a lot of parents want to believe their kid has a substance use disorder. If you are a parent of an adolescent struggling with addiction, look for a comprehensive treatment center. It's good for individuals who do not have a substance use issue to hear about substance use. However, I think a comprehensive program will look at developmental trauma or some type of adverse childhood experience a kid had. I believe those things are the driving issues in terms of why most kids end up in treatment.

I have seen parents try things that work for adolescents. The contract is one of the most effective things I've seen regarding families getting better through their own actions. Kids really struggle when they've been working in a residential setting to get better, and Mom and Dad have not done anything. Mom and Dad don't believe they are to blame. They think they don't have a role in their child's issues. When you have a kid who has worked so hard, and he is doing what he is supposed to be doing, but Mom and Dad haven't put the oxygen masks on themselves, a lot of resentments and problems can happen.

Parents may try some things on their own that definitely do not work. One thing is grounding them. Saying, "My kid's grounded, so I'm going to pull away his Xbox. I'm going to take away the keys to the car and not allow the kid to use it." Families will try to pull things away from kids—like privileges and allowances—and make them do chores to make them listen. Those are all good things I do with my kid. "If don't eat your dinner, you're not getting dessert." All of those things are really good things and probably work for a lot of kids, but, in the long term, it may not.

For some kids, it won't change their underlying issues. For myself, that kind of thing did not change the issues I had with my parents' divorce. There may be some benefits. If you tell them they are not allowed to go to the prom this year because they got a D in science and math, okay, that's a good punishment. However, that's not going to permanently change someone like me who still has not accepted the fact that I was there for my parents' divorce. My dad was never around and my mom was probably a non-medicated bipolar. I never knew what I was going to get when I came home during the day or at night. Pulling away my car keys was not going to fix that. They're all well-intended actions, and they all serve a purpose, but they're not going to resolve the larger issue.

DUAL DIAGNOSIS

Oftentimes the kids have a dual diagnosis—an addiction issue along with a mental health issue. There are many ways to handle a dual diagnosis in adolescents when there is another issue besides recovery, whether that's depression, anxiety, or another mental health issue. At Family First we have psychiatry services on staff. If the kids need medicine to manage their anxiety, their depression, ADD, bipolar, or some other issue, we absolutely administer that. While we're not a pure twelve-step-based program, some kids come in and pick up *Alcoholics Anonymous*, also known as the "Big Book," read the doctor's opinion or the first 164 pages and the realize, "Holy cow, that's me." We get them sponsors. We start working on the Twelve Steps, and we get them dialed in and on the road to recovery.

Additionally, the bulk of our kids come in and need to work through their behavioral health issues. A large portion of them suffer with anxiety and depression. In our program we try to get kids to understand what's happening with their bodies. We establish some self-agency, do some breathing exercises, talk about getting into bad situations and how they're going to handle it. They can start to feel their body. The reality is, and we're very realistic with this, while a lot of families want to believe their kid is fixed by coming into treatment, we remind them that there's a long road ahead. The kid is going to detonate when he comes home. There's going to be an issue and it may be in the first twenty-four hours, maybe in the first few days. Whatever it is, generally, there will be a problem.

What Happens After Treatment?

Our goal is ultimately to avoid getting them back into a residential treatment program. The goal is to give that kid some proper wraparound services—psychiatry, therapy, self-agency. We work for a healthier family system. We work for gaining an understanding of how Mom, Dad, and kid can interact with one another. We provide all the supportive services so we mitigate the chance of that kid flying off the handle to the point where he needs another residential program.

In order for parents to avoid pitfalls in the treatment process, avoid thinking that after thirty days your kid is completely fine. Another pitfall is the parents not doing their own work. The way in which a kid gets better is when he is brought into the fact that he needs to get better. I can assure you that most likely the kid can tell you what is wrong with Mom and Dad. Mom and Dad may not want to hear it. However, if they are not brought in and that kid is going to go back to the same home, good luck. This takes a village.

There are certain common benchmarks and occurrences parents maybe might not be aware of and might need help seeing. First off, parents should stick to their gut. First and foremost, if you think something is wrong with your kid, something is probably wrong with your kid. Parental intuition is better than any. Parents just have it. As a parent, when you know that your kid is different, don't blindly turn yourself away from it. The biggest and most common things that I hear from families are a new set of friends, grades gone to crap, and isolation in the room. More today than ever before we are dealing with gaming disorders like Xbox or some other sort of computer gaming issues. Kids are isolating because that is a great outlet for their anxiety, any sort of social anxiety disorder. They can create their own world in the safety of their own room. They can actually have friends and they can get coins, get the various levels, and build this whole world without leaving their own bedroom.

As far as other signs, for some kids it's giving up athletics. It can be that they are not going to church anymore. It can be that they were part of the robotics team at their middle school and now that's gone. Whatever sort of activity or hobby it was, if they were a musician and they played the guitar all the time and now that's done, these are all benchmarks. Typically, what we see with a lot of these kids is they are hanging on. They can manage for a certain period of time, and then boom, they detonate.

I always see this with families. I had a mom reach out to me recently, saying her kid is participating, coming to dinner, and being honest with her. My response to that was, "Yes, because he knows you are on to him and he is about to get sent to treatment. So, now he is trying to hang on and show you how good he is. That will work for a week." I guarantee these kids can hang on, but the wheels will come off. No doubt about it, those wheels will come off because nothing has changed.

Hanging on does not mean the problem is getting any better. Some kids start cutting. Whether that's the superficial cutting, where the kid says, "Mom and Dad, these are not cuts that need stitches," taking a dull object and drawing some blood. Whether it's on their leg or arm or wherever on their body it is, it's a relief. There is also loss of weight. As well, Mom and Dad typically know how much vodka's in the bottle and start to see that as a benchmark.

A lot of families have cameras now. A mom recently told me her kid is going down to the kitchen a lot at two o'clock in the morning and asked me what's going on? My answer is your kid is smoking pot every single day. He's high as heck and has got to get clean. They are wondering why he is going into kitchen, thinking that he may be going through a growth spurt. No, he's not, and that's not okay. I don't say, "Wake up, lady." I say, "I understand why you are asking. It's okay to not know what these benchmarks and occurrences are. It's clear as day for me because I'm a drug addict. I know what your kid's doing. You never experienced that so I can understand why you have questions." There are benchmarks to see and to understand, and recognizing them is a step toward the kid's success.

DIFFERENT WAY TO RECOVER

There are many ways for adolescents to recover. There is not just one answer. I'm a twelve-step program guy (AA or NA) and I got out from under with a lot of help from Alcoholics Anonymous, and a lot of outside help. I don't believe AA is the sole way to get sober. I had to resolve issues outside of the rooms. AA is great for some people, but it's not great for all people. I know people who have done it in other recovery programs and in other ways. For example, deciding to work out. They work out and it changes their life. Different things work for different people. If it works for you, do it. Who am I to judge?

In my experience, outside help, in a roundabout way, ended up having a monumental effect on my sobriety. My AA sponsor, a bus driver named Angel, helped me get sober and helped save my life. Angel told me, "I don't care if you live on Park Avenue or sleep on a park bench." What he meant by that was, socioeconomically or where you come from, whether you went to Harvard or you never graduated from the seventh grade, doesn't affect your chances of becoming an addict. I believe anyone can be an addict because I believe that in all of this, in life, we are all looking for a quick fix. The reality is, I believe, you need to put the work in to get results.

With anything in life, if you put the work in, in terms of doing whatever you can do to help your depression, anxiety, or substance use disorder, I believe you can get the results. Those results may come quickly, or they may come slowly, but I do believe they will always materialize. I really believe that for everyone. The fact is, the longer someone is in treatment, the greater the results. Now everything in healthcare is very expensive, so socioeconomically you could make an argument that someone who can afford treatment can subsequently keep their kids in treatment longer and therefore the odds are greater. I believe there's always a gap. There is a gap in healthcare and education. We see it with our inner cities in terms of resources being more plentiful. They are more plentiful in Winter Park, Florida, than they are in Skid Row, Los Angeles.

However, I have seen all sorts of people recover from all sorts of horrible situations, socioeconomically, no matter where they are on the gamut. I've seen people get better who I thought would never be able to get better. I believe with adolescents, if you look down on the surface, they come at you with their middle fingers up, and they also come in simultaneously very scared.

Measuring Success

A lot of kids come to Family First with substance use disorders, and a lot of them come to us with mental health issues. Kids come to us, for example, with an anxiety disorder, but they have never done any drugs. We don't look at success rates in terms of sobriety. We look at success rates in terms of whether or not our kids need to move into a higher level of care. We follow kids for sixteen months, post discharge. We look at what percent of kids need to go back into either a residential program or an acute psych hospital (usually, if they need to get stabilized under the Baker Act).

We monitor that, and 84 percent of our kids do not need to go back into a higher level of care. That means 16 percent need to, and that's not a failure. Most of our kids go home after their ninety-day stay with us. Ninety days is our average length of stay, and I can guarantee you 100 percent of those kids have had issues when they have gone home. What the 84 percent number tells us is, 84 percent of them are now able to manage their issues at home through Mom, Dad, a therapist, psychiatrist, coach, wraparound services, whatever source of help they have, without having to go into a higher level of care.

For the parents and families of adolescents struggling with addiction, know you are not alone. There are different ways to get support. Parenting is the most important job we have, but there is no manual for it. If you're struggling at home, you are not alone. Church groups do really well with this, and so do therapeutic settings and school systems. The communal portion is there so you're not alone. It is there so you can reach out for help when you may believe you are deficient.

I'm deficient with my little kid in terms of how I help his speech and his inability to self-regulate. He has bad tantrums. I need to reach out to others for help because I don't know how to help him. I knew that in my gut. If you recognize that, if you are a mom or a dad, and you know in your gut that something is wrong with your kid, look to the community of resources. If you don't ask around and get help, you would have never known something was wrong.

Adolescents don't have to hit bottom to understand the concept of recovery. People come into a congregation or a church in order to change their lives for the better. They have a job, pay a mortgage, have a car note, and are productive members of society. They didn't hit bottom, but they came in and found Christ and ever since they have been crushing life. I think anyone can put the shovel down at any time. I believe some people have high bottoms and some people have low bottoms, and I believe when you have felt enough pain, you change. And that pain is unique to each individual person.

I'm the last person in the world to judge and say that you need to go out and feel a little more destruction. The only time you hear that is from an old school AA guys who say, "Well, maybe you need to go out and have another drink." I believe that ideology is good for some, in that they might need to have another drink to realize that they cannot safely drink. I had to experience that personally years later in my own recovery. I forgot about my pain and suffering. I don't believe it was necessary, but I believe it happened for a reason. I needed to go do a little more research—I call it research and destruction—to realize I cannot safely drink like other people. It could be that you cannot safely manage your anxiety without your medicine. Whatever it is for each individual, maybe they need to realize that. I'm not encouraging that. It might be that maybe a little more pain is necessary, but it's not a requirement by any means.

When I went into treatment, I knew I had a progressive substance use disorder, and I looked up at that wall with the Twelve Steps, and said, "Yep, that's for me." Well, I was in treatment with a bunch of kids who had just been smoking weed and doing stupid things for six months. I'm not minimizing that, but when you put those kids in a treatment center, and tell them twelve-step meetings are the way, those kids are going to roll their eyes and think, *what are you talking about?* That kid is right. He doesn't belong in that program. He belongs in something that's going to properly address mental health.

What Happens When Adolescent Enter Adulthood?

Adolescents who struggle with addiction will be dealing with issues as they age. Dealing with issues as we age is universal to all people—yearning for love and acceptance from others, wanting to be successful, wanting to be content, and wanting to be happy. I don't think any of that is unique to the adolescents themselves versus substance use disorder. The manifestation of a lack of such is brutal to the psyche and adds wrinkles in the problems adolescents face as they get older. Meaning, if I'm not feeling those things and most people don't do what I do (which is go and get as much cocaine as I can and blow it up my nose as quickly as possible). That's not a normal reaction.

I would say the yearning and thoughts for things in terms of wanting to be a success, wanting to be accepted, whatever that is, are the same as any normal person. The difficult thing is the end result of not getting that need met. You know the kid who is suffering with mental health issues? Well, you have got to be really careful because the suicidal ideations may very well turn into an action and God forbid something happens. The kid who doesn't suffer with that might get really sad, but they have ego strength. Even though they had a bad week, they know they will be okay next week. With the addict or the person who suffers from underlying mental health conditions, the end result could be a lot worse. My issues were more substance use than they were mental health, so for me it was more similar to situational depression. I'm a firm believer—and I think this also holds true with kids who suffer from mental health—that if they go back to drinking or not taking their medicine, they will slip back into some type of manic break or bipolar disorder. That doesn't change because it's five years, ten years, twenty years, or thirty years removed from that last episode, of that last drink. The harm that can come as a result is just as evident as if it was yesterday.

Conclusion

I believe ultimately, the only thing that matters is what works for you. The best way I can describe it is I remember when I was in high school, I used to ask people how long they studied for tests and exams. How long did you study for that? How long did you work on that? I realized as I got older that those were stupid questions because ultimately, that kid could be an astrophysicist, and it could have taken him five minutes. I know I'm not wired that way, so why am I asking that guy what worked for him? While I'm interested in what works for others, I can guarantee you that my approach and my handling of things looks different than yours. If you tell me you are actually an atheist, and being an atheist works for you, I have no problem in that, but that's not my way.

Basically, as a loving Christian, I care that my fellow man is feeling good and is happy. I think that is fair. If you are happy and you are enjoying your life, that's how you should live it so long as you are not hurting someone else; you are good, and you're feeling good. Even if you don't believe in God, that is okay. An individual can succeed in their recovery apart from God. I would be too egotistical and single minded if I said they couldn't. I don't know if I am right, but from what I have seen, I believe people can get better without relying on God. I'm okay with that although obviously I believe you would miss out on the many other benefits of a personal relationship with God. Those include the certainty of your place in heaven, walking through this life with God, experiencing His joy, peace, mercy, love, and forgiveness in this lifetime and for all eternity.

Families should know it will take a lot of work for their kid to get better. Understand this is a marathon and not a sprint. I want to provide hope that it's an absolutely beautiful thing that your kid is having these problems today. You may not look at it this way. However, your kid can get into a supportive environment, not only in their own house, but also within a residential program around other kids. Your kid can get help while they are malleable, and they can make a progressive positive change rather quickly. It may seem like the end of the world that you're having this problem if your kid is only thirteen or fifteen. However, I was a high-school dropout. I got my GED out of Minnesota, and then I ended up going to college and getting a very high-paying job at a tier-one investment bank on Wall Street.

I'm not patting myself on the back. I am pointing out all that happened because I was intervened on early and because the village wrapped around me and helped me. Ultimately, that senior year or junior year I failed meant nothing, really nothing, in the long run. What a beautiful thing we were able to get that out of the way on the front end rather than suffer years later through all this destruction and damage in my twenties and thirties. If you think it's hard now, I can assure you with very good confidence that if your kid does not get help, and the problem continues, it will be even more difficult later.

Look at it as an opportunity and reach out to those families who have been through it before to help give you hope. I've walked through it myself and being intervened on and getting help at seventeen years old is, to this day, the greatest experience, joy, and gift in my life. I'm talking above the birth of my child and a woman I married whom I love, and I'll tell you exactly why. Because if that had never occurred, I never would have had these subsequent things in my life, ever. When I put on the oxygen mask and got help for myself after two suicide attempts and horrible high school years, and came out the other side thinking I've got the most blessed, greatest life I could ever possibly live in, I know it was only as a result of early intervention. So, early intervention is the greatest show on earth. You may not feel that way in the midst of your child's misery, but thank God you're handling this today and not later.

SHORT-TERM & LONG-TERM
TREATMENT CENTERS

The Power of Transformed Lives: A Long-Term, Faith-Based Treatment Center Director's View

By Douglas Lidwell

I believe addiction is all about a break of the interpersonal relationship, first with the Lord and secondly with one another, and when we can reestablish those relationships, those struggling with addiction have a much stronger chance, a much greater opportunity, of getting through this thing and coming out the other end in a positive way.

Faith Farm Ministries

Faith Farm Ministries is one of the oldest and longest-running addiction recovery centers in the nation. We have three campuses across South Florida, roughly 450 beds and no clinical element. It is a completely faith-based, discipleship-based recovery program all about finding freedom through Christ. The program is ten months long and is completely free to those who come here seeking recovery. Faith Farm Ministries is paid for through a thrift store model. The people who come here work in thrift store operations, in the kitchen, and do other maintenance. There is a lot of working, building good habits, and getting up with alarm clocks. Residents take classes, build a good work ethic, and form a relationship with Jesus Christ, learning to hear His voice and get inner healing for the wounds that are causing their addiction. It is a pretty complete approach, barring the political element.

Faith Farm residents are between the ages of eighteen and sixty. They are from every corner of the country, from every walk of life, every denominational background, and every ethnicity. They come here to seek recovery through a relationship with Jesus Christ. Our campus is all men, but Faith Farm Ministries has a small women's program at the White Beach campus. At our Fort Lauderdale, Florida campus, we have up to two hundred men. It's roughly 50 percent white, 35 percent Black and about 15 percent Latino, but that varies from month to month.

People coming into the campus program have all different frames of mind, from excited to resistant, and are from of all types of backgrounds. We look for those who are desperate or at the end of their rope, at rock bottom, and just desperate to have somebody please fix this. These people want to develop a relationship with the Lord. Other people come in because Mama said if they don't get help, she's done with them, so she kicked them out the door. We don't get too many people who have been court-ordered, but it does happen occasionally. No one can court-order someone to get recovery, but they can be court-ordered to come to Faith Farm. I think the biggest advantage we have is that we are free. You don't have to have insurance. You don't have to spend any money. A lot of these places are $30,000 or $40,000 for a thirty-day stay. We have nearly a year-long program that is completely free.

We are entirely supported by our thrift store operations. We do not have a development director receiving six and seven figure checks the way similar ministries do. We're supported by the donations of the people in our community of furniture, clothing, and household goods, and then people coming in and shopping at our stores and buying these items. That means we're always working hard just to pay the bills. We don't always have the money that's necessary for maintenance on our buildings, vehicles, and so on. Our biggest challenge is probably just raising revenue. This is a free program, and we want it to always remain a free program. We rely upon the Lord to provide, and He always has. We're very grateful for that.

We started nearly seventy years ago. At that time, it was explicitly alcohol, and then through the sixties and into the seventies, the drugs started creeping in. Now, if we get somebody who is only an alcoholic, we don't see that as a big deal. If someone is only using crack, we can deal with that. Now, with the heroin and the other opioids, Fentanyl, designer drugs like Flakka and others, it's the gamut. You used to be able to almost pick out by ethnicity what drugs somebody was on, but now it's everywhere and there are no barriers.

We are incorporated as a church so we are not held back by healthcare laws or medical restrictions. We have a partnership with a local clinic where the men go and get their needs taken care of, and we treasure that. We don't have a clinical element. Anybody who comes into Faith Farm needs to go through a detox before they arrive. They always say they have, and that's not always factual, but they say that they have.

An ongoing issue we face is the push to legalize marijuana and normalize the use of it. This is a huge mistake in our culture. It's a huge problem. We believe marijuana is the gateway to the hard drugs. We get guys coming in with the mindset that marijuana is perfectly acceptable, normal, and even desirable. That is just absolutely false. It can often lead to bad places. This cultural issue is causing problems. We don't see a lot of legal issues other than the cultural shift to legalize marijuana, and I expect that eventually they'll try to legalize other drugs, as well.

The men have almost always been to other rehab programs before coming to Faith Farm and have tried other ways to get sober. Sometimes this is their first program, but most of them have been through what we call the South Florida Shuffle, going from programs to rehab to a halfway house to institutions, jail and back out again. Some of them have been doing that since their mid to late teens. For a lot of these guys, their career is in addiction, in programs, and they know the system.

THE TRANSFORMATION

This transformation and relationship with God can occur right away, after a week, or after several months. It varies according to an individual's spiritual background. Roughly half of the men were raised in church. Sometimes that's an advantage because they already know the Lord and they are somewhat familiar with the Word. Other times that's a disadvantage because they've got a lot of feelings toward religion to unlearn before they can just enjoy a good relationship with Jesus. At times, it's easier when you have somebody with no knowledge of this and who is fully willing to say, "I know absolutely nothing about the Bible, nothing about God, nothing about salvation." Sometimes these guys are easier because they don't have any preconceived notions. There is a wide range. It's every denomination. We get people whose only concept of God is a Catholic concept, or their only concept is a Lutheran concept or Presbyterian or Baptist. They put God in a box, and they think He is this way, and must be this way, because that's what we've been taught, but that's not the case.

The transformation occurs over time from the day they arrive. They're taught their new identity in Christ, even if they're not yet saved or born again. We teach them what an identity in Christ looks like as a son of God and an agent, an ambassador of the Kingdom of Heaven. We begin teaching them journaling and hearing the voice of the Lord for themselves, so the Lord can minister to them as they go through this process. We teach them to distinguish between the voice of the enemy, the voice of the flesh, and the voice of the Holy Spirit, and to journal those things and to keep track of them.

Accountability

They are held accountable at every turn, not just on misbehaviors but little things. If they are withdrawing or isolating, we ask them what's going on. If they are acting passive aggressively, we ask them what gives them permission to be that way. We look for those ministry opportunities, not necessarily as disciplinary issues, but as ministry opportunities to call people out on their behavior.

Several times in each of the four phases of the program the men will get peer reviews. They will sit down with their class, which is somewhere between fifteen and thirty people, and the class will be asked to choose who is the spiritual leader, who has the best work ethic, who is the most relational, and who is easiest to get along with. Then, who is the least spiritual guy, who has the least work ethic, and relationally who is not getting along with folks. The class calls them out on those things. If you're this really spiritual giant and you're constantly in your Bible, but nobody in the room has that much of a relationship with you, there's an issue there. You get called out on that by eight or nine guys in your class and you realize there's an issue, and you need to work on it.

We build this type of accountability over time, and this brings a transformation. As a preacher, I would love to be able to tell you it was because I preached a perfect message and someone just got it so a transformation occurred, but that's not it. The steady drip of the Word of God anointed and spoken to them, as well as the interpersonal relationships, brings a transformation. I really believe addiction is all about a break of the interpersonal relationship, first with the Lord, and second with one another. And when we can reestablish those relationships, they have a much stronger chance, a much greater opportunity, of getting through this thing and coming out the other end in a positive way.

Relationships

We strongly believe in establishing interpersonal relationships, and we try to stay on top of the latest research on this subject. Recently, research came out of Europe with laboratory animals. It showed laboratory animals that are given cocaine-laced water will become quickly addicted to it. Then a control group is left in that environment and another group is put into an enriched environment with other rats, toys, puzzles and games. It showed that the other group will learn to ignore the cocaine-laced water and go back to pure water by reestablishing those connections with others in their community. It certainly suggests that addiction is a lot about being connected to others.

Part of the reason people turn to drugs is because of the pain of being disconnected, first from God and then from one another. We like to say that people do drugs because drugs work. What they work for is numbing or eliminating the pain of living in a fallen world and in what we call the yuck of life. The way the world is now is not the way it was when it was created. Our society is not the way it's supposed to be and, at times, that carries over into our relationship with the Lord. None of us have grown into the one that we are supposed to fully be. That causes forms of pain. Everybody has defense mechanisms and ways to compensate for the pain of just living.

None of us were raised by perfect parents. Our parents should have been wonderful people. If they were not, meaning that they were at work all the time or they were not there for our ball games, we feel some kind of pain or rejection. Often the quickest way to numb that pain is to go to drugs and alcohol. Others do the same thing in a different way. They will go to work. They will become captains of industry, and we'll praise them and call them successful businessmen. Others will get wrapped up in sports, ministry, or other forms of getting this dopamine release in the brain. The only difference with our guys is that they happen to have turned to drugs and alcohol, which is more destructive than some of those other behaviors.

Do you become successful in the program when you first learn to turn away from drugs and alcohol, or are you successful when you stick to it? There are different ways to measure success in recovery. Success can be not picking up drugs or alcohol one year after you leave our farm. It can be considered a success after five years or ten. It is a success to stumble and then to remember your relationship with the Lord, remember the tools, then reapply them and come out of it before you hit rock bottom. I would love to say that after ten months at the Farm, you are done and you will never touch it again. Unfortunately, that is not the case. No recovery program is a panacea, a remedy for all things. After you leave Faith Farm you are not done. What Faith Farm and other folks in recovery do is teach people the habits and tools, and hopefully the relationship with the Lord that they need in order to be successful in the future. If they quit doing those things, what they learned at Faith Farm will no longer work.

Work the Program

A program works as long as you work the program. When you stop working it, it doesn't work anymore. It's just like if you're on a medication. It works as long as you're taking it, but if you stop taking it, it doesn't work anymore. That makes perfect sense to us. Somehow people think they are going to go attend a thirty-day, sixty-day, ninety-day, or even a ten-month program, and suddenly they're going to be done. That's not the case. It's something you're going to have to work for the rest of your days. Continually grow your relationship with the Lord, be involved in church and be in your Bible, be in prayer and worship and apply the tools you learned at the Farm or at some similar program.

People return to Faith Farm. We often see people come back for a second or third run, and we see that the more of it they get, the stronger they are. At some point there was an idea that we would no longer take repeaters, but we actually see people come out a lot stronger once we've seen them a couple of times, so we don't discourage that.

I'm almost always wrong about knowing if people are going to make it when they come in. We have people who show up and we might think they're not going to make it, but then they do really well. Others that I think that are going to be champions fall by the wayside in short order. Every time I get a feeling about success, I'm usually mistaken.

It comes down to you. You have got to want it. I think the only person we can't help is someone who doesn't want help. Not everybody wants it. All they really want is a lack of the consequences of their drug use, a lack of the financial consequences, of legal consequences, and of the destruction of their relationships. They want to still be able to use drugs, but not have people have a problem with that. We can't help those folks. When these guys come in and think their issue is crack, but they can still smoke weed, they're going to smoke weed and then, within just a few weeks, that's going to lead to being right back on crack again.

Moving Forward

We always want to support our loved ones, especially when they are in a desperate way. It is really hard to see your son, your daughter, or your husband or whoever that is, just destroying themselves with drugs. So just out of love and compassion, you are driven to help. You let them stay on the couch, you let them eat in your home, and you let them shower up. Every single time you do anything that prevents them from spending what little money they have on living, you're letting them spend it on drugs. If you are a family member of a person struggling with alcohol or drug addiction, do not enable them in any way. The only help you can give to the addict in your life is a ride to detox, or a ticket to a treatment program. If they're not ready to do that, then say, "I'm sorry. I love you so much, but you cannot stay in my home." Say, "No, I will not feed you unless it's the drive thru on the way to detox." That's the only help you can give them and that's really hard when it is your baby, or your husband, or even your parents. It's really hard to do, but it's the only help you should give.

When a person comes home after the program, be willing to acknowledge what they have been through. If you have experienced addiction, even if you haven't experienced it, try to acknowledge that they have been through this process. A couple of years ago we had a man from a very large Greek family. The family would come over for church and then they would stay and all eat. One day, they invited our fellowship over to eat lunch with them. It was a big, loud Greek family. They were all talking at once and one of them asked me, "What should we do for Rodney when he gets home?" Somehow the entire family heard the question and they all quieted and turned and looked at me and I said, "Just don't be Nazareth." One of them was a pastor and he understood that immediately.

Don't be Nazareth. Luke 4 and Mark 6 tell the story of when Jesus went to his hometown… They weren't willing to accept Him as Messiah. They questioned and asked, "What is all this Messiah stuff? Isn't this the carpenter's son? Aren't we married to his sisters? Aren't his brothers here with us?" Then Jesus said, "A prophet gets no respect in his own town and because of their lack of belief. He can do no great miracles among them."

What we see is the men come through the program for nearly a year and go through a transformation, but the last time the family interacted with them was when they were stealing Mama's lawnmower or lying in a pool of their own vomit. They are still very wary and shy of this person who has hurt them. When the dog has bitten you, you're very cautious around it for the rest of his days. I encourage people to acknowledge that your loved one has been through a transformative process. Be open and willing to treat him as such instead of treating him like the criminal and drug addict he was when you saw him last. That's very difficult for folks to do when that has been their life experience.

The Lies We Believe

Diving a little deeper, we have an exercise in our program called Houses. It is a tool for people to go back through their early life and talk about the major life events that occurred. An example of one person's story of rejection is, "I was wearing shorts and didn't want to put pants on, so I threw a fit my dad finally said, 'Just get in the car.' We got out into the woods, and not even twenty-five feet in I caught a thorn on the back of my knee and it scratched me. I started bleeding. What happens when a three-year-old sees blood? I screamed bloody murder and my dad got irritated and put me back in the car, drove back into town and dropped me off in my front yard. He looked at my mom, shook his head, and said never again, turned around, stomped back to the car and drove off. My three-year-old mind interpreted that as the most important person in the world doesn't like me and doesn't want to be with me, and there is something wrong with me. I'm not man enough. I experienced rejection there."

I have my own set of stories too. I'm from Illinois and in the spring time for about two and a half weeks, morel mushrooms grow up in the forest. If you have the talent for going and finding them, you could gather those up, soak them overnight in salt water and fry them up in butter. They're delicious. My mom loves them. I was three and a half years old and I can remember one day, it would have been late May, my dad had come home from work and we were all in the front yard. My grandparents lived right next door. He handed off his lunch bucket to Mom and said he was going to go out and get some mushrooms. I was three and a half years old and I just wanted to go with Dad, so I threw a little bit of a fit. He said, "All right, fine! Go change your clothes and get to the car." I felt rejected by my dad, however that wasn't true. My dad was just frustrated with a kid throwing a fit and he wanted to get his wife some mushrooms for the dinner table, but my mind interpreted it in a certain way and this inserted a lie into my thinking. Not a conscious thought, just an assumption about myself that was false. Over time I developed coping mechanisms for that assumption about myself. That, and a thousand more stories just like it, affect what we call a personality. It is what I now call my mushroom story, and we all have many of these kinds of stories. I was not molested or abandoned or beaten or abused. It was a simple issue of throwing a fit and Dad being irritated. But that's all it took for the enemy to insert a lie in my way of thinking and my personality.

The Houses exercise helps you go back to these stories and find the lies you believe. When you find the lies, you can ask the Lord, the Holy Spirit, to bring truth to that. He'll fix it right there on the spot. We teach our men journaling and hearing the voice of the Lord from the beginning, so they can get to the truth that will set them free when they find these lies. Through this process you begin to question all sorts of things. Are you shy? Just because you're naturally shy? Or was that a coping mechanism for you from a story of yours? Are you overbearing just because you've got a big booming voice? Or is that something you developed on purpose to keep people at a distance because you believed that if they get close, they wouldn't like you. We have so many different personality traits. We have to wonder, are they actually the way you are? Or are they defense mechanisms we developed to deal with our past experiences?

This concept of the subtle lies we believe is immensely painful and doesn't leave us. The lies are so subtle and they form the way we think. It becomes a pattern and a habit. The style of thinking we have is colored by all of these things we've come to believe about ourselves that simply are not true. Maybe they were true at the time, but they're not true now. If people were in a desperate situation in their youth, they may have been in danger then, but they're not in danger now. When the Holy Spirit speaks to you and brings truth to these lies, it is the same concept we teach. This concept goes into our entire approach to recovery, which helps people learn about these wounds. We've taken the Houses concept, and we developed it further. Now we have an inner-healing model that we use throughout the entire program. It's not just this one exercise.

The program is designed with four ten-week phases. We don't move you on to the next phase until we feel you're ready to move on. If you still have not grasped what we're teaching in a ten-week phase, we will not move you to the next one. We will give you multiple opportunities and more and more time, as long as you're trying. You don't have to have gotten it yet, but we really want to see that you want it and you're trying. However, if someone is just being disruptive, and perhaps even affecting the program of their classmates or the other people around them, we will invite them to seek recovery elsewhere.

The four ten-week phases start with an orientation phase when you're just getting settled in, getting your job assignment, learning the rules and the history of Faith Farm, and discovering some facts about chemical dependency. We call that Phase One. Each phase and each class builds upon the previous. There is a strong progression through the phases. By the time someone gets to the end of Phase Four, they have learned boundaries to protect their sobriety, and they are planning a transition for going back out into the real world.

We look very sharply at their transition plan—where they're planning to go, who they're planning to be with, and who is going to be around, as well as how they're going to pay their bills and what their budget looks like. We look at all of these things in the weeks leading up to their graduation. We've had people whose plan was to go back home and live with their parents in the basement where they were before, where they would drink themselves into a stupor every night. We tell them this is not a healthy plan, and that they're not ready to move on. They have to change their plan before we graduate them. What we saw just seven years ago, was about 90 percent of the guys, upon their graduation, left to go back to wherever they came from and a few would stay on. Now, probably 90 percent of them will stay on in one way, shape, or form. We have three different ways that graduates can stay on with us for a longer term. They can stay on and get a little bit more before they move on to what comes next. We are really strong on people not going back to the conditions they were in when they left. Very few people are strong enough to go back to that. It's critical. People who think they're going to go back to the same living situation and people that perpetuated their drug use, and somehow this time they're just not going to use, are fooling themselves.

A lot of these guys, because of what they have been through in their addiction, have been through hell, almost literally. They have missed opportunities with education and with their career. They have experienced broken relationships, and some of them haven't seen their kids in years. These things are really hurtful. Once they are a few weeks clean and sober, we get to see their genuine personalities come out. We are always so struck by how good our men are. How talented, able, and smart they are. They are genuinely good to be around and it's a joy to speak with them. That's not the experience of their families and loved ones. We get to see the man their family hasn't seen since they were children. All of those missed opportunities and the penalties they have paid for the misbehavior are real tragedies. For those who don't make it, relapse, and potentially lose their lives, that's another huge tragedy, but I see tragedy in every one of them who has been living their lowest potential for so many years.

Neither my wife nor I have ever suffered with addiction. Addiction ministry was not something we planned to do. We never made a decision to get into addiction recovery. Within weeks of me getting saved, I was called into the ministry rather dramatically and suddenly found myself ministering primarily to people who struggled with drugs and alcohol. That wasn't a plan. It just showed up. I then started teaching a class at a program called Teen Challenge, which is a nationwide addiction recovery program. I was teaching at their location in Illinois in Esther House, a women's center across town. When we found out about Faith Farm and learned they were looking for a pastor, it just seemed like a perfect fit because we're very well suited to that form of ministry. We can genuinely love people without taking on their burdens. That can be very challenging for a typical pastor who's very soft-hearted and isn't used to losing people. When things go well, you get people for about a year, and then they go out of your life again. You have to be able to genuinely love all people and then say goodbye to them in one way, shape, or form.

I think God has to be in the middle of all modes of recovery, even if it's a completely secular approach, the ones that have nothing to do with the Lord. I think His heart gives people yield, even if they don't know Him yet. He is using all these different forms to guide and direct those people into a greater state of health. I believe there is a place for secular programs, even if it is only breaking through denial, the first of the Twelve Steps. A lot of these thirty-day programs are designed to do just that, help the addict break through denial and get the addict in touch with another recovery program, whether it's NA or AA or some other twelve-step approach. The Lord can use all of them in the same way He uses doctors every day to bring healing. If people work with them, they work. We definitely see people who attend one of those thirty or forty-day programs, walk out the other end, and be okay. That would suggest to me that they might not have been in genuine addiction, and maybe they were in chemical dependency. There is a big difference.

Chemical dependency is just what it sounds like. You've been abusing a substance for so long your body becomes dependent upon it, and if you don't have it, you're sick. What you see is when someone detoxes from that drug, they are done with it. The people who are dragged into the detox, get clean and sober, and then go back to the drug have an emotional driver to that behavior. That's when you know the real addiction has kicked in—when people have paid a price and it has cost them something—whether it's months or years of their life behind bars, a DUI or two, a broken marriage, or a lost job. When people experience consequences for their drug or alcohol use and keep doing it, they're in addiction.

There are ways to communicate with kids to warn them of the dangers and consequences of addiction. For kids who have not experienced drugs yet and have not had addiction problems, the last thing I would tell them is don't do drugs. Telling someone not to do something is the surest way to get them to do it. Adam, "Don't eat the fruit of this tree." What did Adam do on the very next page? He ate the fruit of the tree. If I say don't think about a black cat, you just thought about a black cat. You're never as hungry as you are when you're on a diet and trying not to eat.

Instead, I would tell them they need to be informed and look at the consequences of these things before even thinking about getting involved. I would show them before and after pictures of people who've been on methamphetamine, crack cocaine, and other drugs. I would say, "I know you're almost sixteen and looking forward to getting your driver license, but can you imagine having your driver's license taken away from you for the next eight years because you have had three DUIs? It is going to cost you five, ten, or even fifteen thousand dollars to get that back. I would talk about the consequences of drugs, so they can make an informed decision and say, "No, that's not something I would want to do." That is the correct way to warn kids about drug addiction. Simply making something forbidden makes it attractive.

There are good ways to talk to kids who have started doing drugs and who are starting to experience some of those consequences. These things start out small and then progress. At one point, what might have been sneaking a beer behind the barn too soon becomes needing to have a case every night, or a glass of vodka by the bed so that you can take off the shakes when you get up in the morning. What might have started out as just a joint with your buddies as you're cruising around, can become selling yourself on the streets just to get crack cocaine. Very few people stop where they are. Almost everybody progresses, and what they think they can handle today is going to get to a place where they cannot handle it in the future. So, I would turn to that twenty-year-old and say, forty-year-old you is standing next to you, and he wants to tell you something. Will you listen? What he wants to tell you is, "Man you're about to make my life a whole lot harder. Please don't."

Addiction can happen to anyone, no matter the variations of life experience a person has had. A year and a half ago I had two men sitting next to each other in class. One day one stood up and told the story of his upbringing. He was raised on a private island off the coast of Georgia by a dad who was an extremely successful CEO and made lots of money. His first car was a limo. He was raised rich and he told the story of feeling as if he was rejected by his dad because his dad spent so much time at the office and was so involved in working. He felt as if his dad demonstrated his love by trying to throw money at him rather than genuinely spending time with him. It was heartbreaking.

Sitting next to him was a man that grew up in the hood. He told his story. He and his brother came back from school and they had to wait in line to get into their own house. They lived in a crack house and were raised by a single mom. They had two different dads; his brother's dad showed up regularly, but his dad was never around. He would sit by the phone, but his dad never called. He talked about feeling rejected by his dad because his dad was involved in his business, which of course was selling drugs.

You have two men. One is just as white as snow and raised rich, and the other was African-American and raised very poor. They could not be any more different, but they had the exact same wounds. It is surprising how alike we all are when we get away from the misbehaviors to cope with addiction. They are such good men and we love them so much.

What we all have in common is a feeling of rejection. In my mushroom story, I believe what I felt there was rejection. There is rejection in that story and hundreds of other stories like it. All my life, I believed in some way, shape, or form I was rejected. Rejection is very painful. The man who grew up on the private island felt rejected because his dad was a captain of industry. The man sitting next to him who grew up in a crack house felt rejected because his dad didn't come around. In some way, I think this describes the human condition. Adam fell and covered himself with leaves and hid. When the Lord came looking for him in the garden, he said, "I was afraid because I was naked, so I hid." (Genesis 3:10)

There is a belief that there is something wrong with me and I'm no longer worthy to be in my Father's presence. That wound in the Garden of Eden is what addiction is the solution for. Drugs and alcohol are not people's problems. Drugs and alcohol are people's solution to their problems. Their problem is the pain of feeling rejection in so many different ways. The stories are all different, but the wound is always the same. We all feel like we've been rejected by God, rejected by our fathers, rejected by our brothers and sisters, our mothers.

Those feelings aren't always true. They are lies. However, that is what we have come to believe and simply assume about ourselves on a subconscious level. When we track those things down and receive truth, we can get genuine healing so there is no longer a need to cover up the pain with drugs and alcohol. Jesus is the solution to this. He has made the way for us to be rejoined with the Father. He is the Spirit of truth and the Spirit of wisdom. His Holy Spirit gives us the truth so that we can enjoy this life. He is the author and the finisher of our faith. He's the only one who makes us worthy even to be in union with the Lord and be worth being together. When people get ahold of that relationship and begin to understand their new identity in Christ, begin to get the healing for these wounds, of roots of rejection, they will no longer suffer from the fruits of rejection.

Addiction is a family problem, not just a personal issue, because addiction is a byproduct of problems in relationships, separation of relationship with the Father, and the separation of relationship with one another. Within this problem there will be people who are affected, whether they're alive or whether they have died, and for the people who are alive and associated with the addict, they have to begin to understand that they are not separate from the problem. They also have a problem.

Many people feel like a person in their family has a problem, and he needs to get help. As soon as he fixes his life, the family and the relational problem will be fixed. That's not actually true because, as you've seen with the Coronavirus, we've all come to this broad epiphany that we are connected. We are connected at our core. You don't live on an island. You can't even pretend to live on an island. People in the Brazilian rainforest got Coronavirus, and no one knows how it happened. On this planet, we are all connected. In your families, you are designed by God to be in a relationship with Him and to be in relationship with one another. When a person in your family has addiction, you are affected, and it's very important that you begin to seek help yourself.

My wife was in a relationship when she was young with a person who had an addiction. At the time, one of the most helpful things she heard when that person was trying to get recovery was, "Heather, you need to take care of yourself." That's the best thing you can do for the person you love. Almost every person who goes through addiction has a codependent partner in their addiction, someone who is enabling them. A person is dysfunctional in the addiction with them on a codependent level.

Most of the time family members have no context and no idea what to do for themselves in this problem. Organizations like Al-Anon and Celebrate Recovery are there to help people understand the issues that come out of the family to create an addictive mindset. I would say for the person who has a loved one seeking help for addiction, it's equally important that the family members go seek help for codependency and understand appropriate boundaries.

We need to make sure we're not Nazareth when the person comes homes to recovery, but to be accepting and loving. However, we also need to have boundaries. It's absolutely appropriate for you to be able to watch that person be accountable and have accountability systems. That's what you should expect. It's okay to question your loved one about their boundaries and make sure they're continuing to work their program. Not that you have to stay on top of them, just have transparency in your relationships so everyone understands we're all fallen, and we all need recovery of some kind. I need recovery for codependency and the addict needs recovery for addiction.

Once they understand it's a family disease and must be walked out by everybody involved, there's a lot of good support that will help the person in addiction. We have many family members in denial. They do not believe they've done anything to enable. They don't want to look at their own problems because the effects of their codependency are not as visible. They're not as obvious. You know, we believe when the people around us fall to addiction, that's their problem. We had nothing to do with that. That's not really true because people really rarely fall into addiction in a vacuum. We all need restoration in Christ on so many levels. You've also got to deal at some point with the family problem, or else you're only dealing with half of the problem.

My wife Heather and I have been with Faith Farm Ministries for seven years. Though it's been very challenging and sometimes gets old in that it's difficult to continually try to pour into people what they need in order to survive, we feel blessed and like we're very well suited to it. When it starts getting hard on us, we get away just by ourselves to talk through it and rely on each other in that way. It's a very challenging ministry, and one you've got to be called to. It can't be a job. If it ever gets to where it's a job, you're done.

We strongly believe that's the case with us. We've seen some amazing transformations. We have someone now who has never had a legal job in his life. His entire career has been using and selling drugs. He grew up really rough without a dad. His only role model was the drug dealer on the corner who was a cousin of some guy. He followed in his footsteps, picked up the business and grew it, making it bigger. He's been in and out of prison numerous times, and so on. Now when you speak to him, he is just the most wonderful guy; he knows the Lord and loves the Lord. He's ministering very strongly to the students who are coming up behind him. It is a genuinely transformed life. Those kinds of successes are extremely reassuring and what encourages us and keeps us going. We would not trade seeing the transformed lives and the unbelievable privilege of watching God at work. We see firsthand the miracles God is doing in giving people their lives back, freeing them from the bondage of addiction and putting them back on the path to loving Him and seeing the joy, beauty, reality, and peace that comes with a life transformed by God. That is something that is both priceless and precious to my wife and me. We are grateful that God continues to use us to help those in need.

A Higher Power Is the Healer: A Long-Term, Faith-Based Treatment President's View

By Pasco A. Manzo

Why Do People Abuse Drugs?

For many years I have been around those who abuse and are addicted to drugs and alcohol. The questions asked by them, their families, and those providing care are always the same. Why do people abuse drugs? Why can't I just stop? Is drug addiction a disease? Why do some people become addicted while others do not?

There are a variety of reasons why people abuse drugs. Initially, they want to feel good. Most abuse drugs to produce intense feelings of pleasure. The initial sensation of euphoria is followed by other effects, which differ depending on the type of drug used. For example, with stimulants such as cocaine, the *high* is followed by feelings of power, self-confidence, and increased energy and concentration. In contrast, the euphoria caused by opiates, such as heroin, is followed by feelings of relaxation and satisfaction. These feelings help drug users mask their problems and true emotions.

Drug users want to feel better on the inside, do better on the outside, or get better health.

Inside: Many users suffer from social anxiety, stress-related disorders, and depression. They attempt to lessen these feelings through drugs. Any of these mood disorders can also cause a relapse in those recovering from addiction. Loneliness, childhood wounds, and growing up in dysfunctional environments are also reasons people use drugs to fill the void.

Outside: *They want to excel.* The pressure to chemically enhance or improve cognitive or athletic performance often plays a role in initial experimentation and continued abuse of drugs, such as prescription stimulants or anabolic/androgenic steroids. *They want to fit* *in.* Adolescents are particularly vulnerable here because of the strong influence of peer pressure. Teens are more likely than adults to engage in risky or daring behaviors to impress their friends and express their independence from parental and social rules. Yet, what often begins as recreational use can become an overpowering addiction.

Health: Legally prescribed medication is being abused in massive amounts. A common misconception is just because a medical doctor writes a prescription for drugs it's okay to take them and they are safe. Medical marijuana is also included in this list. The fact is that prescription drugs can be extremely harmful and as equally addictive and dangerous as illegal drugs like crystal meth, cocaine, and heroin. Unfortunately, prescribed drugs are not always properly monitored by the doctor and discontinued before a patient becomes addicted. Doctors now write prescriptions by the billions. I am astounded when I look behind the pick-up counter at a drug store and see how many prescription orders have been processed. Additionally, prescription drugs can easily be purchased on the street or online.

Street drugs make it easy to address one's inside, outside, or health issues. A bag of heroin can be purchased for five to ten dollars and amazingly you can get an *introduction bag* for only one dollar!

Alcohol has long been a socially accepted and legal vice. It is not just available in liquor stores, but grocery stores, drug stores, restaurants, airplanes, trains, sports events, and elsewhere.

Addiction can begin with a young person being curious and experimenting. The situation starts out most often with a lesser drug like alcohol or marijuana, but far too many times it leads to heroin, cocaine, and strong addictive prescription medication. Most say, "I will never use heroin," or, "I will never shoot heroin into my veins." No single factor can predict whether a person will become addicted to drugs. Risk for addiction is influenced by a combination of factors that include individual biology, social environment, and stage of development. The more risk factors an individual has, the greater the chance that taking drugs can lead to addiction.

ADDICTION

Let's look at the word addiction. The origin of the word **ad-dic-tion** stems from 1595–1605 Latin *addiction* (stem of *addictiō*) a giving over, surrender. The root word is "addict," in Greek it is "*diké*," justice, rights. Something like "*adiktoi*" could mean, "those not entitled to rights," therefore slaves.

Merriam-Webster Dictionary states: "Addiction is a compulsive need for and use of a habit-forming substance (as heroin, nicotine, or alcohol) characterized by tolerance and by well-defined physiological symptoms upon withdrawal. Broadly: persistent compulsive use of a substance known by the user to be harmful."[1]

Dictionary.com states: "The state of being enslaved to a habit or practice or to something that is psychologically or physically habit forming, as narcotics, to such an extent that its cessation causes severe trauma.[2]

A *British Dictionary* states: "Addiction is the condition of being abnormally dependent on some habit, especially compulsive dependency on narcotic drugs."[3]

According to the government's 2018 National Survey on Drug Use and Health, over one hundred sixty-four million Americans age twelve and older—nearly 61% percent of population—use illegal drugs. One hundred thirty-eight million of those used alcohol and almost thirty-nine million used illicit drugs. The National Institute of Health estimates two million Americans on prescribed opioids are in danger of turning to the black market for a stronger fix.[4] Substance abuse refers to the harmful use of psychoactive substances, including alcohol and illicit drugs. Psychoactive substance use can lead to dependence syndrome, a cluster of behavioral, cognitive, and physiological phenomena that develop after repeated substance abuse. It typically includes a strong desire to take the drug, difficulty controlling drug use, and persisting in drug use despite harmful consequences. Additionally, a higher priority is given to drug use than to other activities and obligations, tolerance of the drug increases, and sometimes there are withdrawal side effects.

The power of substance abuse and addiction distances individuals from their parents, siblings, spouse, and even their own children. Their friends become alienated as bridges are burned while they seek to satisfy their addiction. Their integrity, dignity, pride, self-respect, and self-esteem slowly shatter. Their dreams, career, and all aspects of normal daily life dwindle as their newfound addiction takes precedence.

1...Merriam-Webster, 2020
2...Dictionary.com, 2020
3...Collins Concise English Dictionary 2020
4...National Survey on Drug Use and Health: Summary of National Findings, 2010

Most Common Myths Associated with Drug Addiction

Myth #1: Drug Addiction Is the Individual's Choice

Most people believe that drug addicts have the choice to use drugs or not, and that their addiction exists because the addict allows it to. This is not true. When drugs are consumed by an addict, the brain is *hijacked*, which affects the addict's ability to control the level of their drug use. Addiction should be thought of as a brain disease, which causes the addict to think they must comply with its demands to survive. Often addiction opens the door to stealing, lying, neglecting responsibilities, and causes other risky behavior to satisfy the addiction. Psalm 103:3 says, "He (Jesus) forgives all our sins and heals all of our diseases."[5]

Myth #2: Only Individuals with No Willpower Are Addicted to Drugs

Some people think only weak-minded individuals develop addictions. The fact is the levels of dopamine in the brain get altered from substance abuse and generally take twelve to eighteen months to readjust. One of the reasons for Teen Challenge New England & New Jersey's high recovery rate is its fifteen-month program and optional six-month apprenticeship.

The Mayo Foundation for Medical Education and Research reports: "People of any age, sex, or economic status can become addicted to a drug. However, certain factors can affect the likelihood and speed of developing an addiction."

- *Family history of addiction.* Drug addiction is more common in some families and likely involves genetic predisposition. Having a blood relative, such as a parent or sibling, with an addiction, puts one at greater risk.
- *Being male.* Men are more likely to have drug problems than women. However, progression of addiction is known to be faster in females.
- *Having a mental health disorder.* A mental health disorder such as depression, high anxiety, attention-deficit/hyperactivity

---

5...*Psalm 103:3, NLT, Tyndale, 2020*

disorder, or post-traumatic stress disorder may cause addiction to drugs.

- **Peer pressure.** Peer pressure, primarily for young people, is a strong factor in starting to use and abuse drugs
- **Family issues.** Difficult family situations or a lack of parental bonding or supervision may increase the risk of addiction.[6]

Myth #3: Drug Addiction Is A Hopeless Condition

Once an alcoholic or drug addict, always one. Not true. Proverbs 13:12 says, "Hope deferred makes the heart sick, but a longing fulfilled is a tree of life."[7] *Help* and *hope* are available for every addict. Teen Challenge New England & New Jersey has seen countless people remain clean and sober for many years, breaking the power of addiction and never going back to abusing substances. Our *Changed Lives* books series offers stories from many who have broken free from the bondage of addiction and is proof that the power of Jesus Christ offered in our program can help anyone who desires freedom and a new life.

Addiction is no stranger to the rich and famous. Rush Limbaugh got hooked on Oxycontin. Glenn Beck is a recovering alcoholic, as is Elton John, Eric Clapton, Anthony Hopkins, Judy Collins, Mel Gibson, and many more. Tiger Woods is a recovering sex addict— perhaps Warren Beatty and Wilt Chamberlain also, among many more. William Bennett's gambling habit was all over the news. Oprah Winfrey acknowledges she's a carbohydrate addict. For Julia Cameron, it was alcohol and drugs, just as it was for Mackenzie Phillips and Carrie Fisher. Former President Obama was addicted to nicotine.

Drug and alcohol detoxes, treatment centers, drug-counseling, and even jail time help in the recovery process, but for many addicts, they do not have a lasting effect.

Addiction has so many faces today. It can be anyone from anywhere. Stereotypes are gone for good. One in five who take legitimate prescription drugs for pain relief wind up buying illegal drugs to kill their pain. The examples are endless. A thirty-seven-year-old mother of three children who has back surgery and is prescribed

---

6...Mayo Foundation for Medical Education and Research, Drug Addiction (substance use disorder), Staff, pages 9-10, 2020
7...Prov. 13:12 NIV, Biblica, 2011

oxycodone. An NFL player breaks a bone and is given a fentanyl patch. A professional financial broker starts taking Xanax to reduce stress. A nurse has a root canal and is prescribed Vicodin. A college student dealing with the stress of exams gets Adderall.

Psychiatrist M. Scott Peck, MD, a self-confessed nicotine addict and author of *The Road Less Traveled*, offered his perspective in a lecture, "Addiction: The Sacred Disease." Dr. Peck's thesis was communicated as follows:

At birth, humans become separated from God. Everyone is aware of this separation, but some people are more attuned to it than others. They report a feeling of emptiness, a longing, what many refer to as "a hole in their soul." They sense that something is missing, but don't know what it is. At some point in their lives (often quite young) these sensitive souls stumble across something that makes them feel better. For some it's alcohol, for others it's sugar, drugs, shopping, sex, work, gambling, or some other substance or activity that hits the spot. "Ahh," they sigh, "I've found what's been missing. This is the answer to my problems." They have discovered a new best friend—*their drug of choice*.

Peck pointed out that the alcoholic is really thirsty for Spirit, but he settles for spirits. Alcohol is simply a form of cheap grace, as are all addictive substances. What we humans really long for is a connection to God... alignment with the Holy... re-union with the Divine. It is a deeply spiritual hunger—a longing to go home again, back to Source. But we're confused about what we're really hungry for, so we go looking for love in all the wrong places. We reach for anything to take the edge off, to smooth out life's rough spots, to help us make it through the night.

Most residents who enter our Teen Challenge program agree that no matter what drug they used or how high they got, nothing could ever fill that void. In fact, often it only seemed to get deeper. Only when they responded to the opportunity to accept Jesus Christ as Lord and Savior did they attest to their void being filled.

Is there hope for the addict? Is there an answer for addiction's tight grip? Is there a power stronger than the power of addiction? Can you or your loved one become free from the control of addiction and live a productive life? *Absolutely yes!*

When Paul the Apostle asked his rhetorical question, "Who shall deliver me from this terrible state that I am in?" He answered it with, "Thank God! The answer is in Jesus Christ our Lord." He understood human nature as he also said, "In my mind I really want to obey God's law, but because of my sinful nature I am a slave to sin."[8]

He is the One who can free those trapped. He is stronger than any addiction! *There is a higher power… His name is Jesus Christ!* At Teen Challenge our twelve-to-fifteen-month residential program has proven to work again and again because of the *Jesus Factor*. He is the central focus, who can and does break the power of addiction. The program is designed to assist the resident in dealing with their issues and re-entering society as a productive and healthy person. But our success rate would not exist without each addict forming a personal relationship with Jesus Christ.

A study submitted by Brian J. Grim and Melissa E. Grim entitled "Belief, Behavior, and Belonging, How Faith is Indispensable in Preventing and Recovering from Substance" reviews the voluminous empirical evidence on faith's contribution to preventing people from falling victim to substance abuse and helping them recover from it. Their study shows that:

Religious beliefs, practices, and ministries not only provide succor and solace to those in need; they provide tangible, valuable resources that can help prevent and address substance abuse. In addition to the effective role of spirituality, congregations and faith-based institutions are particularly effective in community mobilization and timely response to crises. Faith communities are adept at facilitating quality group interactions focused on overcoming past negative experiences, which are often drivers of the emotional and spiritual despondency that feed mental illness and substance abuse. This study found that volunteer addiction recovery groups meeting in congregations across the USA contribute up to $316.6 billion in savings to the US economy every year at no cost to taxpayers. Grim and Grim find 84 percent of scientific studies show that faith is a positive factor in addiction prevention or recovery and a risk in less than two percent of the studies reviewed. They conclude "that religion and spirituality are exceptionally powerful, integral, and indispensable resources in substance abuse prevention and recovery; faith plays a key role in treating the mind, body, and spirit.[9]

---

8   Romans 7:25 NLT, Tyndale, 2015
9   Grim & Grim, 2019, Online Journal of Religion and Health

ADDICTION: CHASING THE CURE

The cure for addiction is a fleeting thought for the addict and often short-lived. It is a dream with holes of hopelessness. The addict knows how to chase the urge to get high. In fact, for most, the chase is a part of the high. I have been around addicts when they are in this chase to get their drug of choice. Nothing and no one will deter them until they have achieved their desired goal. For the most part, an addict wants to be free, but this turnaround can only come when they stop chasing their high and begin to chase their cure.

We teach our residents that they must chase the cure with the same determination as they chased their drug of choice. To bring lasting change, an addict must be set free from the power of addiction. We have to address the whole person—physical, mental, emotional, spiritual, and behavioral. Change has to come from the inside. Telling them to cope with their addiction and that they will always be an addict brings no hope to them or their loved ones.

Teen Challenge has found the cure for addiction, and it has been proven again and again over the last sixty-plus years. That cure is the *Jesus Factor*—a relationship with Jesus Christ. His love reaches them at their worst, giving hope no one else could give. The One who created us knows how to fix us. As one chases after Him rather than their drug high, He can be found. He doesn't discriminate against city, country, color, culture, status quo, language, male, female, young, or old. He says, "Come to me, all you who are weary and burdened, and I will give you rest. Take my yoke upon you and learn from me, for I am gentle and humble in heart, and you will find rest for your souls. For my yoke is easy and my burden is light."[10]

Our program is twelve to fifteen months, giving the necessary time to create structure, teach discipline and responsibility, and help residents to rebalance their lives. They acquire self-worth and value, changed behavior and attitude, and life skills. They attain GEDs and receive clinical counseling and life coaching. They rebuild relationships with loved ones. The proof that the Jesus Factor is the answer is in the lives of everyone who walks the aisle of graduation

upon completion. If you or anyone you know is struggling with addiction, the power to heal, deliver, and change comes from a relationship with Jesus Christ.

---

10   Matthew 11:28-30, NIV, 2011

Quotes from Former Teen Challenge Residents/Family

Scott O. - IT Professional

"As I reflected on my own journey through Teen Challenge, I saw how necessary it was to go through each stage and phase of the program. With every challenge, there was only opportunity for victory. Long-term treatment was what I needed. It worked for me and it has worked for so many others."

Allison C. - Wife/Mother

"I remember the day I found out my husband was addicted to methamphetamine. My whole world turned upside down in a moment. I tried everything I could to help him, everything from flushing his drugs down the toilet and throwing his paraphernalia away to begging and pleading with him to get help and attempting to bring him out of the places he was. He wasn't the same person I married. Meth had taken over his life. There were many sleepless nights spent wondering if he would live another day. I found myself feeling alone with nowhere to turn for help except to God."

Craig J.

"The first ninety days at Teen Challenge were some of hardest days of my life. The chiseling process is painful. Change isn't easy. I wanted to leave the program daily, sometimes hourly. The first time I was in the Massachusetts Center, I walked into the multipurpose auditorium and there was huge sign that read "Now Is The Time." It was confirmation that this was exactly where God wanted me and that He would be with me through this tough process."

Enzo R.

"Deep down inside I wanted a new life. I wanted to change and I needed a relationship with Jesus. When I entered the doors of Teen Challenge, I immediately felt the presence of God. I remember feeling relieved and like I was finally home. Immediately the Spirit of God was all over me. I was in His presence and felt His grace and love saturate me in every chapel service and in every room. I couldn't escape His love. I repented of all I had done and the chaos I caused in my life and the lives of others. I was humbled and broken that the

Lord forgave me."

Emma M. (Bloom Adolescent Home Graduate)

"Arriving at Teen Challenge Bloom Campus, I was met with more love and kindness then I had ever expected. The women on staff cared about me in a way only possible through the love of Christ. Through the uncomfortable counseling and self-reflection, I was finally able to see myself in a new light. I finally laid my life down in a humble attempt to start over and cleanse my heart and soul of whom I chose to be."

Emma M's Parents' Perspective

"God used Teen Challenge Bloom to radically change our daughter. That statement is the conclusion of what has been the toughest three years of our parenting lives."

WORK CITED – MANZO

"Addiction – Wordreference.com Dictionary of English." WordReference.com, 2020, www. wordreference.com/ definition/addiction.

"Addiction." *Dictionary.com*, Dictionary.com, 2020, www. dictionary.com/browse /addiction.

"Addiction." *Merriam-Webster,* Merriam-Webster, 2020, www. merriam-webster.com/dictionary/addiction.

Grim, Brian J, and Melissa E Grim. "Belief, Behavior, and Belonging: How Faith Is Indispensable in Preventing and Recovering from Substance Abuse," *National Center for Biotechnology Information, Springer Journal of Religion and Health*, U.S. National Library of Medicine, 2019, www.ncbi. nlm.nih.gov/.

Mayo Clinic Staff. "Drug Addiction (Substance Use Disorder). *Mayo Clinic*, Mayo Foundation for Medical Education and Research, 2017, www.mayoclinic.org/.

"New International Translation Bible," *Bible Hub: Search, Read, Study the Bible in Many Languages*, Biblical Publishers, 2011, www.biblehub.com/.

"New Living Translation Bible." *Biblegateway.com: A Searchable Online Bible in over 150 Versions and 50 Languages*, Tyndale House Publishers, 2015, www.biblegateway.com/.
Peck, M. Scott MD, "Addiction: The Sacred Disease." Further Along A Road Less Traveled. 1991, USA.

"Results from the 2010 National Survey on Drug Use and Health: Summary of National Findings." *Substance Abuse and Mental Health Services Administration*, 2014, www.samhsa.gov/.

A Short-Term Treatment Center Owner's View

By Joe Bryan

I've run a successful treatment center for over forty years, and I'm happy to share with you some of what I've learned.

My first experience with a treatment center was part of a day of *firsts* when I was just nine-years old. It all started in a Ford station wagon traveling to Eagleville Hospital in Pennsylvania. The hospital was nine hundred miles away from my home at the time. The station wagon was somewhat new, but it broke down thirty miles into the trip! We finally arrived at Eagleville Hospital, which had recently been converted from a tuberculosis hospital to an alcohol treatment program. That day, it seemed like a large scary building to me.

I didn't realize it at the time, but that day changed the course of my life. I had three major *firsts* that day. I saw my first treatment center, I heard about Alcoholics Anonymous for the first time, and I met my father for the first time. I did not know at the time that my father was a recovering alcoholic, nor did I know what a big part all these *firsts* would play in my life.

Years later, when I was attending college in Tallahassee, my father asked if I wanted to go fishing with him and his friends in Naples, Florida. Since I was floundering at FSU, I thought, "Why not go fishing? It will clear my head and then I can go back and finish school." Upon arriving I learned that all of my father's friends on the boat were sober and members of AA. But others on the boat *should have been*. After we were underway, the first mate had a seizure from running out of booze. He had assumed, like many fishermen, we would bring plenty of alcohol, and he paid the price for his mistake.

After that memorable fishing trip, I started working for my father at The Beachcomber Recovery Center. I moved there and I began to witness many things for the first time. My father put me to work and I started out at a slow pace. However, soon I was doing more and more. I worked in nearly every position. I did maintenance, I was a driver, I was a breakfast cook, I was a fill-in/back-up chef, and tech; I did whatever needed to be done. Those first years I was around the patients virtually twenty-four hours a day since I worked *and* lived at The Beachcomber.

During this time, I was able to truly learn what patients expected and how they thought. Also, I was able to see firsthand how the health, outlook, and behavior of some improved as a result of the treatment they were receiving. I also observed the opposite in others, as there were as many negative as positive changes. I was also able to finish school and get my undergraduate degree.

My work experiences at The Beachcomber as a young man played a fundamental part in shaping me and giving me the ability to do the job I would eventually hold as CEO/Owner of The Beachcomber. To be the CEO of a small treatment center, first you need to understand your patients, but you also need to carefully select and support your staff. Your staff is very important. It is vital they know you support them, but it is also important to make certain they do the right thing.

For example, I had a director of therapy who told a patient information that wasn't true. Then after discovering his mistake, the he did not apologize or admit his error. His pride prevented him from being honest with the patient, so I had to let him go.

Besides having a good staff, the *quality of treatment* must be a priority for a treatment center to stay in operation as long as we have. My father's philosophy in decision-making, which I have continued to follow, (such as a new idea, change of procedure or policy, etc.) was, "How will the change help the patients get sober?" Quality patient care must always be at the forefront. However, the process of creating and maintaining a quality program is a difficult task. I have added to my father's philosophy that *everything is important.* Many things can add to or take away from our efforts, so obviously it is important to identify those things. Some important components to a smoothly run program are:

1. Take care of your staff.

2. Take care of your patients.

3. The group is more important than the individual.

4. Little things matter.

5. If you promise a patient something, you better come through.

6. Tell the truth. A patient can see a lie a mile away.

7. Treat everyone equally—this includes staff and patients.

8. Never let patient buy lobsters, etc.—*no special treatment.*

9. Fix things quickly and if not, explain why it cannot be done quickly.

10. Don't make any threats or set boundaries unless you will follow through. (For example: "If you do that again there will be consequences.")

11. Staff the facility to fit the needs of the patients. Keep a tight patient-to-therapist ratio. At The Beachcomber we have six therapists for sixteen patients.

12. Hire therapists with different views and specialties. You need a competent team of therapists who can handle many different personalities, not automatons.

13. Always ask regarding changes to patient treatment, "Who does this help? Does this help the patient get sober?"

14. Have a family program and an aftercare program.

15. Understand addiction.

16. It's *we,* not I, when it comes to treatment. Everyone from the CEO to the cleaning staff have a part in helping the patient.

17. Listen, listen, listen to staff and patients and don't be defensive. Accept criticism. Ask patients about their stay. I don't want to hear good things only. I want to know what went wrong and what needs to be fixed.

Why are consistent rules important and why do we do all these things and more? It's because we need patients to trust us, and that trust must be earned. Once they begin to trust us, we have the chance to get to know the real person and, thus, can truly help them on their road to recovery. Trust helps people open up and allows them to let their guard down, and it's a connection many patients have never had. To gain trust, everything matters. Sometimes this can even include what you wear and drive. Patients watch everything you do. So, if you drive up in a very expensive car, some patients think that your business is all about the money, which is something they have probably seen all too often. Decisions made regarding patients should never be based on money. It is important for the group to see that your program does what it says and treats everyone as equals—again, no *special treatment* for those with more money. All the rooms are the same, everyone eats the same food (obvious exceptions include special meals required for medical or religious reasons). I could go on, but everything matters.

The staff of a facility should also be treated equally. They should also be informed of the challenges we are meeting and seeing in the future. I learned from my father that some treatment programs had too many staff meetings that had nothing to do with patient care. Therefore, the only scheduled meetings we have are to discuss patient status. I also learned from him that it is important for therapists to be given support, education, and time off because their job is mentally stressful. It is important to back up staff and not to allow patients to break rules, threaten others, or disrupt groups, just because they are paying cash. Your staff, like your patients, must believe in what you are doing. The CEO must be involved in treatment, must listen to his staff, and must be willing to admit he is wrong or made a mistake, if he has.

For example, I once had the idea to expand to twenty-two patients. (We are a sixteen-bed facility.) The more patients we had, the more money we would make. We filled all the beds, even had a waiting list at times, but I could tell the program had changed, and not for the better. All I could think of was adding more patients, and slowly but surely, the program began to show the stress of too many patients. Fortunately, I realized I was allowing money to undermine the quality of treatment and made the decision to go back to sixteen patients. The cars, trips, and early retirement I had thought of were now just dreams, but I was happier and so were the patients and staff.

I personally talk to many patients to find what worked for them and what did not. How were they treated? Was the room adequate? Were the therapists helpful? Was the food good? Were all needs met? Were any needs ignored? If they needed help, did they receive it in a timely manner? In asking these questions, the patients realize you truly care about them. So, when someone asks me what is the most important objective of The Beachcomber, I have to say it is *all important*—from delivering cigarettes and fixing the air conditioner to seeing a counselor that day, if asked. Be true to your word. If a patient is disrupting the group and unwilling to change, a transfer may be in order. Always treat everyone equally.

WHAT I'VE LEARNED ABOUT ADDICTION

Here are some of the other things I've learned firsthand through the years from running our treatment center, about those struggling with addiction.

- Those who have the lowest success rate will be the ones who have been in multiple treatment facilities already. Also, those individuals who have what we call the *least amount of treatment or recovery capital,* such as life skills, place to live, education, financial backing, family backing etc. will do worse. The more support the individual has, the better chance of success. Also, certain drugs have less chance of success. Meth and crack seem to take longer inpatient treatment to have a chance for success. It seems there are advantages for patients in the age range of twenty-five to sixty. The younger ones probably haven't felt enough pain yet to be ready to quit, and the older ones may think they are too old, so it's not worth changing. These are broad generalizations and obviously anyone can have success in treatment if they are willing.

- The most important thing in someone succeeding in rehab today is if the individual is tired, worn out, spiritually empty, and willing to do whatever it takes. They must have admitted they are incapable of successful sobriety on their own. The most successful ones have realized they have reached the end of their rope and they need help and assistance to recover. They are desirous of that help and assistance.

- I think the biggest obstacle standing in the way of people's sobriety lies with the addicted individual who has difficulty with spirituality or has other issues such as trust, past traumatic experiences, past treatment experiences, and possibly other issues.

- For family members dealing with someone struggling with addiction. We believe a *tough love* approach is the first message that needs to get across. The addict must see and feel the consequences of their actions in order to understand the full scope and severity of the problem. It doesn't mean you have to cut the addict out of your life. It just means you are refusing to enable them to continue in the same destructive behavior.

Most addicts who are not completely surrendered to the concept that their addiction has overtaken them and they need help, will come up with every excuse possible to not go in for treatment and get help. They will say they cannot leave their family, their job, or their responsibilities. We always say there are a thousand reasons not to go in and there's one reason to go in. That reason is to save their lives, futures, families, and jobs, which they will certainly lose if they continue in the pattern of addictive behavior they have fallen into as a regular way of life.

Sometimes I ask myself why I am still working in treatment as there are so many hassles, requirements, and obligations involved in successfully running a viable treatment center that really helps its clients in an ethical way with integrity, genuinely putting their clients' interests first.

For example, the Department of Children and Family Services came to The Beachcomber, did an inspection and license test forty-four years ago when we started and then every year since. Then after forty-four years, we didn't pass the fire inspection one time and were downgraded to a temporary license. In order to receive permanent status again, we ended up replacing all the cabinets on the premises, repainting the whole inside, replacing a few windows, upgrading two new doors to fire code, as well as getting a new fire extinguisher, two ceiling retardants, and a new door between all rooms. All the work was finished in thirty days. When the inspectors returned, the building inspectors passed us, but the new fire inspector didn't. Then we were on a second temporary license, which is all DCF (Department of Children and Families, the regulatory body for treatment centers) will give. My brothers, who own the facility along with me, were very worried and called me frequently to express their concerns. The fire department wanted a new stairway outside from second floor to the first. I responded to their request, and after repeating myself, I lost my patience and my temper. Ultimately, the fire department passed us. It felt like a basketball game with three seconds left in second overtime, where the lead changed twenty times, and we have the ball down by one.

So, why do I still do this? While experiencing all these frustrations in the course of the couple of months, three former patients called to thank us for the help they received at The Beachcomber, which allowed them to reclaim their lives and truly live again. The genuine gratitude they expressed to us was priceless. I'd work three more lifetimes to hear even one of them respond that way. Another gentleman who, before coming to treatment, had lived on the street for a month and did things he was not proud of, came by on his one-year anniversary to thank us. He's been working and is back with his family and going to meetings. He has a sponsor, has gratitude, and prays for guidance.

So, why has The Beachcomber not changed dramatically over our forty-four years like many others have? Because we have kept the quality of the program as our number one priority. Details are important to us.

Unfortunately, a treatment center can make a lot of money without offering a quality program, without good outcomes, and without all of the things I mentioned. Shamefully, so many struggling addicts are victims of shoddily run, money-first treatment centers and their sobriety, recovery, lives, and futures are negatively impacted. We want patients to get sober. That is our number one goal and priority, not profit. Everything we do revolves around that. Our reputation is our most important advertising tool. So, if you ask me why is The Beachcomber such a good program? My best answer: we believe *everything matters* as we help our patients to attain sobriety!

SOBER HOMES & TRANSITIONAL LIVING

Sober-Home Owner, Therapist

By Kerry Roesser
LMHC, LPC, NCC, CAP, SAP, CRC, CRRA

The following provides an overview of sober housing for individuals with substance use disorders and examines the role housing plays in remission and recovery. The *compilation* comes from more than fifteen years of experience that includes owning and managing sober living houses and a substance use disorder and mental health treatment facility, practicing in several states as a licensed provider and specializing in substance use disorders, supplying clinical supervision for those seeking state licensure, and supporting those with substance use dependence, as well as their families and loved ones, as they educated themselves about the pitfalls of the disease of addiction.

Sober Housing Terms

In clinical settings, words matter. Therefore, it is essential to introduce the many names for sober housing. There is halfway house, recovery home, recovery residence, transitional living, sober house, and sober living. These are the most commonly used terms for housing. Although I am not of the opinion that each term has a distinctly different meaning, others might disagree.

In some geographical areas and among different clinical and recovery communities, these terms may have different meanings. The word *halfway* was used to indicate a person was *halfway* home. Traditionally, this term was used to describe a post-incarceration midpoint or halfway home from inpatient substance abuse treatment. People commonly refer to sober living houses as halfway houses. For the sake of simplicity, the term *sober living* will be used throughout the chapter.

FEDERAL REGULATION & INDUSTRY
HOUSING CERTIFICATION

Often people with substance use disorders, their families, and loved ones are surprised to learn that there is no formal regulation of sober living houses. This is due to the Federal Fair Housing Act of 1968 that makes it unlawful to deny housing to a person or group of people because of a disability. Under federal guidelines, people with substance use disorder are recognized as having a disability. This can cause friction among governments and sober living homeowners. At the local and state level, governments try to circumvent the law through the use of the *unrelated adult* statute. This statute can be misused by local or state government officials in a thinly veiled attempt to violate the rights of people with substance use disorder. The laws state that no more than a specified number of unrelated adults, usually three to five, are permitted to live in one apartment or in a single-family home. Therefore, in order to operate with more than three to five unrelated adults, you must apply for special permission called *reasonable accommodation*. Some governments automatically approve reasonable accommodation requests because they know it is difficult to circumvent federal law. In fact, I was among a group of sober living homeowners who used the Fair Housing Law to file for protection against a town in Florida. The lawyer, James K. Green, successfully argued our case and has successfully argued many others such cases using various laws.

While Federal law prevents a requirement that sober living be licensed, a national organization offers voluntary certification. In Florida, a statute passed that made it illegal for state-licensed substance abuse facilities to refer clients to sober-living homes that are not certified. This was the state's attempt to gain jurisdiction over sober living. If argued in court, it is likely the statute would be overturned. However, that would require an expensive lawsuit, so to date the statute has not been challenged.

INDUSTRY PITFALLS

Unfortunately, the organizations that certify sober housing often have limited funding. I am of the opinion that, due to the lack of funding, they provide little oversight and do not have a well-functioning system of checks and balances. In fact, when I have complained to the local organization about nefarious operators, I was told that the organization is "not the police." Employees are not held to screening regulations and are not well monitored. Some have been caught up in webs of corruption. One inspector was arrested and charged with the crimes that the organization is intended to protect. There are conflicts of interest and each officer appears to have his own agenda. One of the officials is rumored to own his own uncertified sober-living home. Conversely, there are some that put in hard work for little compensation. However, the danger remains in that public perception is that certified housing is a well-monitored home. Some of the worst offenders I have seen were certified. I advise families not to use certification as the criterion for determining the legitimacy of a sober living home environment.

What to Look for and Expect in Sober Living Housing & Costs

Referrals to sober living are made through several avenues. The most common is through the facilities where clients are being treated. Be cautious about these referrals. It is not prudent to rely on treatment facilities, including detoxes, for referrals. They may offer options based on business relationships rather than what is in the best interest of the client. In my experience, if a client does find his own option, and the center finds out, the client is advised by the treatment staff of a *more suitable* option. When this happens, beware! These *options* can be those where the center has a *referral relationship* with the home. Insist the staff be clear as to the reason they chose a particular sober living home and verify what they are saying.

The best way to determine suitability is to be an advocate and ask questions. Here are a few examples. Ask to see the rules. Is it single-sex housing? Are *couples* allowed? What are the credentials of the owner? How long have they been around? Is the drug testing billed or included in the housing cost? Are they *required* to attend treatment that is billed to insurance? Were you asked if you have insurance? Is the cash pay price the same as if you have insurance? What is the relapse policy? Is it zero tolerance? Are they housing MAT (Medically Assisted Treatment) clients? Is the property owned by the owner of the sober living house or is it being rented? Is there a house manager and, if so, can you speak to him or her? Do they call you if your loved one relapses? What is the process for a relapse? Is insurance covering all or even part of the rent? If so, then beware!

Sober living is very rarely covered under an insurance policy. You may be told that rent is *reduced* or *waived* if you have health insurance. In most states, this is illegal as it is a form of enticement and, even if allowed under state law, can still be insurance fraud. If a person is using health insurance for outpatient treatment and he/she is living outside of a licensed facility, the insurance can only pay for outpatient services. Insurance does *not* pay for rent. If the client is not being charged *reasonable and customary* rent or is being forced into attending outpatient treatment in order to live rent free or with reduced-rate rent that is not available to people who do not have insurance, they are committing a crime in most states. Those clients are rarely invested in treatment if they are incentivized. Often high-paying policy holders are given latitude for drug and alcohol use. Some of the laws around this are state laws and may vary. Some are federal laws. It is best to contact your insurance company for more information.

Having you or your loved ones using insurance for rent creates an ethical and legal dilemma. There needs to be more supervision and/or a longer treatment stay, yet there is no money for rent and/or the family is no longer willing to provide financial support. This is understandable. This makes it tempting to allow the crimes to be to committed as long as the help is provided.

Regardless, besides being wrong, there are a few major issues with this behavior. One is the first principal in addiction recovery is honesty. It is imperative that the providers, families, and loved ones model the behavior they expect of the person with the substance use disorder. In my experience, if you or a family member are attending outpatient treatment and not paying sufficient or any rent, outcomes are not good. This practice supports the insurance companies' excuse to deny claims and shorten stays at the higher levels of care. *Please* do not allow this to continue. A person can work and pay for sober living. Unfortunately, abuses have happened on both sides, and many of the abuses led to harm and death for those with substance use disorders.

At the onset, sober living homes offer similar things. They have rules for behavior, curfews, and provide some monitoring. Most expect clients to engage in twelve-step recovery and get jobs. The environment allows residents to practice coping skills and make behavioral changes necessary for long-term sobriety. The most basic expectations of the homes are cleanliness, regular maintenance, proper oversight, zero tolerance for using drugs, which includes alcohol, and operation by caring, ethical, experienced service providers.

The residents have formal house rules. Residents have to initial or sign paperwork stating they understand and will abide by the rules. The residents are expected to complete chores and adhere to curfews. In most of the homes, adherence to a program of recovery is expected and is a condition of continued housing. In addition, a house manager or the owner will administer urine tests (hopefully observed) to ensure clients are free from a wide variety of drugs, which includes alcohol. House managers may ask residents to submit to tests on suspicion, randomly, or even several times per week. If a resident uses drugs or alcohol, the penalty that was stated in the rules will be enforced. Good houses do not waver from these rules. The resident will return to treatment at a higher level of care or make other arrangements, but he/she cannot live at the house and must leave and go to a safe place. Sober living does not have to adhere to federal HIPAA or state privacy rules. This means the family can be and should be called, and the decided upon next move-in should be taken.

The initial costs of sober living can vary greatly. Usually the first payment includes the first and last weeks' rent and an administrative fee. After the initial fee, there is an ongoing weekly fee. Some might charge a month at a time. This means that for many, the initial cost may be prohibitive. In addition, there are very few, if any, government subsidized sober homes. As previously mentioned, insurance rarely pays for sober living. Housing is not considered to be *medically necessary*. This means that the fees are paid by private pay options. Either the person coming out of treatment or his/her family or loved ones have to pay. This may create an unfortunate barrier to entry if money is not available.

The Essential Role of Housing in
Sustained Remission

Appropriate housing can be an essential component of sustained remission for many reasons, but it is not always seen as such, as is the case with insurance companies. First, sober housing is inexpensive in comparison to the addiction treatment levels of care. Insurance companies would see higher success rates and reduced costs if they paid for sober housing. Second, research supports ongoing monitoring as the most effective way to ensure continued remission.

Two great examples of sustained remission are the medical and aviation fields. In these fields, the percentage of success is significantly higher than in the overall population of people with substance use disorder. The statistics are presumed to be high because of the strict monitoring that is mandated for five years. As with many diseases, five years is the *magic* number to where a disease is considered to be in full remission and, in some cases, cured.

Third, sober living can provide a safe haven as families return to a state of homeostasis. During the critical early years, there may be significant changes. Some family members may not be able to let go of resentments. Sometimes couples may break up or, if married, they might divorce. They may remarry or move. There are minor and major changes.

In recovery, it is important to have support when there are significant life stressors. Fourth of the many important reasons for sober living is the time to focus on and engage in a program of recovery.

At this point, you may be more confused than before you started this chapter. The question still remains. Is sober living essential for you and/or your loved one? If sober living is important, then why? Is there a way to tell who will do well? The answers to these questions are simple in theory, but people have a difficult time with the execution. As noted, the first part of the chapter summarized the basics or, as my company is named, the *Foundation*. The text is dry, but important. The second part is the heart of my journey. After more than fifteen years of twelve-hour days, I have easily exceeded Malcolm Gladwell's controversial ten-thousand-hour mark. According to Gladwell, ten thousand is the number of hours it takes to become an expert in something. Gladwell states that if you working at something for three hours a day for 3,333 days, which is nine years, you will hit the mark of expertise. Some argue that the mark is significantly less. Gladwell's ten thousand hours is a benchmark I surpassed more than eight years ago. The second half of this chapter is about my observations and my thoughts on what works and what doesn't, what helps and what harms, and what can help keep addiction in remission.

COMMON QUESTIONS & STATEMENTS
FROM LOVED ONES

The following common questions and statements made by families and loved ones may offer some insight into the belief systems held by the family and provide ways in which they might heal.

1. **My loved one is *different* than the other people who are here.**
   Translation: He is from a better family and is not as bad an addict/alcoholic. He is *special*.
   Underlying: We have guilt and don't like him associating with *these* people.
   Manifestation in the client: Entitlement coupled with low self-worth.
   Intervention: Lots of love and support/test the cognitions. Challenge the concept that *more than* means *better than*. There is a need for education on the disease of addiction and the role of the family.
   Possible Result: The client will manipulate the family by telling them what is *wrong* with the people, in order to be allowed to *not* fulfill his commitment to sober living.

2. **He has *tried* the Twelve Steps, but it does not work for him or he does not like them.**
   Translation: Twelve-step recovery is *cult-like*. We agree somewhat. We don't see the point.
   Underlying: Trust issues. Secrets in the client and, probably, the family. Fearful of loved one becoming a *God freak* and/ or viewing the family in a less flattering light. Client has not engaged in Twelve Steps. He has gone to a few meetings, but not engaged in the program.

Manifestation in the client: Abandonment and trust issues. The Twelve Steps work for so many but won't for me.

Intervention: Offer information and research about the efficacy of Twelve Steps. Let the client express his dissatisfaction openly in order to challenge his cognitions. Review the principles behind the Steps. Offer to meet with him to discuss twelve-step recovery. (This usually encourages him to attend!)

Possible Result: The client will try to use this to not attend meetings and will begin to *live his life*.

3. **His therapist said not to help him financially.**

    Translation: We are unsure of what to do. We are afraid of hurting him. We do not have the means to help, but we feel shame about that.

    Underlying: Fear of financial strain causing him to relapse. Fear of making mistakes that hurt him.

    Manifestation in the client: Resentment if the family has the means but will not help. Insecurity. Entitlement.

    Intervention: Explain enabling. Explain that there is no research on what they were told. They have a right to do what they want and it is fine to make that clear to the client, but do it with conviction and for the right reasons.

    Possible Result: If a client gets help in active addiction but not in recovery, he may decide that relapse is rewarded. Reward remission not return to use.

4. **We will do whatever we can to help.**

    Translation: We are scared. We want to be able to do something, but nothing is *working*.

    Underlying: We realize we don't have control.

    Manifestation in the client: Play on the fear. History of trying to make family feel guilty.

    Intervention: The loved ones should engage in the Twelve Steps or therapy, but they rarely do. However, this one of the most successful ways to help their loved one.

    Possible Result: If the family members work on themselves, this can have a very good outcome.

5. **He got addicted because of an injury or he was self-medicating.**
   Translation: He is not a *real* addict.
   Underlying: They feel guilty and want to believe it is not their *fault*.
   Manifestation in the client: *Secretly* harbors the belief that he is not a *real* addict or the opposite and is shamed at the truth of his disease.
   Intervention: Teach about the disease of addiction. Work on shame. Family support.
   Possible Result: Client begins to understand the disease and sees the precursors that existed before he used harder drugs.

6. **My other children are not *problems*. They are *good kids*.**
   Translation: We are good parents. Only he/she is the problem.
   Underlying: We did not cause this. He/she is just a *screw-up*.
   Manifestation in the client: Feels *less than*. Further reduces self-worth. Increases shame.
   Intervention: Explain family roles and how each child grew up differently despite being in the same home. Educate on addiction.
   Possible Result: Client begins to become more comfortable with his understanding. He extricates himself from the family enmeshment.

As for the most common and most important question I get from families, it is some form of...

7. **Can you tell if he/she will do well?**
   The answer is "maybe." Research shows that there are *six main predictors of outcome*. I included two more related to age I consider important. The predictors are in no particular order.
   a. Presence and/or level of psychiatric issues.
   b. Presence and/or level of legal issues.
   c. Presence and/or level of support of loved ones (including friends).
   d. Ability to define goals, specifically noted are educational and vocational goals.
   e. Level of engagement in a program of recovery.
   f. Strength of self-efficacy.
   g. Age at time of treatment.

h. Age of first use (includes alcohol).

First, awareness of new or pre-existing mental health (psychiatric) issues is paramount. Although mental health issues *do not* cause addiction, they may not remediate once addiction is in remission. In some cases, they may become more pronounced. If your loved one presents with a mental health concern or has a diagnosed disorder such as bipolar, depression, or anxiety, it is imperative to be properly treated and, if necessary, medicated. This is not the time to *let him make it on his own*. It is important that someone act as a case manager. To some extent this may be a service offered in very solid sober living homes. Although, eventually the family needs to take responsibility or the sober home staff needs to be compensated for medication management. This goes beyond the scope of a sober home's responsibilities.

Second, pending serious legal issues that may limit his freedom will reduce his ability to remain sober. This client will need special encouragement and attention throughout the legal process.

Third, I encourage loved ones to work to let go of any anger and/or resentments so they can be genuine and supportive. This can be difficult but can be accomplished through therapy, Al-Anon, or other free groups. The person with the substance use disorder cannot fix other people's resentments. Both must learn to hold healthy and loving boundaries without fear and anger. Remember, family and friends must support remission more than they support return to use.

Fourth, when one cannot envision a bright future, it leads to being devoid of hope. A lack of goals, especially educational or vocational goals, contribute to hopelessness. Goal setting is a learned skill. The Department of Vocational Rehabilitation has many services and excellent testing centers, all of which are free when documenting your disability. One, of which, is addiction. This is another important step in the recovery process.

Fifth, the most important predictor of success is solid engagement in a program of twelve-step recovery and being around recovery people. I cannot stress enough the critical importance of the Twelve Steps. In study after study, the Twelve Steps trump every other recovery methodology, including treatment in facilities. This is a foundation upon which all else is built. This is where a client begins to understand his role in the management of his own disease. He learns that he is able to keep the disease in remission through his actions.

The sixth predictor of success is self-efficacy. The difficulty is that self-efficacy ebbs and flows. If a person is not in supportive housing, then, at times, he or she will have to rely on sheer willpower. Willpower will not work over time. Not for anyone. If you have ever been on a diet, you understand a little bit about craving. By the way, I am not suggesting that dieting is the same phenomenon of craving that a person with this disease experiences, but it may be relatable. For example, when you want to eat something during a diet, you may begin to *crave* it. You decide to just eat *a tiny bit*. You may be able to stop, or you may eat the whole thing. You may feel guilty. You may feel ashamed. In the morning, you swear off sweets or whatever it is and continue with your day. If you have another bite, then so be it. It does not ruin your life. Unless, of course, you are a food addict, then it is back to the disease. The person with a substance use disorder does not have that luxury of making that *mistake*. He or she cannot have one tiny bite. You have to imagine having to be perfect during a diet or whatever you are using to relate. Some days are easier than others. Sometimes you decide those extra pounds are not so bad. Some days your self-efficacy wanes. The unsteady resolve makes this difficult. Sober living is a place where you are surrounded by people feeling the same way.

The final predictor is age-related. There's research indicating that a percentage of people diagnosed with a substance use disorder experience a spontaneous remission after age 35. This might indicate that when an individual over 35 is still in active addiction his or her recovery is more immutable. When an individual is under 21 years old, he/she has a reduced chance for sustained remission. This may be due to hormones or impulsivity. As for age of first use, those who used prior to age fourteen, including alcohol, are at a higher risk of relapse. People meeting these criteria may need extended stays in a sober living environment. Those who are dependent on family for support should have a strict boundary regarding the requirement for sober living. Unfortunately, families of the very young appear the least likely to have firm boundaries.

The conclusion is that sober living provides a place to strengthen the factors predicting success. The resident can practice coping skills and learn to manage emotions without drugs and alcohol. They can develop confidence, and that translates into self-efficacy. They will be around sober people, attend twelve-step meetings, learn to set goals, do chores and keep commitments, learn to deal with disappointment, and love themselves, but not through another's eyes as intimate relationships are discouraged. Often, family members encourage such relationships. Beware of this. This is another predictor of failure. Relationships can be hard when both partners are healthy, let alone when one or both people are so vulnerable.

Essentially, these suggestions offer simple solutions, but many times they are ignored. The complexity is the family dynamic and the self-worth of the client. Remember, time is one of the most important factors in recovery. The longer a person stays sober or engages in treatment, the better chance he will continue to do so. Managers and/or owners should be licensed or credentialed professionals. Being a former addict may be helpful, but it is not enough, just as being a person with diabetes does not mean you are qualified to treat diabetes.

The information I offered is backed by research, yet people still ignore the advice. The most frustrating observation is that between three and six months, the client begins to think he is ready to be on his own. He manages to convince his family of this. Sometimes it is due to cravings and at other times naivete. Regardless, *why do the families support this*? Nothing is more disheartening. With so many deaths, it is imperative that recovery is supported.

If I can get any point across, I hope it is this one. If you have control over finances, then *do not* allow them to leave sober living. You will balk at this, but I suggest approximately two years. It takes at least this long to develop healthy coping skills. This is especially true for the very young. The young men I worked with who stayed one and a half to two years are sober after many years. Some went to college. They got great jobs. They healed their relationships with their families, and most of them fell in love.

My pet peeve about addiction treatment is the use of the term *enabling*. Addiction is a disease that you cannot disable, therefore I don't believe you can enable addiction. This does not mean you give money to a person to buy drugs, nor should you allow them to live in your home and use. That is not enabling. It is just nonsensical.

I believe in offering alternatives that makes sense. One example is that you can say he can go to treatment or leave home, but you cannot use drugs and alcohol in my home. At any time, or if a person relapses, once, or many times, it is fine to say you will not pay for treatment. Instead he can go to a place that is state run or one of the sober places in the mountains. If there is not money for treatment, you can help find options, but only if he is invested.

In conclusion, my heart goes out to the friends and families of the seventy-two thousand people who overdosed only last year. This does not include the alcohol-related deaths. Neither does it include all of the other drug-related deaths and incarcerations, nor the deaths unrelated to opiates. Hundreds of thousands of people have suffered unimaginable pain. Substance use disorders are destroying a generation. There are more orphans from the opioid crisis than from the AIDS crisis. There were more overdose deaths in one year than during the entire Vietnam War. What was the response? One, we continued to legalize an *innocent* drug (marijuana) across the county.

Second, in November of 2018, in the midst of what was one of the most severe years of the crisis, the FDA approved, Dsuvia, an opiate that is ten times stronger than fentanyl. It is possibly the strongest painkiller ever made. All of this while I watched the best families destroyed by the deaths of their children. I heard a mother screaming in agony upon hearing the news about the death of her son. I have bargained with God at the bedside of a boy who overdosed before he was old enough to drink. I have witnessed hospital staff ask an overdose victim to leave the hospital. when he arrived clinically dead three hours prior. I've heard EMT's complain because they had to Narcan people "too many times." I have picked up the phone at 3:00 a.m. to inaudible words coupled with screams from a young girl who just found her boyfriend dead. I lost my best friend in the world, who I worked with side by side to build our business, a person I loved to my core. He protected me and loved me and made my life and the world better. He was in the most indescribable emotional pain, and had endured unspeakable torture, but was able to transcend his pain and live without resentment as he responded to everyone he met with love and compassion.

His name was Patrick "PQ" Quinn, Jr. and he taught me the final, and most significant predictor of success for treating addiction.

I will share with you his thoughts and his words. He told me that what saved him was forgiveness. He said we needed to let people know we trusted them and we could forgive them. We need to do this over and over, despite what they had done. The families that showed the most love did not always have the best outcome. Many wonderful families lost their children, siblings, and spouses although I believe their love kept their loved ones alive for as long as they were able to fight. I think the families who *enabled* their children but lost them, have more peace than those who did not *enable* and lost them anyway. I believe the disease of addiction is a test of our humanity. To show compassion for those who suffer with a disease that we cannot see can be difficult. How can we have compassion for those who are talented, good looking, sensitive and smart? Do these people really have an invisible disease? A disease that causes a person to isolate and to deny needing the most essential elements in life— Love. Touch. Kindness. A disease that is made worse by a lack of connection… One that is remediated through love, forgiveness and acceptance… So, above all, despite the statistics, the research and the peer-reviewed conclusions I shared, my best advice comes from a high-school dropout, who was often *inappropriate*, who could light up a room with his infectious smile, but who spent years in a dark prison and that is this… *To forgive without ego and to love, and to do both with all of your heart.*

Washed Clean by God's Grace
35 Years an Addict: A Long-Term, Faith-Based Transitional Home Owner's Perspective

By Pastor Craig Nichols

My Story

Growing up was quite difficult for me and involved a lot of confusion. I experienced fear and loneliness, not doing well in school, and quickly turned into a dysfunctional child with parents who had troubles of their own. Amidst trouble and turmoil, at the age of twelve, I attended a church where I gave my life to Christ. Shortly after, I was told by the man I believed to be my grandfather, who struggled with alcoholism, that my dad was not my real father. I was devastated and numb, felt abandoned, and was left completely confused! At the same time, we moved from Canton, South Dakota, to Sioux Falls, South Dakota, where I was introduced to alcohol for the first time. The initial numbing effect quickly advanced into a blackout!

Little did I know this was the beginning of a thirty-five-year, full-blown addiction. Living a life as an addict was extremely difficult and, for me, the three stages of addiction progressed very quickly. The first stage was all fun, the second included both good and bad, which progressed quickly to the third stage, all bad. At the age of sixteen, I was admitted to my first local treatment center and soon after that, a state training school in Plankinton, South Dakota. I was released at eighteen years old, still longing for the numbing effects of alcohol and drugs, which led to my first overdose. A combination of alcohol and methamphetamine led me to my first near-death experience.

Physically and mentally, I was losing my mind, waking up repeatedly confined in straightjackets, jails, and mental institutions. It felt like complete insanity! Alcohol and drugs had taken over my whole life.

I met and married my lovely wife Nikki, who has been in recovery herself for seventeen years. She came to the realization on her own that the drug life was not what she liked or wanted. Raising our five children—Bradey, Craig Jr., Dylan, Nathan, and Colton—and having a family became her priority. We will be celebrating twenty-eight years of marriage this year. I'm so grateful she stuck with me every step of the way. Raising five boys with a full-blown-addicted husband led to a lot of chaos and turmoil in the family.

Eventually, there came a day when I was faced with the reality that our five children, who were all exposed to the drug and alcohol lifestyle, were beginning to experiment with drugs themselves. I became a broken man looking at my five children addicted to meth, alcohol, and marijuana. I realized the devastating effects my own addiction had on every aspect of my children's life including their mental, emotional, spiritual, and physical lack of well-being!

A Spiritual Awakening

At one point, my wife moved in with a relative to get away from the fear-driven lifestyle. I was tired, alone, and scared. I was broken mentally and spiritually, and barely breathing physically. I got on my knees that dark and lonely night and surrendering completely to God. Something lifted that night, clearly. I had a peace within and a purpose in life for the first time in my life. Wow, the power in brokenness!

I spent about six months living in a bus, seeking direction from God and building a spiritual foundation through Jesus Christ. It was in that time God gave me a clear idea of what I believe He wanted me to do with and for the rest of my life. There, in that bus, Washed Clean Addiction & Recovery Ministries was developed.

I sought out spiritual advisors to help me along my journey. A few had a tremendous impact on my life. Pastor Al Peratt was the first man God put in my life. He was then the head pastor of Set Free Ministries. (Today he is head chaplain of Volunteers of America Dakotas.) He has done many great things in recovery at Keystone Treatment Center and lectures around the United States. He invested in me and I will be forever grateful. In May of 2018, I became licensed to minister the gospel with his direction. He is a true brother in Christ, and I would not be where I am today without his guidance and time invested in me.

The second man, my uncle and pastor, Doug Weinzetl, is a great man of God who prayed over me throughout the thirty-five years of my addiction. He remains a great influence in my life today. Doug has also been involved in Washed Clean Ministries from the beginning. Thank you, Doug!

The third is my great friend, Jack Alan Levine. I got ahold of a couple of his books early on in my recovery (*My Addict Your Addict* and *Don't Blow It with God*) and fell in love with reading them. I have read every book he has written, some of them three to five times over. They gave me hope, inspiration, and teaching that fueled my mind and changed my heart. Thank you, Jack, for your dedication to helping others.

I encourage you to find people in your life to help you. Find people who will pray, listen, and encourage you on your journey.

WASHED CLEAN: OUR APPROACH TO RECOVERY

At Washed Clean, we take a different approach to sobriety. We believe no one can truly recover without first opening their heart to God. Once you make the connection, the strong and unbreakable bond, you will be less likely to feel the urge to fill up with something destructive again. You can finally be free.

Washed Clean Ministries provides a spiritually-based, transitional living home for people coming from treatment centers, prison, and the community. Guests typically spend eight to twelve months here, depending on which stage of recovery they are in. We help people not only kick addiction, but also help them reintegrate into society in safe and healthy ways.

Our program is run in a highly-structured facility with support staff available twenty-four hours a day, seven days a week, to help with accountability. Spiritual advisors, mentors, and life coaches are on hand to help clients with their specific needs.

Our goal is to help addicts get themselves *washed clean* so they can spend the rest of their lives in deep connection with God and serving a higher purpose!

As Washed Clean developed, God gave me a clear vision that spiritually-based, transitional living was needed desperately in the Sioux Falls area. We saw guys coming out of treatment centers and prison, who ended up relapsing right back into treatment or prison.

The recidivism rate at the South Dakota state prison was 83 percent, and at the local treatment centers, only about one of ten were staying clean after leaving treatment. These were staggering numbers for me to see.

Most often people coming out of prison and treatment end up going back to the same environment they came from, with no spiritual foundation developed in their life. They often turn back to what they know best—drugs and alcohol—and that lands them back in treatment or prison. We meet them at the door and begin the journey with them. Accountability and structure are needed. We also believe in the Twelve Steps of Alcoholics Anonymous to develop a stronger spiritual foundation.

We have a fifty-two-week, twelve-step recovery group that meets weekly, to help ensure all people get through the Twelve Steps. We also have a weekly Bible study that helps to build a spiritual foundation and gives direction for a better way to live. We do a lot of service work in the community, helping churches and other businesses with a wide variety of things, to create a better place to live.

We bring in a diverse selection of speakers on a weekly basis to provide alternative perspectives and a better understanding of how others have achieved sobriety and kept it. We also work with local employers to secure job placement for the guys coming into the transitional home. We try to meet each person where they are and walk with them on their journey by providing them with spiritual advisers, mentors, pastors, and many resources in the community to help individuals with their specific needs.

We recommend staying in the transitional home for eight to twelve months to provide structure and accountability that will better their chances of staying free from addiction for life. Avoiding people, places, and things are key for sobriety. We meet weekly to assess where they are with their steps, their goals, and their spiritual journey. We have seen great success with the group home dynamic that helps people coming out of addiction. Many people who come here have shared that there's something different here—the presence of God, the love, the care, and the individual interaction with me, the staff, volunteers, and other residents.

THE TRUTH ABOUT ADDICTION

Addiction doesn't discriminate against age, gender, or the color of your skin. What matters most is that you're broken and ready to surrender your life to Christ and walk in a different direction. It's a matter of are you done with your addiction? Are you done with the pain?

Oftentimes, kids who are enabled, sheltered, and given everything growing up struggle harder to grab the concept of letting go of their addiction. We had a guy here 64-years-old who had everything as a kid, was brought up very sheltered and spoiled, but still got addicted as a 14-year-old and has dealt with this all his adult life. His parents never smoked or did anything. But he still became an addict and, unfortunately, today all of his children are in active addiction.

Of course, we want to stop kids as early as possible from heading down the path of self-destructive addiction. We want them to get ahold of sobriety early in life, as young as possible. But everyone has their own breaking point, maybe it's prison or jail, an institution, or perhaps they have had a taste of the addicted life and realize it's not a place they want to go.

The majority of our residents are 35 and older, although we have had younger adults, as well. The world is getting to be a tougher place to live in and I've noticed younger kids are growing up in some pretty dysfunctional homes, with a lot of trauma, perhaps from their family situations. For many of the younger generation, their parents are so lost and addicted and living a tough life themselves, and kids are being brought up in that atmosphere. There's also a lot of divorce, which can lead to feelings of abandonment. Kids can often feel just lost.

In order to recover, people need to experience a moment of clarity in their lives. I had many in my addiction recovery process. Our job at Washed Clean is to develop and provide a curriculum and programming that keeps addicts moving in a positive direction once they hit their bottom and have surrendered. We walk with them the best we can, but unfortunately, there are so many distractions in the world today. Hence, the necessity of our long-term programs of ten months or a year. If we can keep them in the atmosphere of recovery as we do, where they are surrounded by other Christian brothers all trying to achieve sobriety with biblical principles, guidelines, and structure, it becomes a complete transformation of life. It doesn't happen in just 30 or 90 days.

In the first month a resident comes to Washed Clean, they get a job in the local area and start to earn a paycheck. Sometimes they think they have it all figured out at that point and we have to say, "Slow down you're just getting started. Don't leave before you get everything you need." We work on to rewarding them and encouraging them. At three months, they really feel like they've got it all figured out, but the work is really just beginning at that point! We try to keep them focused and remind them they're not ready to leave; they need to get the whole Washed Clean experience in their lives before they leave. Getting them through the Twelve Steps (of AA or NA) is also part of what we do. Many times, you see guys come from other treatment facilities and I always ask, "You've been to treatment two, three or six times but have you been through all Twelve Steps?" Most have been through five of them in prior treatment programs. Out of eighty guys, one guy will raise their hand and say they've been through all Twelve Steps. So one of our goals is to get them through all Twelve Steps.

A lot of guys really don't have a purpose in life. Service work and getting them involved, whether it's building a large wooden cross or playhouse for a church, or painting, just keeping them active, is key. When they have too much time on their hands, things can go south. As the twelve-step program so accurately remind us, "We have a thinking problem not a drinking problem," So, keeping the mind and body occupied is critical to recovery.

Social media, like Facebook and Instagram, can also be a huge obstacle in people's recovery today. People go into treatment or prison and they get their phone taken away for thirty days or ten months or a year. When they get out and get that phone back in their hands, and all their old contacts and friends are still in that phone, it can be a major issue – past girlfriends, past boyfriends, drug connections.

Another major factor to people's recovery is employment. There is a lot of opioid and meth addiction in Sioux Falls and other areas, as well. So, if we send our guys to work and other people there are using, it can be a problem. Obviously, they have to get to the point where they are able to say "no." But, in the initial phases of their recovery, is not good for them to be working in an environment where they know there's a guy or two getting high in the bathroom. As addicts, they certainly know who's using and who's not. They may be able to resist for a time, but, believe me, if I were working in that kind of setting, sooner or later I would give in and use again. Especially early on in the recovery process. There is so much of that out there, which makes it hard.

We encourage those who come into Washed Clean to seek a complete transformation of life. They have to learn to choose new friends. We bring them to a good Bible teaching church where they can develop new friends and meet people who they can learn to trust and share life with. It can be confusing coming out of the dysfunction of addiction, where people lie, steal, and cheat them. It can be scary to find people who are good for them because it is contrary to what they know.

I remind people who are struggling with addiction that our minds have been mired in darkness for so long that renewing the mind is very important. Our minds are messed up from addiction, whether it's five years of addiction or 35 years, like me. The mind is so distorted, spiritually and mentally, and just not living. Physically, addiction is tiring, as well. What worked for me was a lot of Scripture reading. I often tell people who struggle in the beginning of recovery that they may not understand it all in the beginning, but keep reading and things will start to make sense in your head. Then your heart will start to change. We keep encouraging them to be in the right readings, whether it's the Bible or other inspirational books. That's where I found freedom in my life. Today we give those particular books to every new guy who comes through our doors. You have to have good reading that makes sense and then you can relate it to Scripture. It works for our program. Also, being around other people who have gotten through addiction, seeing what they're doing, and walking with them, is critical to the process of sustained recovery.

To family members, I would say you have to let your kids go a little bit while setting boundaries. I have five boys. It's hard, but usually the family members are not those who can help the addict. It is often someone else God puts in their life who can make that connection. Enabling them is not the way. You have to let them find their path, but it's hard to step back and do that as a parent and let that process happen. It's hard for me as a dad, but I just pray that God puts somebody in their path they might relate to, or they pick up a book they can relate to. A lot of guys I've worked with have family members, moms and dads, who were struggling with drug and alcohol themselves. In many cases, the whole family unit is addicted. Many times you're dealing with parents who have been living with addiction for most of their adult lives. So, we have to work with the families, as well. Sometimes parents are divorced or families are blended. By the time the addict hits bottom and want to change their life, there's a lot going on and it can be very confusing.

I believe everybody can get the concept of recovery and be healed at some point in their lives, no matter how far down they've gone. I work a lot with the homeless. For some of them, unfortunately, it has become a way of life. Homelessness has almost become an addiction, as well. I didn't understand this before I started working with the homeless, but it has become apparent to me now. You can give them everything and every opportunity, but homelessness is all they know. You can come and share the gospel and the Steps, but it's so far from reality for them. Homelessness is sometimes the only thing they know and for someone to tell them they can have this new life and new reality, well, it just doesn't make sense to them.

You just don't know who will respond to the message of a better way of life and freedom from addiction. You can give somebody an opportunity to change, you just don't know if they will respond. Until that individual is ready, it's not going to work. Unfortunately, they can go to treatment ten times, they can get the tools that treatment offers, AA will lay the spiritual tools at their feet, but it's up to them to use them! It's a choice each person has to make for themselves. We encourage people to make that choice. We hope and pray that they want it. It's having a place like Washed Clean where they can be met at the door, loved, respected, and be around other people who are trying to live the same life they want is a big encouragement for them. I also ask them to look at the bottom line, which for addicts is often jail, institutions, or death.

I ask, "Are you tired of being in prison in your own mind?" "Are you tired of that type of life?" I understand that because I was never comfortable in my own skin. I share with them there is a better life available for them! I share my own experience with addiction, what my life looked like to other people, then what it is today. What a difference! They can see the difference in my life. Hopefully, they will see a guy who went through 35 years of drug and alcohol addiction, but has come through it and this is where he's at today. So, if there was hope for me, then there is hope for them! I tell the guys they can be the one person who makes it. Not everybody makes it, but you can be the one!

Today, I know for sure God comforts us in all our troubles. Thus, we can comfort those in trouble with the comfort we ourselves have received from God (2 Corinthians 1:3). Today, I know this is made possible through Christ.

THE EXPERIENCE & TRANSFORMATION FROM MEN AT WASHED CLEAN MINISTRIES

Denny McCoy, resident of Washed Clean

After 40 years of addiction to alcohol, cannabis, and meth, I was sick and tired. I drove around Sioux Falls looking for a good, safe place to seek help. I knew Pastor Craig Nichols from our mutual using together in the past, so when I heard about Washed Clean, I went to speak with Craig. After our conversation, I felt that this was a great choice for my recovery.

A lot of people don't complete programs because they do not have a support system in place to hold them accountable, and they don't know God. Without the spiritual aspect of recovery and trust in Christ, the odds are against you. The frequent house meetings with our peers give much-needed support, as well. Some of the obstacles include driving past old neighborhoods and landmarks with old connections, and acquaintances that aren't really friends. You must have a good support team to prevent you from *slipping back*. Most addicts need more than thirty days to get freedom from so many years of abuse. A long-term commitment (ten months to a year) gives a person a hand up instead of a hand out. You need to make the effort with God as number one and have people to hold you accountable. You can succeed, if you really want to remain clean and sober, one day at a time!

I believe the success of Washed Clean Ministries is due to the spiritually-based, hands-on management, including personal accountability, responsibility, and family support. People tend to fail by letting idle time, no hobbies, and self-pity lead to *stinking thinking*, and returning to old habits. Instead, we need to do things differently, work hard to achieve something positive, and regain self-respect. If people are ready to be totally honest with themselves and others, they need to invest the time and effort to make it happen. It is worth it!

When you are seeking a credible place, look for an organization's cleanliness and friendliness, and trust your first impressions. My face-to-face meeting with Pastor Craig was instrumental in my decision to come to Washed Clean for the long-term. Washed Clean is a ministry not a state or federally-funded organization. It is smaller, on a more individual scale. The residents have more accountability and the opportunity to form real, long-term friendships. Having more freedom and responsibility (such as a job) along with Bible studies and projects complements the more personalized attention, and spiritual self-awakening. Trust also aids in the transition to a life washed clean from addiction. Washed Clean made the difference for me!

Aaron Gruenwald, former resident of Washed Clean

Many of us have lost our sense of reverence, awe, and wonder. These, once found, can spur on our recovery. A proper, right-sized sense of self develops with our new focus upon God and our spiritual development. Being as honest as we can, we face reality—not in fear but with engagement to address the pressing issues of our life. We befriend the real instead of attempting to escape. We face damage we have caused and sustained. The *God concept* requires that I clarify my ideas about God and how I relate to Him. I attempt to find what God's will is for my life. Scripture guides me here. I believe God is just and desires for me to be in relationship with Him. Doing so makes us friends with God and this is deeply healing to me. It is a covenant based on love and discipline. Many keys to recovery come through an understanding of the God concept.

Barriers to recovery include past people, places, or things. People in active addiction may distort natural and healthy instincts. We express them often with reckless, destructive behavior. When we are in sobriety, we can begin to experience unaltered moods and instincts. We have the choice of expressing them honestly to meet our needs. This leads to positive change and authenticity.

TWELVE STEP PROGRAMS

Alcoholics Anonymous: A Path to Freedom

By Mike W.

My Qualification

My name is Mike and I am an alcoholic. My sobriety date is April 9, 2013 and I haven't had a drink or drug since then. This is a pretty amazing statement given the condition in which I came into recovery. God is at the core of my recovery and Alcoholics Anonymous got me on track and keeps me on track today.

I had my first drink at the age of three. I would pull back the tops of my dad's beer cans just enough to sip what I could. I got drunk for the first time in sixth grade. I drank a bit more in high school and really kicked off my drinking career in college. I became a heavy drinker in my twenties and graduated to cocaine in my early thirties. I quit doing cocaine in my late thirties and replaced it with vodka. I became an all-day, everyday drinker, which led to my physical dependency on alcohol.

I went to my first rehab in 2004. It was a twenty-eight-day program. I made it twenty-six days, relapsed twice, and then was kicked out. I wasn't ready. During this time, I was introduced to Alcoholics Anonymous. I wasn't ready for AA either. I could not imagine a life without drinking.

During one of the many AA meetings I attended during rehab, I heard from a gentleman who shared he had been sober for over twenty years. I didn't understand why he was still going to these meetings. My interpretation in that moment was if you haven't figured out how to stay sober after twenty years, you're never going to figure it out. I truly wasn't ready for AA let alone a life in recovery.

By 2011, I was drinking vodka all day, every day. I would pass out around 9 p.m. and wake up at 1 a.m. going through withdrawals. I would get up, take a few drinks, and work my way back to sleep. My day would eventually begin around 5:30 a.m. being woken up again with the shakes and cold sweats. Vodka was the cure for my condition. I needed to drink to function and I saw no way out of this. I prayed every day for God to make it stop. I truly did not know what the cure would be for me. This went on for well over a year.

The End of My Drinking Career

In April 8, 2013 this all came to a screeching halt. I had been sick for several days, throwing up continuously and eventually began throwing up blood. My wife, with the help of a very good friend, was able to finally get me into detox.

It is hard to share this part of my story because I do not remember much of it. In the weeks preceding this, I was prescribed Ativan to help me stop drinking. The Ativan was supposed to help stop the shakes and sweats. That didn't work, so I began mixing the Ativan with alcohol, which created blackouts. I do recall sitting in an empty lot on the eighth of April with a Mountain Dew bottle full of vodka. I could remember a time when I could "drink my way over the hump" and begin to feel better. I couldn't do it this time. I remember being in physical pain. I threw the bottle away, went home, and got help.

I spent four days in detox. I had an endoscopy and ultrasound to see what kind of damage I had done to my esophagus, liver, and kidneys. By the grace of God, the drinking had not yet caused any irreversible, long-term damage on my body.

During my time in detox, I experienced managed withdrawals. The detox center kept me on fluids and small doses of anti-anxiety medicine. Even so, my mind was racing. I had so much anxiety and fear of what would happen next. I had a job that I wanted to keep, but I was in no condition to function. My wife spent the four days in detox by my bedside. I could see the fear in her eyes and hear it in her voice. I was in no condition to be of any support or security for her. All of this was extremely overwhelming.

I did know this, for the first time in years, I did not want a drink. I did not crave a drink. I did not think about a drink. This was encouraging, but I didn't trust it would last. I didn't know if I could quit permanently. I didn't know what that would even look like. As fearful as I was, I did have a glimmer of hope.

I left the detox center on Thursday, April 11, 2013. When my wife and I joined each other in the car to head home, she asked if I had a plan. All alcoholics have a plan and I was no different. The problem with my plan was that I came up with it. My best thinking and planning are what landed me in detox. As I shared my plan with my wife, she began to cry. She wanted me to go to a thirty-day program and that was not in my plan at all. Deep down I knew that was what I needed, but in my head, it didn't seem practical. There had to be an easier, softer way.

After leaving detox, instead of driving home, my wife drove to a nearby Starbucks where we met with my mom, dad, and recovering alcoholic, Jim. I had met Jim in a blackout the previous Monday, but other than that, I didn't really know this man. Given my condition, I do not remember much of the meeting except for a few life-changing comments. Jim started off by telling the four of us, "Mike is in no condition to make any decisions on his own. We need to treat him like an infant." My first response was anger. I kept it inside, but I was hot. How dare he say such a thing in front of my wife, as well as my mom and dad. He doesn't know me! During this internal burst of anger, a wave of surrender came over me. It was the first of many gifts from God. I understood and knew Jim was right. I may have been without a drink for three days, but I had no idea how to manage anything.

The Beginning of a New Beginning

After this meeting, Jim took me to his home group AA meeting. The meeting was held at noon and it was packed. Driving to the meeting my head was a mess. I cannot begin to describe the overwhelming feelings of anxiety, dread, and fear. I was incapable of stringing a thought together let alone expressing anything in words. It was a quiet drive up until Jim asked me what was going on in my head. All I could do was shrug my shoulders. At that moment, Jim began to tell me his story.

In that moment, a warm, comforting wave of hope came over me. Another gift from God. As Jim told me how far he had fallen, he also shared with me a way to get back up. He shared with me how much richer his life was. Jim continued to share his story, all the muck, all the grime, and then all the rewards and all the joy that came from being sober. The dread I was feeling at the time was replaced with the same glimmer of hope I had in detox.

Over the next few days, arrangements were made for me to go off to The Florida Recovery Center in Gainesville, Florida. I knew absolutely nothing about this facility. There I met Dr. Huckabee, a doctor at the Center and in recovery himself. He is a very smart, kind man who took the time to help me better understand the disease of alcoholism. I never believed it to be a disease. I drank because I liked it. Then I drank because I needed it. I always held the position that I got myself into this on my own. Bad choices, a lack of discipline, and the absence of self-control kept me in this condition. Dr. Huckabee helped me understand that this disease allowed the reward centers in my brain to like alcohol more than a non-alcoholic. In its simplest terms, if everyone felt as good as I did when I drank, they would drink and crave alcohol as much I did.

Dr. Huckabee was another gift from God and another brick laid in the foundation of my recovery. I reminded myself that my body likes alcohol way too much for me to be able to manage and drink like anyone else. If I could just control myself not to drink, the disease would never kick in. But, how could I control my mind that seems to be obsessed with the drink?

The next 36 days were spent in rehab in Gainesville. I learned a lot about alcoholism and addiction. We were also required to attend AA meetings throughout our stay. I still wasn't quite getting the purpose of AA, but I wasn't really paying much attention to that part. In rehab I was focused on giving up control and learning how to deal with life without alcohol. Now that I knew my body responded so much differently to alcohol and my brain couldn't shut that off, I came to grips with not picking up a drink again, although that concept still didn't seem achievable.

Rehab is somewhat of a fake environment where everything is controlled, and you are kept busy. People would throw fits, confrontation would arise, but there was always the opportunity to break it down and learn from it. You visit with counselors on a regular basis, so you do get to work out a lot of baggage that you carry in with you, but the environment itself isn't like real life. The amount of counseling and coaching available in rehab isn't sustainable outside of rehab. This worried me as I prepared to leave. How could I replace this on my own?

Before leaving rehab, I spent time going over a plan for life outside. There really wasn't much to plan. The plan that was created for me was to attend ninety AA meetings in ninety days.

This did not seem like a very in-depth plan for success and I was not a big fan. I certainly wasn't looking forward to hitting AA every day, but I didn't have any other alternative and I certainly didn't want to start drinking again. So, it began.

ALCOHOLICS ANONYMOUS

Alcoholics Anonymous was started in 1935 by Bill Wilson and Dr. Bob Smith, two alcoholics who couldn't stay sober on their own but discovered by the grace of God (or a higher power) and the community of others, they could quit drinking entirely.

Alcoholics Anonymous is one of the most widely known organizations worldwide. AA has a presence in 180 nations, an estimated membership of 2.1 million people, and an estimated 60,143 groups in the US alone.

With a reach as far as this, most people have heard of AA and most have their view and opinions of AA. I was no different. In hindsight, my views were based on my own fears, insecurities, prejudices, and a lack of knowledge and experience with AA. My feelings, centered around negative ideas, like: *My circumstances or story are different. AA doesn't really apply to me. The people in AA aren't like me. They wouldn't understand. I don't belong here. These aren't my people.* Some people struggle with the idea that AA is like a cult. Another hang-up is the God factor in AA, and I didn't want to hear about that.

However, I didn't have any other choice than AA. I didn't want to go back to drinking and I didn't know how to do this on my own. I had to surrender my prejudices and begin my ninety meetings in ninety days. It took a few meetings to get over myself and realize that it was exactly where I belonged. These *are* my people and we have a lot in common. I heard one incredible story after another. People shared their stories of shame, guilt, sadness, perseverance, resilience, hope, and victory. I heard these stories and was amazed at how similar they were to my own. The meetings began to feel like home and I became very comfortable. I found myself picking up on ways to handle situations that had always baffled me in the past. I learned ways of handling anger, frustration, fear, and anxiety.

As it turned out, all the problems that made me feel unique, quirky, and crazy, a lot of people have the same problems! The solutions I heard in the meeting would come back to me throughout the day as my way of thinking began to change.

AA uses chips (similar to poker chips) to mark the achievements of people in recovery. I got my white chip at the first meeting, and the thirty-day, sixty-day, and ninety-day chips followed. We traveled a little during my first ninety days and I went to meetings on the road. I got my sixty-day chip at a sunrise meeting on the beach in Delray Beach, Florida. I visited the Worm Group in Key West, Florida, and got a fishing worm as a visitor.

AA has a language of its own and it is most certainly a cliché factory. Here is what I learned about AA in those ninety days…

One day at a time / First things first / Time takes time / Keep it simple / One is too many, a hundred aren't enough / We'll love you until you learn to love yourself / Write a gratitude list and count your blessings / Keep coming back / It works if you work it.

My favorite… You can't be too dumb to get AA, but you can be too smart.

I have heard some of these before, but never in context. I used to think *one day at a time* had no meaning. As I went to AA meetings and heard this, it drove me nuts, but time in AA taught me context. The cliché not only makes sense now, but it provides relief. I used to struggle with the idea I will never be able to drink again. That is way too much to handle. If I live one day at a time, I only need to worry about today. I don't have to drink today, and tomorrow will take care of itself. It clicked and I continue to apply this thinking to many areas of my life.

How It Works

AA is comprised of meetings that are based on the book *Alcoholics Anonymous* often referred to as the "Big Book." The first 164 pages of the "Big Book" outline our common struggle as alcoholics and our inability to stop drinking and manage our lives. It also provides the solution to quit drinking and live a fulfilled life. When I first read this book, I was amazed how much it described me and was I comforted that there was a solution.

The core of AA is the Twelve Steps of Alcoholics Anonymous. These can be found in chapter 5 of the "Big Book" of *Alcoholics Anonymous*:

Remember that we deal with alcohol—cunning, baffling, powerful! Without help it is too much for us. But there is One who has all power—that One is God. May you find Him now! Half measures availed us nothing. We stood at the turning point. We asked His protection and care with complete abandon. Here are the steps we took, which are suggested as a program of recovery:

1. We admitted we were powerless over alcohol— that our lives had become unmanageable.
2. Came to believe that a Power greater than ourselves could restore us to sanity.
3. Made a decision to turn our will and our lives over to the care of God as we understood Him.
4. Made a searching and fearless moral inventory of ourselves.
5. Admitted to God, to ourselves, and to another human being the exact nature of our wrongs.
6. Were entirely ready to have God remove all these defects of character.
7. Humbly asked Him to remove our shortcomings.
8. Made a list of all persons we had harmed and became willing to make amends to them all.
9. Made direct amends to such people wherever possible, except when to do so would injure them or others.
10. Continued to take personal inventory and when we were wrong promptly admitted it.
11. Sought through prayer and meditation to improve our conscious contact with God as we understood Him, praying only for knowledge of His will for us and the power to carry that out.
12. Having had a spiritual awakening as the result of these steps, we tried to carry this message to alcoholics, and to practice these principles in all our affairs.[11]

Whether you are an alcoholic or not, I believe the Twelve Steps are important and a template for everyday living. We all need to recognize what we can control and what we cannot, and accept it. There is a Power greater than us and He is the One we need to surrender to everyday. Confession is powerful and necessary to relieve all the guilt we carry. Make amends to those we have harmed.

---

11   *Smith, Dr. Bob, Bill Wilson. Alcoholics Anonymous, 4ᵗʰ Edition, 2001*

Stay in constant contact with a Higher Power. Even secularists believe in the power of meditation. Continue to make amends and clean out our hearts and minds (confession). Last, but very important, help others who are struggling.

As the book says, this is a tall order. Key ingredients to adhering to the steps is being open, brutally honest with ourselves, and accepting progress, not perfection.

I Don't Believe in God

A large hurdle for some and a big criticism of AA is the idea that God, or some religious component is behind the Twelve Steps. God is the core of AA. God is mentioned 134 times in the "Big Book." This is a spiritual program. I do believe in God and He is the One who brought me into and keeps me in recovery. But believing in God is not a requirement to take your first step. The only requirement to be part of AA is the desire to stop drinking. Many atheists and agnostics have walked through the doors of AA, have found their way into recovery, and have stayed in recovery. The spiritual aspect is very real and is addressed in the "Big Book" in chapter 4 titled "We Agnostics." "To one who feels he is an atheist or agnostic such an experience seems impossible, but to continue as he is means disaster, especially if he is an alcoholic of the hopeless variety. To be doomed to an alcoholic death or to live on a spiritual basis are not always easy alternatives to face."[12]

This is a grim reality for many alcoholics and the "Big Book" continues to describe the depths of this reality. "Lack of power, that was our dilemma. We had to find a power by which we could live, and it had to be a Power greater than ourselves. Obviously. But where and how were we to find this Power?"[13]

The "Big Book" of *Alcoholics Anonymous* is about solutions so it does not leave the non-believer without hope. "Much to our relief, we discovered we did not need to consider another's conception of God. Our own conception, however inadequate, was sufficient to make the approach and to affect a contact with Him. As soon as we admitted the possible existence of a Creative Intelligence, a Spirit of the universe underlying the totality of things, we began to be

12   Smith, Dr. Bob, Bill Wilson. Alcoholics Anonymous, 4th Edition, 2001
13   Ibid.

possessed of a new sense of power and direction, provided we took other simple steps."[14]

It continues with words of encouragement and affirmation that this is a program designed for each individual and it is not cookie cutter. It is far from a cult in the sense we come to our own terms with our recovery and our own relationship with God or a Higher Power. "When, therefore, we speak to you of God, we mean your own conception of God. This applies, too, to other spiritual expressions which you find in this book. Do not let any prejudice you may have against spiritual terms deter you from honestly asking yourself what they mean to you."[15]

Many also are strong believers in God yet challenge this position as watering down the concept of God and His power. This I can assure you is not the case. "Remember that we deal with alcohol—cunning, baffling, powerful! Without help it is too much for us. But there is One who has all power—that One is God. May you find Him now!"[16]

Steps for Success

Alcoholics Anonymous is a program of action. It is up to the alcoholic to get out of it what he/she needs to get out of it to stay in recovery. It is important to keep in mind that meetings are run by recovering alcoholics. A lot is said and shared that is beyond the "Big Book." But with an honest, open mind, you can figure out what works for you and what doesn't. Advice given to me and repeated often is, "Take what you can and leave the rest."

AA is a simple program. We alcoholics, however, will take it and complicate it. There are only twelve steps, but somehow, we manage to create so much more out of it. A statement I heard early on was, "You can't be too dumb to get AA, but you can be too smart and miss it."

Read the "Big Book!" There is a cliché that says, "Meeting makers make it." Meetings are a great way to stay connected with the fellowship and learn from others. But if you don't know the "Big Book," you won't know whether what you hear in meetings is true

---

14   Ibid.
15   Ibid.
16   Ibid.

or not when it comes to the program. The "Big Book" established the basis of AA. The AA experience is much more rewarding and enriched knowing the history and context in which it was formed.

As you read the "Big Book" find a "Big Book" study (there are certain meetings that focus specifically on the text of the "Big Book"). If one isn't available, research the beginnings of AA and the stories behind the "Big Book." Context helped me better understand the whys and ways of the Twelve Steps. I do believe the "Big Book" is divinely inspired and there is power in the book for both believers and non-believers.

Another part of the AA program is to have a sponsor to walk you through the steps. A sponsor is someone in recovery who has experience working the steps, generally someone who has some time in the program. This can be a challenge for many. A sponsor may tell you things you don't want to hear. They are charged with calling us out on our crazy ways of thinking. They are a mentor and they teach us a new set of rules to live by. Like any other walk of life, there are good ones and bad ones. You can gauge their ability quickly by asking them about the steps, where they are in the steps, and how transparent they are with their own program. You may outgrow your sponsor, or you may find you just don't mesh well. If necessary, get a new sponsor; it's allowed! Don't use this as an excuse to say AA doesn't work. AA works for millions, but it requires rigorous honesty and openness, as well as a relentless drive to not drink.

During my first exposure to AA, I didn't understand why one would continue to attend AA meetings after so many years in recovery. The Twelve Steps are instructions how to live life on life's terms. As I live, I will continuously have confessions and new amends to make. I must be diligent in treating others with respect and handling situations, so they are productive for all. It is important to continue to learn new ways of handing certain areas of my life, and the fellowship of AA is a big contributor to that. Continuing to engage with AA and attend meetings also allows us in recovery the opportunity to exercise the twelfth step: "Having had a spiritual awakening as the result of these steps, we tried to carry this message to alcoholics, and to practice these principles in all our affairs."[17]

---

17   Ibid.

Why Does AA Work

AA is unique in comparison to any other program in the sense it is led by alcoholics in recovery. There aren't any *official* positions held by anyone. As already mentioned, the only qualification for membership is the desire to stop drinking. There are no dues to be paid and there are not any attendance requirements. What makes AA work is the ability to share and hear others share their experience, strength, and hope. As simple as this sounds, there is a lot of power for both the one sharing and the one listening. For the one sharing it is exercising the Twelfth Step.

This is the premise, *in order to keep it, you have to give it away.* For the alcoholic to share and work with other alcoholics, it reminds us of where we once were. It keeps us humble and reminds us of the cunning, baffling, power that alcohol has over us. For the alcoholic who is hearing this for the first time, it brings a feeling of hope. It is also very comforting knowing that other people have been just like us and are now on the other side.

Our Higher Power ultimately gives us the strength to persevere. At times, life will deliver hard news or hard times, and our first inclination is to go back to our old ways. In situations such as these, our Higher Power can help us recognize this pattern of behavior and help us take different steps such as calling our sponsor or going to a meeting. These types of actions interrupt our old patterns of behavior and will keep us on the right track.

A WORD OF ENCOURAGEMENT

Alcoholism and addiction are scary for the addict, as well as their family and friends. As much as the family doesn't understand why their loved ones do what they do, neither does the addict. So many want to quit but cannot and do not know what to do.

The Big Book of *Alcoholics Anonymous* is an incredible resource. For the alcoholic it helps us to better understand our condition and find hope in a cure. It also is the first time we will read about our condition and realize we are not the only ones who suffer. We are no longer on an island by ourselves. We are not crazy.

For the loved ones of the alcoholic, it provides an explanation and clear description of what we are going through. I would read the "Big Book" to my wife because it helped me put in words where I was and what I was experiencing. Sharing the "Big Book" with her helped her better understand my condition, and we were able to walk through recovery together. My wife read numerous books on addiction and alcoholism, but didn't find anything that helped her understand my condition any better. Most left her feeling hopeless and helpless. After reading the "Big Book," she was relieved and full of hope.

Alcohol is cunning, baffling, and powerful to the alcoholic. Alcoholism is cunning, baffling and powerful for those we alcoholic's love. AA is a place where the two can meet, begin to understand, and work toward recovery together.

I pray for the alcoholic who struggles, I pray they will see it through, so that the promises of recovery will be a reality:

"If we are painstaking about this phase of our development, we will be amazed before we are half-way through. We are going to know a new freedom and a new happiness. We will not regret the past nor wish to shut the door on it. We will comprehend the word serenity and we will know peace. No matter how far down the scale we have gone, we will see how our experience can benefit others. That feeling of uselessness and self-pity will disappear. We will lose interest in selfish things and gain interest in our fellows. Self-seeking will slip away. Our whole attitude and outlook upon life will change. Fear of people and of economic insecurity will leave us. We will intuitively know how to handle situations which used to baffle us. We will suddenly realize that God is doing for us what we could not do for ourselves.

Are these extravagant promises? We think not. They are being fulfilled among us—sometimes quickly, sometimes slowly. They will always materialize if we work for them."[18]

Editor's Note: Also submitted anonymously, the next chapter is about Narcotics Anonymous. While the two programs (NA and AA) virtually mirror each other on the same principles, foundation, and operation, it is always recommended that those struggling with alcohol go to AA and those struggling with drugs go to NA. Even though the pain of addiction and destruction caused by addiction is the same, it is most often easier to relate to people who are going through the same experiences with the same substances.

18   Ibid.

Narcotics Anonymous: A Road to Recovery

By Alice H.

What is the Narcotics Anonymous program? "NA is a nonprofit fellowship or society of men and women for whom drugs had become a major problem. We are recovering addicts who meet regularly to help each other stay clean. This is a program of complete abstinence for all drugs. There is only one requirement for membership, the desire to stop using. We suggest that you keep an open mind and give yourself a break. Our program is a set of principles written so simply that we can follow them in our daily lives. The most important thing about them is that they work."[19]

These words from the book, *Narcotics Anonymous*, also known as the "Basic Text," still ring true for me thirty-seven years later. I am an addict in long-term recovery from substance use (drugs) disorder and bulimia. After a tumultuous relationship with another using addict, I found recovery in 1982 while trying to save him. I was so unconscious about my own disease that a loving God used this man to break through my very deep denial. When I first got clean, I thought I'd never fit in because most addicts there were IV heroin users. You see, I had never shot up, did not have tattoos and had never been in jail, unlike most of the folks there. Many longtime members deemed me not most likely to succeed in staying clean. Resistance, rebellion, and resentment ruled my life, being in direct conflict with how you gain success in the program.

The First Step of Narcotics Anonymous levels the playing field. Here we are powerless over our addiction (not a specific substance) and our lives have become unmanageable. Oh boy! I could certainly relate to that! My life and second marriage were a mess. I was full of self-hatred and desperately seeking a multitude of substances and behaviors to fill the terrible void that was at the core of my addiction. I never wanted to feel any emotions and pursued everything to numb myself out. Learning about the first step allowed me to relate to the disease of addiction, the insane thinking that goes with it, and the disasters that happen when we use any substance to change how we feel.

---

19   *Narcotics Anonymous, Sixth Edition, Page 9, What Is the Narcotics Anonymous Program?*

Why NA Works

Narcotics Anonymous is a spiritual, not religious, path that each member can define for themselves. This guarantees that anyone, regardless of their belief system, can have the chance to recover. *"It is important for you to know that you will hear God mentioned at NA meetings. What we are referring to is a Power greater than ourselves that makes possible what seems impossible."*[20]

Connection is the opposite of addiction. This is evidenced by the addition of the word *we* in the Twelve Steps of Narcotics Anonymous. This reminds us we are never alone if we remain in the recovery process. In NA, we talk about the therapeutic value of one addict helping another being without parallel.[21] The best evidence of this is the sponsorship bond. The sponsor shares wisdom, experience, strength, hope, and knowledge with his or her sponsees. Sponsees often return the favor by sharing back to their sponsor freely what has worked in getting better. Giving back and being of service to others continues to be a way to heal ourselves. Oftentimes sponsees become sponsors themselves. Giving freely and sharing what they have received and beginning to teach others.

MY STORY

Healthy relationships were a mystery to me until a few years into recovery. My current husband and I met in 1984 at a recovery meeting in Connecticut that I helped start. We started dating two years later when we went to a Stevie Wonder concert. Since that day, our relationship has blossomed into a marriage of thirty years that is based on love and mutual respect.

The final tenet of my personal philosophy is focusing on the importance of family and friends. I have grown, struggled, and have been most joyful in my marriage and friendships. A relationship commitment is one of the most important elements to have in one's life to fulfill the growth process. Living with someone else through love and disagreements is one of the most powerful teachers in life. Finding what you love in terms of work and committed relationships are important elements of living the good life. Freud said the task of the individual is to resolve the questions in two areas: love and work.

---

20   *IP No. 22, Welcome to NA*
21   *Narcotics Anonymous, Sixth Edition, Page 18, How it Works*

I would agree that a major part of spiritual fulfillment comes from being happy in both domains.

Addiction Ruins Careers

Before recovery, I was not the best employee. Years of working the Twelve Steps of NA has changed that so much so that I created an in-service program about *Addiction in the Workforce* that has helped hundreds of addicts. Now, as a recovery coach, my expertise is working with those who suffer from both substance use and eating disorders. My passion lies with helping others achieve long-term recovery from whatever keeps them from enjoying a full life. I am a daughter, sister, wife, friend, employee, artist, and a recovering woman. Through living and internalizing the spiritual principles of the Twelve Steps, the ability to be a better person in all these roles is happening.

My story is one of achieving lost dreams and healing ruined relationships, all while working to maintain a career. Addiction destroys dreams, and one of mine was to be an artist. After a long break from creating artwork, I started painting again after the death of my sponsor, who was an artist. When I paint, I always feel a powerful reconnection with her.

Why I Keep Coming Back to NA

Longtime engaged NA membership assures us we are never alone. When difficulties in life happen, we always have a choice. We can either fall into the depths of despair or choose to stay in the recovery process. I have learned that I can survive my worst fears and grow instead of leaving a path of destruction.

Over the past fifteen years, those worst fears came true. My loving sponsor died. I got laid off from work. My husband had a catastrophic car accident. He then developed liver cancer. Living in the Steps with daily prayer and meditation got me through those terrible times.

And it is not just my own prayers. Having long-term recovery gives me the opportunity to know many addicts around the world. The prayers of these addicts helped me through the grieving process, the job search, and the many days in the Intensive Care Unit watching my beloved husband almost die from his injuries. I never felt alone and never had the desire to self-destruct. Prayer got my husband out of the hospital and back to work in seven weeks. The doctors say he is a miracle, and I know that was the power of a loving God at work in our lives.

Later we had to cope with serious medical issues yet again, but once again were strengthened by the prayers of our NA friends and family. Optimism feeds my spirit. By staying in the moment and continuously asking a loving God for help, I can walk through times of uncertainty.

As my late sponsor used to say, "Whatever happens, a loving God will help me go through it." Based on my own experience in recovery, I have the knowledge that I will be okay no matter what. Every day I thank God and NA for the power of prayer in my life because I'd be lost without it.

Gifts of Recovery

Millions are part of the recovering communities across the world. Yet this was relatively unknown when I began my own journey of wellness. The problem remains that many people still don't know that recovery is a reality.

Even though I am now sixty-seven years old, I was a candidate for recovery at the age of twenty. My reasons for continuing my use of alcohol and drugs were many, the biggest one being that I was a well-respected healthcare professional. Stigma plus fear of judgment and discrimination were barriers to asking for help. It took many years to be okay with revealing my history of substance use despite helping thousands of women find and maintain recovery. To quote a friend, "My past is now my biggest asset."

Everyone talks about the drug epidemic in an almost a hopeless way. Overdoses and drug use tragedies make headlines—recovery successes not so much. Since hope is a catalyst for recovery, the freedom to share one's journey goes a long way in making it okay to ask for help. What a wonderful world we could have if more humans knew about this miracle and had the tools to pursue wellness.

Who can impact a recovery movement better than people on their own path? Recovering people can tell their stories, raising awareness of wellness-based pathways and healing. This trend allows more individuals and families who struggle with substance use disorder to find a better way to live. Getting the word out about NA can create a tidal wave of hopefulness. Together we can ensure that no one misses a chance to find restoration.

I have recently connected with NA on an even deeper level as current technology allows me to attend online meetings from all over the planet. The thrill of sharing my story in Iran, a country that as an American would be difficult for me to visit, drove home that recovery is possible worldwide. NA is truly a viable program of recovery!

A note about Anonymity: The author chose to remain anonymous to adhere to the spiritual principle in the Twelfth Tradition of NA which states: "Anonymity is the spiritual foundation of all our traditions, ever reminding us to place principles before personalities."[22] Remaining *faceless* allows the reader to relate to the story and emotions while protecting both the addict and the NA program as a whole. For more information about Narcotics Anonymous, go to www.na.org.

---

22   *Narcotics Anonymous, Sixth Edition, Page 61, The Twelve Traditions of Narcotics Anonymous*

ADDICTION CHURCHES

THE RECOVERY CHURCH MOVEMENT

BY PHILIP DVORAK

MY THOUGHTS ON ADDICTION AND TREATMENT

Everyone struggles with immediate gratification in our society, but for an addict or alcoholic it is much more significant. There are traits that are amplified in addicts. There are habitual sins and things that other people struggle with, that are similar to what an addict or alcoholic would struggle with, but for addicts there is a difference. There is this invisible line that, somehow, they've crossed, and it's become a compulsion, an obsession that is beyond their control.

I've had my own journey and my own struggles, like many. My brother struggled with addiction for over 30 years. I have worked in treatment centers for a while and, from what I have seen, one of the greatest problems is that we do not have a clear definition of what the problem is. Since we have these disagreements in the addiction field on what addiction is, we have a disagreement on how to properly respond and how to properly treat it. So much of the time at treatment centers is spent proposing ideas about what are the best practices and interventions, when we should be more focused on looking at evidence. For the most part, treatment centers don't say, if faith-based treatment has the highest results, we should be encouraging that. Instead, decisions are based on the opinions, the feelings, and the biases of the individual staff members and clinicians. When someone has a faith-based background, encouraging their faith has huge resiliency factors. We should be looking at evidence and know that people recover better when we do this, and we take that and encourage it. I have seen some treatment centers encouraging treatment in that way, but I've also been in environments where decisions are based more on the opinion of a particular clinic, rather than any evidence.

I am a man of faith and there are instances where it becomes hard to employ faith because of the biases of treatment center owners and staffers. The brilliance of the Twelve Steps is the ability to get through to an addict who isn't a man of faith, who, in that moment, is not willing to accept faith. Many treatment centers and facilities still embrace the twelve-step process, yet there are some exceptions now as I believe the attack has gotten stronger against twelve-step programs. However, the Twelve Steps are still seen as one of the most effective forms of support and treatment available to their patients. The Twelve Steps, in its brilliance, is really a pathway to Jesus. It has Christian origins. I have had a spiritual awakening as a result of the steps, being born again, and I have rarely seen someone who dives into the Twelve Steps, surrounded by a Christian community, who does not fall in love with Jesus.

No facility can truly measure success. The reality is, staying sober for the rest of one's life and never having any relapse treatment until the day they die, is not possible to measure. No facility can truly measure that because we would need a lifelong longitudinal study, which we don't have the ability to do; there hasn't been one done at this point. The statistics many treatment centers give, which measure the completion of care, usually varies from 70% to 90% of people completing the recommend length of care, but I don't think that is what most people care about. Success is a life change, a life transformation. The problem is if you compare it to other chronic conditions that have a level of freewill associated with them, if you compare it with a compliance for a diabetic to eat healthy and take their insulin, to do what they are supposed to do, to maintain and balance their diabetes, I would say we see very similar results. It's very difficult for any treatment center to give a number that measures success. If a treatment center says this is the number of our success rate, the center is probably being deceptive, or trying to give a number because that is what people want to hear. They want a number, but the reality is, you can't really give a number.

In this moment, my feelings are that we are seeing lower success rates than we have in the past. The further we move away from twelve-step-based treatment, move away from allowing people to integrate their faith, and move away from these types of interventions, the more we are going to see a continuing lowering of the stats. If we don't encourage sponsorship, we don't really encourage account-ability. If we don't encourage community as part of the entire treatment plan from the very beginning, when the people are discharged from treatment, I believe we will continue to see a lowering of long-term success rate.

We're seeing people go into treatment multiple times, not just once, and many who relapse again in a short period of time. They had the knowledge and heard the message, yet still relapse after treatment. The most simplistic way to explain this is deception from the enemy, believing lies about what recovery can be. Currently, we are seeing a huge push to focus just on the biology of addiction, purely on the disease of addiction, and to ignore the spiritual components. We are seeing people looking to treat a physical, mental, and spiritual condition simply with medication. People are believing and accepting that the only way to stay sober, in particular those who struggle with an opioid(opiate) addiction, is for them to be maintained on some other substance for the rest of their life. I don't believe that to be true. I believe that is deception. I believe that is something, which in the long run leads to additional harm. It also leads to a belief within the recovery community that you can't truly recover, and that somehow people who believe in abstinence-based, long-term recovery are being closed-minded.

Currently, there's a push for people to be accepted in recovery who are on medical marijuana. Or a push for people in recovery to be considered sober and clean if they are on Suboxone or Subutex, depending on what fellowship they are a part of. They want to consider medical marijuana as a form of addiction treatment. The mindset that you can't really recover without one of these substances for the long term is, for many people, destroying the concept of long-term non-medical-based recovery, which is possible. We see it happen all the time. Often, people are looking for an easier, softer way and if we present them an easier softer way, they take it. The problem is, it's not easier and it's not softer and they end up dying.

Many people I personally minister to and counsel, unfortunately, pass away and die. This has to stop. We lose millions. Not to diminish the seriousness of the current Coronavirus pandemic, but worldwide, we lose over three million people every year to addiction. If you combine both alcohol and drug addiction, its closer to four million people every year. The statistics are staggering, and that's not including addiction-related suicide and car accidents. In the United States, we are losing substantially more people to addiction than we have from this Coronavirus. Now, that might not stay the same, and they are certainly different. I'm not trying to diminish anything, but we have been living in a pandemic for over a decade. It's decimating to the addicted population and we are seeing them die at an insane rate. We are losing an entire generation and we're not providing good solid options.

We have to do something; we can't lose an entire generation of people. There are days recently where I lose three people in a single day, people who die from the disease of addiction. We pray with them, but we have to do better. We don't have a good comprehensive system. It affects every avenue of our society, from our healthcare system, to our politics, to our laws. We have to look at all these elements, and look at our trade, our borders, and all the different systems that are in place. Instead, we look at it from one little pocket. We look at one little thing and say that the answer is a pill. We know it's not going to be good enough. We need a more comprehensive look at the entire system and we need to be able to put safeguards across the board.

When I first started working in the treatment industry, there were lots of alcoholics, some marijuana users, random drugs popping in and out, some cocaine and crack. It was rare that you found the heroin addict or an opiate addict. Then pills came on board and the opioid-addicted populace exploded. Once we started restricting opiate prescriptions, heroin overtook that population. Then Fentanyl, Acetenyl, and other synthetic opioids took over. Now that that is getting restricted, meth is on a surge again. If we only do one piece, if just the water moves, the river flows in a little different direction. We have to look at it comprehensively if we are going to really make a difference. It's not those people; it's our children, it's our brothers and sisters. It's something that effects every single one of us at this point.

How Do We Solve the Problem?

In order to begin a comprehensive approach to solving this problem, we should start by focusing on prevention. We need to put more energy into the prevention side of things and not in the sense of what we have done in the past where prevention was just education-based. DARE statistically increased drug use in the people that went through the program, instead of having the predicted effect. The drug education piece is not what we need. Good prevention is encouraging the family. Prevention is making sure the family unit can stay together. If you look at what happened to the American family, you can see that helping the family is of primary importance. What laws, what rules, what things can encourage and support the family? How do we allow families to have time to parent? What can we do that encourages a family member to stay home? What can we do in the systems that, instead of hurting the family unit, help the families? Currently we have tax codes and other things that can hurt a marriage. When is it better financially to not get married? This is devastating to culture. The first thing we can do is focus on prevention and ask ourselves how we can address large-scale prevention. We have kids at risk. It is not education at that point in the intervention, it is getting kids involved in things we know are resilient factors. Preventive factors, things we know can help, for example getting kids involved in extra-curricular activities. We should encourage the things that have been cut from public-school systems – the arts, band, and sports, as well as many others.

We have to look at a whole restructuring, beyond the family, we need to look at society as a whole. We need to secure borders, look at our ports, and look at how items are being shipped into our nation. People are ordering drugs online, on Wish, on Amazon, and through other websites and affiliates. They know how to do this. It flies under the radar and it comes through the mail. Those elements need to be addressed.

We also need to have a look at places who have had success with creative solutions. What are we offering people who are not using? We are not decriminalized; we are not legalizing use, but are we offering amnesty? Are we offering opportunities for people to receive treatment? What programs have worked? Are drug courts effective? If they are, how do we implement them on a larger scale? What can we do to truly rehabilitate and treat? At the moment, our prisons are full of addicts and alcoholics, and those addictions are the primary reason they are there.

Our healthcare system is burdened and taxed because we don't have good standards. We don't know what these standards are. Treatment centers don't know ahead of time how much they are going to get paid and therefore don't know how to properly staff and provide. If they get $30 from one insurance company for someone staying in in-patient care, but they can get $2,000 from another company for another patient staying in in-patient care for one day, for someone with the same condition, the same problem, they can't possibly run a business effectively and ethically. With all that insanity, there needs to be an overhaul of how it works. We need clearer regulations of expectations within the industry as a whole. Additionally, we need to encourage and not discourage the faith-based community to be involved. We need to find ways to invite them into the process. Invite them in, allow them to feel safe, allow them to provide resources in our communities where we have previously alienated the faith-based community. We need to break down that divide.

The way things are now, alcoholics and addicts come into treatment and we do not know if they are going to succeed. Wondering ahead of time if a person will succeed in the program, is cunning and baffling. I often believe that certain people I meet have got a handle on recovery, and that things are looking great for them, then I am shocked when they're the next one in the obituary. At times, I have been able to judge who's going to be successful in a program. I see them make it through the treatment center, but as far as long-term recovery, it's funny and enigmatic. You can think they are going to do it, but you just don't know. The one universal thing is their willingness to surrender, their willingness to deflate their ego, their willingness to allow themselves to become second. The more I see a person willing to say that they can do it and surrender that ego, the better chance they seem to have. However, their willingness to maintain that position of heart, I've never been able to figure; but when they're willing to do that they are successful. That's where the Christian paradigm becomes so successful in the treatment of addiction and alcoholism because that's the core of our faith – dying to self, daily. It's picking up our cross and following Jesus. Our life is not about us, it's about others, it's about God. When a person truly surrenders, truly gets the willingness to say they are going to live with eternity in mind, when they decide to live focused on what matters to God, not what matters to them, it breaks down that need for immediate gratification, to satisfy our immediate, earthly needs. I believe those are the ones who maintain, who stay in long-term sobriety.

We are hurting with the direction of today's health laws and practices, the current direction moving towards more and more medication-based treatments. There is a place for some of those medications. There is a place for long-term takers. However, I have dealt with thousands of individuals and my observation is rarely, if ever, have I seen someone truly reducing the medications with a comprehensive plan of how to slowly remove themselves, or be removed from these medications, by having these medications reduced in a proper way. Typically, the doses continue to increase. I don't feel that most of the people I see are learning how to live abundant lives. It does not feel like they are seeing their own transformation or even a transformation similar to one we see with others who don't choose these paths. However, currently I am seeing the only way to maintain, the only way to get the funding needed, is to encourage medications. I am seeing halfway houses mandating that everyone be on some kind of medication map in order to be in their halfway house. You have people who do not want to be on any medication, having to be on medication. I am seeing health districts not providing counseling for people who are recovering addicts and alcoholics unless they get on meds. It is becoming that they must receive some form of it in order to receive any form of care. There are all sorts of problems with that.

Short term, as part of a comprehensive plan, it may have a place or it may not, but in the long term, there needs to be a comprehensive plan. For instance, right now, in this Coronavirus pandemic, we're on lockdown. Say you are using methadone. You are going the clinic on a daily basis to get your medication because they know if they give you a week's supply you'd die. They know an addict cannot be trusted because the disease of addiction is still active, even though you don't want to admit you're still thinking like an addict. They can't possibly give you a month's worth, like they would with antibiotics. You could sell that off, lose it, use it, abuse it, so they won't do that. What happens when you can't go out during a hurricane, they give you a little extra. If they give you a little extra for an extended period of time, everyone on that dose is now increasingly at risk. What addict or alcoholic keeps their insurance for a long period of time, or follows through on that paperwork needed? Eventually the resource that is providing them with this medication might not be available to them. Now they're in a major difficult situation because they haven't been able to work on the underlying problems and the underlying symptoms. The only way I see medications as an effective form of intervention, is if they are administered with a comprehensive plan of action. No physician writes a prescription says here you go, this is all that is required. What I'm seeing is more and more movement towards this medication-assisted treatment being the standard of care, rather than abstinence being the standard of care. I am not seeing both available. I am seeing a move towards discounting abstinence-based treatment to the point where it is becoming irrelevant.

When people come in with addiction and other mental health issues, either anxiety, depression, trauma, or abuse, it is extremely complicated. There are people who have addiction and a disorder that will need medications, a dual diagnosis. I am not an anti-medication person. There are people who have long-term, clinical depression, and they have tried everything, and medication is the only thing that has been able to help them. They may have made progress with Cognitive Behavioral Therapy, they may have made progress with different kinds of therapies, and they may have made progress in their faith journey, but there is still something they need medication wise. I am not against medications. It is difficult to balance, like the chicken and the egg. You have people coming in presenting themselves as bi-polar and they are not truly bi-polar, they have been abusing crack. Sometimes you have someone who has been abusing who is bi-polar. Differentiating between all that takes a very skilled person, it takes time, and a very comprehensive safety net to be able to navigate. If you take someone off their medication who is truly mentally ill, they can be in imminent danger. We want to make sure that they have the right people around them to navigate that, in the right systems, because we don't want to do harm, we want to help people. What I have been seeing is people who do not have any true occurring condition settling with being on opiates for the rest of their lives, but I have never seen that actually work in the long run.

CHOOSING A FACILITY

When a family is choosing a facility, whether there is a dual diagnosis or not, there should be an understanding of what the facility provides. Look to see if it is based more on clinical care or medical care. I have worked at facilities that provide wonderful clinical care and wonderful medical care, and that was the right place for people with a dual diagnosis. It was the right place for patients who needed an intense detox, 24-hour nursing, medical doctors on staff every day, and psychiatrists to navigate a dual diagnosis. Those facilities create a safe enough environment to be able to say, is this the chicken or is this the egg, and how do we walk through this? Choosing a facility depends on what the patient's particular needs are, then how a facility can meet those needs. If the addict is someone who has a higher clinical or medical need, accreditations need to be looked at. Make sure the facility has a Jayco and other certifications. That is not the only thing a facility needs, because there are hospitals that are not good hospitals, that have those accreditations. There are doctors who are not good doctors who are licensed. The family should look at the next level. They have to do their due diligence and ask who are the staff? What are their qualifications? What online reviews, Google reviews can we find? You have to dig through because there are some facilities who are padding their reviews or paying for reviews to protect their brand. Dig deeper than reviews, understand what you are looking for. For example, if you are looking for a facility with medical care, reviews may not be quite as important. The addict will do a detox and that is okay. You must dig deeper when the person needs more of a spiritual awakening. Look into if they are offering a Christian program and what that program looks like. Is it taking the addict to a meeting once a week and allowing a pastor to come visit them, or is it more comprehensive than that? There are lots of options.

Many clinical facilities range from just detox to stabilization, and then move right to an out-patient setting. The person will come in for three to five days for detox (it used to be longer), then after the three to five days they will move into a residential-type setting or an in-patient type setting for around 25 days, and then move into an out-patient setting and probably live-in transitional living. Ideally, it would be better for a person to come into a clinical setting, go through detox, go through the 25-day treatment program, go into a long-term level of care, then from long term step down into an out-patient setting. I feel that time away from the substance along with good clinical care and a deep connection to God, a deep surrender to God, is what is going to give them the best chance at recovery. The problem is people come into a center, but by the time we are figuring out what is really going on, was it this medication, was this drugs, or if they truly have a dual diagnosis, they are already being discharged and moving to a lower level of care. Then we are changing the medications, doing adjustments, and they are no longer in the safety net where we could really do what is necessary for their long-term success. If we can extend the time the patient has at a higher level of observation, that would be the best.

At long-term programs, most of the time they cannot give medications, because of the way they are licensed. That is not necessarily a bad thing; they are ministries, not clinical facilities. We don't have very many long-term facilities, if any, of which I'm aware that are able to manage medication. This is the severe gap in our system. If someone truly does need a medication, say lithium for their bi-polar disorder, then oftentimes they are excluded from long-term, faith-based facilities, as those facilities do not have the licensing to be able to give or monitor that medication. Then we are left with this constant shuffle between short-term and long-term facilities for people who are struggling.

As far as an aftercare plan, a geographical change can be part of that; there is wisdom there. I have seen, though, that no matter where the addict goes, they are still going to find the same type of people in the same situations if they don't have some good work done. Wherever they are, the key is that they must be in a community surrounded by people who are working with them, and a community where they are being honest and transparent. A true accountable community where they have a therapist, they are working with a program, and sooner rather than later, where they are sponsoring and helping others. They are going to get more help by helping others. They have accountability when they have other people looking up to them and other people relying on them, and they are more likely to stay sober. If possible, the addict should be in some type of appropriate, licensed, structured living. If they are back home, if they can't relocate, there are all sorts of triggers and temptations and it is easier for them to get what they want and, therefore, easier for them to fall. We have to make sure they have a good support network in place as soon as possible. After leaving a facility, you know they are not going to be floating around out there. They need to get busy with their recovery. They need to get busy doing what they need to do, work on the steps and start on inner work.

FRIENDS AND FAMILY OF THE ADDICT

Everyone who is a family member of someone struggling with addiction needs to work on boundaries and do their own work. They need to see a therapist, go to Al-Anon or Codependents Anonymous, or get some good books on setting healthy boundaries. If they don't work on understanding when to say yes and how to say no, if no clear, healthy boundaries are set, they will love the addict to death. I have known addicts who have gotten hips replaced, knees replaced, faked cancer, and done unbelievable things to manipulate their families. It's extremely difficult to navigate those waters. Family members need to do their own personal work and learn how to set those healthy boundaries. Make sure the alcoholic/drug addict understands what those boundaries are. Set clear expectations, clear lines and adhere to them. Don't move them or let them be moved. When the dynamic is not working, I've seen families decide to not make these decisions alone, and to have an outside therapist or coach come in and help them make those decisions.

The next thing I would encourage them to do is collect an inventory of resources. Have that in place so when their child (or other family member) comes to their senses or asks for help, they are prepared. What will you have in place? Know what is available. What options can you help him or her find? If you don't know that, when the addict finally comes to you, you are playing catch up and it's too late. Their motivation changes quickly and it is just too late. Understand what health insurance options they have, know what facilities they can go to, and how much these options are going to cost. Get a savings account going. Prepare for them so when they do come to you, you have more options in place besides government-funded facilities or free facilities. It is better to know your options and have other options already in place, if you can.

Intervention

We don't have to wait for the addict to come to their senses and hit bottom, we can raise that bottom. We can help them become motivated quicker. I have seen families motivate addicts to recovery with a well-planned intervention. I have seen interventions, when done properly and well, be successful. I have also seen horrible interventions go sideways. The difference between a good intervention and a bad one is the thought that is put into it. An example of a bad intervention is when mom, dad, sibling or whoever decides to do an intervention and they do it right then and there. What tends to happen is it becomes a browbeating session. They are well-intentioned, but they proceed without a real comprehensive plan of how to go about it. The addict and their family don't have a clue how to really do what's needed and the addict just ends up down at the community hospital or somewhere for a couple days, then there's nothing in place afterwards. Then the addict loses motivation. They may no longer be physically dependent on substance of choice, but they haven't had any true healing or any true treatment. They go back out and relapse, their tolerance levels are low, and then they overdose and sometimes die.

In a good intervention, they get wise counsel, and they have a good plan in place. It starts with someone deciding they are going to do an intervention, no matter what, and then trying to get a show of support or power. They call every family member and every person that could possibly have a positive impact on the addict. They make a list and ask people to join in. They build a list of people willing to move forward and work on a comprehensive plan. They might even hire a professional interventionist who can help them with this process. When planning an intervention, know the options of placement before ever talking to the addict or alcoholic. Have options. If he is willing to go to detox, plan how the family is going to respond. The plan might be for him to go to detox and then into short-term, in-patient care. Maybe the addict is willing to detox then go into long-term, in-patient care. How will the family respond? Have it all thought out ahead of time. With contingency plans in place, interventions go well.

There are things that a parent, spouse, or family member can look for to signal it's time to think about treatment or interventions.

You can look at the wreckage, the destruction, the lack of motivation. You can look at the results of his or her actions. We all know those signals and we all see them in the life of the addict and alcoholic. There are also exceptions. There are some people who are alcoholics and still achieve. Those are more type-A, OCD-concept alcoholics. There are workaholic alcoholics, they can keep going and binge all weekend long. Typically, it's not as subtle as a teenager who is experimenting and hiding, and once they get their claws in, their addiction advances pretty rapidly. It's a pretty significant move, especially with opiates. If the family member has not accepted they are an alcoholic or addict, they need to work on their own denial and work on their own willingness to accept the reality. For instance, I've had spouses call me up and say, "I don't know if he is an alcoholic." If you are calling me asking the question, "Is he really an alcoholic?" then you need help so does he. There is a reason you are calling me asking me the question. There is a reason you are reaching out. Then they start digging in and explain that he is drunk every single night. They are aware. It's rare that I see someone who is a full-fledged alcoholic who keeps it comfortably hidden to the point where his spouse is really unaware there is a problem. They might be in denial. They might not want to name the problem, but they know there is a problem.

I have an example from personal experience. Until around ten years ago, my family would never refer to my brother as an addict or alcoholic. They wouldn't. They didn't understand that his problem was really about that. They just saw him as a guy who made horrible decisions. They never connected those decisions and the alcoholism. I see that often. Family members won't put two and two together, but the signs are everywhere. The person can't hold a job. They're constantly having illnesses and things related to alcoholism or addiction, but the family can't put the two together. They just wonder why their son keeps heading in the wrong direction and making bad decisions. They're not seeing the problem of addiction for what it really is. There is a stigma related to alcoholism and addiction and people don't want to name the problem for what it is.

RECOVERY CHURCH

Who is successful? Who stays in long-term recovery? Who stays sober? Who stays clean? Who stays? Those whose lights become abundant are those who we have seen surrender. Those who we have seen go through a born-again Christian experience are the ones we have had the most success with. There is a need for stabilization from the medical field, we do need detox, we do need a sort of triage and a re-directing of the bow of the boat from a medical and psychiatric standpoint, and so we do need the treatment centers. We need that, however, what I saw was a substantial gap between the Christian community and the treatment centers and that is where Recovery Church stands. There is a gap between the local churches and treatment centers. There is a gap between the twelve-step fellowships and the churches. We do not need the gap to be there. There does not need to be as much of a divide as people thought there needed to be. We thought we could stand in the middle, be a bridge between the treatment centers, between the halfway houses, between the churches and the twelve-step fellowships. We give people a safe opportunity to explore their faith. A safe opportunity for them to have enough space to have that distance, figure out their faith, and come to know Jesus. That is where Recovery Church has kind of stood. We allow that, and we have seen truly remarkable things take place. We have seen things on a level that I just can't even really explain. We've seen lives transformed.

I pastored Recovery Church for many years and am now president and running it. It is my single full-time focus. I had a calling from God and I basically went kicking and screaming the whole way. God dragged me to it. I see both a comprehensive plan and Recovery Church as needed. Recovery Church is part of a comprehensive continuum of care. I don't see us as the solution. I think that part of the problem we have with how we treat alcoholics and addicts is that we try to compartmentalize everything. I see what we are doing with Recovery Church as part of the journey.

When Recovery Church was started, it was a hobby on the side. We had fun with it. I did not realize how large God's vision was. Within two years, we had eighteen locations. Currently, we are on track for over thirty locations. At this time, I visit as many locations as I can, and they are doing it, and raising up the cycles of recovery.

That's the wind, and the wind for Recovery Church will be there when I am no longer needed. That will be when I happily put myself out of a job.

Our vision is to have a Recovery Church in every city in this nation and beyond. It is a church for addicts and alcoholics, for people in recovery, by people in recovery. A really surprising thing is how people start to feel honest, good, and accepted in the Christian community. When they start to have accountability, feel connected, feel needed, feel appreciated, and be a part of it, it is their church.

When someone comes into the church and shares the gospel of Jesus Christ, others may not be familiar with that. When a person who does not accept it, or is really against it, is there, they are going to continue to be welcomed into the church. Our mission is to see people overcoming addiction, breaking free, and having freedom for life.

I had a man "Crispy" come in and he wanted nothing to do with Jesus. He had a very twisted, abusive, background, along with some spiritual drama. He was a former Mormon, became an atheist, and went to treatment. The treatment center brought him to one of the campuses of Recovery Church. Crispy would come because he would be able to get out, have coffee, and listen to some music. It was better than sitting back at the treatment center. He would come, share often, and thank the Recovery Church for allowing him to be there. He would share that he did not believe in the Recovery Church, but that he felt welcomed. We started to allow him to serve and be a part of our community, before he had gone through a class, and before he had been able to make any progress. He helped with coffee, helped with the trash, and over time he came to believe. He is now disciplining other guys, has sponsees who are sponsoring others, and there becomes multiple generations of sponsors. We got to baptize him; his life has been transformed. He is out there sharing Jesus with as many people as possible. This is the heart of Recovery Church. Think of the story of Doubting Thomas… When Jesus came back, where was Thomas? Jesus met with the disciples and Thomas was right there in the upper room with them. He was right there. They made room for Thomas to not believe. They made room for Thomas to doubt, and they didn't kick him out. Recovery Church is that in-between. We allow room for those who aren't sure what they believe yet. We also have some distinct values. One of the values that makes us a little different than other iterations of Christian recovery is we are unashamedly for the twelve-step process.

We want people in the rooms of AA/NA for a variety of reasons. One of the reasons is the Recovery Church is inept to truly handle treatments of addiction. We don't know how to do that. Another reason the Recovery Church is for the twelve-step fellowships is because we see the Twelve Steps as an amazing pathway that leads to Jesus. There is also the opportunity for discipleship to take place right in the rooms of AA/NA. Oftentimes, especially if a sponsor, or a person who is a believer is in those rooms, there is a mission field there. We want the people who are a part of Recovery Church, like Crispy, to be in the rooms of AA, so when a newcomer needs a sponsor, they are able to sponsor that newcomer. They are able to walk alongside them. They are able to share Jesus with them. The other side of it is that the rooms are effective. For instance, when a holiday comes, AA/NA will have 24-hour support and meetings every hour. When this pandemic came, Recovery Church was starting online meetings, but AA/NA had online meetings every hour on the hour, all over the world, the same day things were locked down. It's a support network. It's not perfect, but there is a system built into place. A system that Recovery Church would rather infiltrate than stand separate from. We want to be a part of re-creation. There are resources and amazing things out there and we see those things. That is one of the reasons we are distinctly different. We don't see ourselves as a replacement of someone's recovery program. We see ourselves as part of a more comprehensive program.

Our growth came from word of mouth, from people who are part of Recovery Church. We do virtually no advertising, besides a few Facebook posts. Growth has been from people who are part of us, connected to us. People came and said that they would love to have this in their town and asked us for help to get it going.

Everyone came to us and is still coming. I don't believe there were any churches that we went to; I believe they all came to us. Years ago, we were doing the first Recovery Church and people were leaving South Florida to go back home and they were asking if we could bring Recovery Church back home to them. We said no, that we had no time for that. They decided to open up a little service themselves anyways, like good addicts, they don't listen, but God honored it. More recently, a couple of fellowships came to us and asked is they could be a part of what we are doing. They asked for us to give them some oversight, some accountability. All of a sudden, we were at three locations. I realized God was saying, Philip, I'm in this. So, I left my job and the Recovery Church agreed to try for expansion. The minute we started saying yes, it just exploded.

Many people who come to Recovery Church, who happen to still be in treatment, are non-believers. The non-faith-based places are the ones who bring the most people. So, most of the people who come to Recovery Church are initially not believers or are very young in their spiritually journey. We're not in the business of creating churches by taking people from other churches or taking people from other ministries. This is Kingdom growth. New people are coming. Now there are people who have had a church history, or who are the wayward son or daughter who will come and be a part of it. There are some Christian programs, and programs with Christian tracks that bring people in, but primarily most of the people are coming from the community as opposed to the treatment centers.

The Recovery Church has a very unique view. There are people in the treatment industry who are faith-based and some who are not. We have people in the church who understand addiction firsthand and some who don't. We have people in the treatment industry who have not experienced addiction, and people in the church who haven't, as well. I am a clinician, a pastor, and have had my own unique Christian experience, my coming to faith, with the exposure to multiple denominations and a broad brushstroke of the Kingdom. I came to faith in a Southern Baptist church. My wife grew up in an Assembly of God church and we got married in a Methodist church. I've worked in Lutheran and Episcopal churches. I'm ordained in the Krishna Missionary Alliance. That experience of God has sanctified me; God has changed me. My walk and my Christian faith has put me in a strange and unique position where I'm able to understand the unique sacredness within different parts of God's Kingdom. I see the beauty and I also see the struggles. I can see and understand that a person is coming from a certain perspective. It gives me a unique insight. My total experience, I believe, puts me in a position to be able to speak to pastors, speak to therapists, and speak to the addict in the street, and try to bridge those gaps. Having the clinical experience and my own personal recovery, as well, and seeing the benefits, strengths, and the weaknesses of both, has put me in a position to be able to see where we don't have to throw the baby out with the bathwater. Where there are things that we can learn from each of these elements in order to have a better understanding.

That being said, one of the main problems is we think that the way we encountered Christ, the way we recovered is the way that everyone else is going to recover. My experience has been that God really speaks in the language of that person's heart. There are some universal truths that are not negotiable. There's no question about that. There are some spiritual laws and there are some physical laws and that's not what I'm questioning. What I mean is God can uniquely speak to a person from their unique culture, from a unique perspective, and He uses a lot of these tools to help a lot of these things be seen. It is God who leads the person to spiritual healing and spiritual riches. I pray no one would miss out on this life-changing experience.

It's A Wrap!

By Jack Alan Levine

WOW! You made it through the book … That's awesome! So, what does it all mean? Well, that's a very individual question. I hope and pray that you have seen undeniable themes emerge from the book. I hope you have gleaned invaluable information for your quest to overcome the struggle of addiction, either personally or as a family member or friend with a loved one struggling with addiction. I was so amazed, as none of the authors had any clue what the other was writing about. Some of them were just asked to share their perspective and others given a specific topic but, at the end of the day, the prevailing and reoccurring messages that came through were:

1. Addiction is a crippling, horrific, life-destroying disease.
2. There is not just one way to recovery, there are many ways.
3. We must focus on the total person: spiritual, emotional, physical, and relational, as we seek to overcome addiction, not just on one area; that will not work.
4. There is hope and a way out! There is recovery and victory over addiction on a permanent basis… It exists… The tools are available to you.

I hope you can see the dedication and hearts of those who have contributed to this book. The authors are people on the front line in the battle against addiction. They have seen way to many people die and so many others lose their life potential, hopes, families, dreams, and futures. It is for this reason that these brave warriors continue to fight against addiction, determined to give everything they have to help even one more person have victory. We pray that person is you!

We hope and pray this book is been a blessing to you and that it will not just be another book you read, but something that will change and transform your life—a book you will take to heart and, more importantly, act upon. Grab hold tightly to the principles and practices in this book. Everything may not apply to you, so just take what you need and leave the rest. Let that be your path to recovery and a life free of addiction!

At the end of the day, all the information in the world is meaningless if you won't do anything with it. But I trust as you read this book you will find what you desire—life-changing, accurate, intelligent, first-hand information from those in the know. I believe we have delivered that. I pray we left no stone unturned in our desire to educate and share with you many different perspectives of the addiction spectrum from many diverse representatives. Many forms, types, and styles of treatment are represented. Our prayer is that after reading this, you would have all the information you need to begin the road to recovery. I truly believe it's all here. So, get started… Make a choice and go forward! That is the only way out!

With all our love and the anticipation of great things to come in your lives, on behalf of all of the authors of this book, we thank you for the time you've invested in reading it. It has been is our pleasure and privilege to have committed our time to help you and those who are still struggling.

I leave you with a quote from the Word of God in Jeremiah 29:11 that has long inspired and comforted me, and I know this is God's desire and promise for you, as well. "'For I know the plans I have for you,' declares the Lord, 'plans to prosper you and not to harm you, plans to give you hope and a future.'"

God be with you.
Jack

AUTHORS' BIOS

Jack Alan Levine, addiction expert, speaker, businessman, coach, and renowned author has spoken to thousands of people over more than thirty years on dealing with and successfully overcoming addiction. A nine-time author, his book *My Addict Your Addict* talks about his battles and victory over addiction. Jack created and developed the *Free for Life Overcoming Addiction* online video program, which helps addicts, their families, and employers deal with the realities of addiction and outlines the clear paths and solutions available to overcoming addiction and truly finding Freedom for Life.

Jack is a sought-after treatment center speaker where his clear-cut message has helped many addicts seek and find the path to recovery. He has spoken at Faith Farm, Teen Challenge, Iron Sharpens Iron, Florida Men of Integrity, Igniting Men, Strongmen, and other conferences and organizations about overcoming addiction. He has appeared as a guest on numerous national television and radio shows discussing addiction and recovery issues, and has articles published in national magazines, newspapers, and websites.

Here are just a few of the comments addicts and their families have made about the impact Jack had on their lives. "Jack saved my life." "He explained to me like nobody ever has." "It was as if he could see inside my soul." "Jack is real. He's been there. He's done it. He knows what it takes." "As a parent he could relate firsthand to my pain and desperation."

Jack worked for some of the top advertising agencies on Madison Avenue on large accounts including AT&T, The US Army, and Dupont. He then started his own Ad Agency and later founded a national television production company where he wrote, directed, and produced hundreds of national television shows and thousands of commercials. In 2002, he sold that company to devote more time to entrepreneurial activities and to help those battling addictions.

Jack consults with companies, organizations, colleges, churches, and nonprofits on educating employees, staff, and clients on overcoming addiction. He is also on the advisory board of the N.O.W. Matters More Foundation, an organization dedicated to educating and helping those struggling with addiction. He is the founding director of Voice of God Ministry, a twenty-three-year-old 501C-3 nonprofit, and served on the board of directors at Oasis Compassion Agency, Changed Lives Church, and now serves at Purpose Church Orlando as Executive Pastor. More info on Jack at JackAlanLevine.com

Raymond Alvarez, MS, LCSW, is a licensed clinical social worker and a qualified supervisor and therapist who was born and raised in Miami, Florida. He received his undergraduate degree at Penn State University in Psychology with a minor in Business. Raymond completed a master's degree in Social Work at Florida State University in 2007 and moved back to South Florida. He has worked with youth, adolescents, and families in primary prevention, in-home counseling, and adults struggling with substance abuse issues. Currently he works as a supervisor in an outpatient facility in Broward County.

Graham Barrett, is the director of national outreach for Family First Adolescent Services. He has also worked at treatment centers and was a management executive, franchise owner, and global banking executive. Graham's eclectic background includes years of experience in the field of mental health and substance abuse treatment, helping people to find the help they need. He has a passion for working with teens and families that comes from personal experience as a struggling adolescent whose life was saved by an intervention. Graham's approach with families is to share his experience, provide resources, and help guide them to the level of care their loved one needs with compassion and consistent support. He is a graduate of Rollins College, a husband, and a father.

Dr. Karl Benzio M.D. is a Christian psychiatrist, board certified by the American Board of Psychiatry and Neurology, and is the founder, medical director, and staff psychiatrist at Honey Lake Clinic. He has held several health system clinical director and management positions to infuse his unique integration of spiritual faith with science to treat thousands. He also writes, consults, and serve as frequent media guest expert and conference speaker addressing the impact of a wide range of behavioral health issues and how to bring God's healing to individuals, families, society, and social policy issues.

Dr. Adam Bianchini M.D. is a nationally renowned addiction expert. After receiving his Bachelor of Science in Biology at Brown University, Dr. Bianchini completed his Medical Doctorate training at Jefferson Medical College in Philadelphia. His post-graduate education includes a General Surgery Internship at Wright-Patterson Air Force Base and an Anesthesiology Residency at Hartford Hospital in Connecticut.

Adam's personal recovery experience led him to the field of addiction treatment where he has served in both medical and executive roles. Until his untimely death from Covid 19, Adam served as the chief medical officer of Origins Behavioral Healthcare and previously was the director of medicine at the Treatment Center of the Palm Beaches. His addiction medicine career spans more than a decade. He also has spoken at many addiction conferences nationally. While serving as medical director and chief medical officer overseeing the medical care in high acuity addiction treatment centers, his passion remains aimed at the spiritual solution of addiction.

Keith Everett Brooks is a minister and certified master neuro-linguistic programming and life coach. He has a bachelor's degree in social welfare from the University of California at Berkeley. He started his professional life as a high school teacher, football coach, and professional dancer. Prior to committing fully to his life's passion, guiding those who seek an inward path to self-discovery, he served as a manager for the city of Cleveland and spent eleven years as a sales specialist for a pharmaceutical company. Keith committed to his spiritual journey thirty years ago and this experience enabled him to tap into the ability to change the world by first seeking change from within. Through extensive study, travel, and guided introspection, he has adopted a much more eclectic perspective about how we each seek to know ourselves. Keith teaches that, "life happens for you, not to you." Self-awareness and being centered in the now are fundamental to our personal evolution.

Keith is also certified as a trauma release specialist and inclusive leadership and diversity consultant, as well as being certified in clinical hypnotherapy, dream sculpting, yoga instruction, Reiki I & II, and situational leadership. He has five years of experience working with clients in drug recovery programs as a life coach and a group facilitator.

Joe Bryan is CEO/owner of the Beachcomber Treatment Center in Delray Beach, Florida. Joe began working at The Beachcomber in 1980, shortly after The Beachcomber opened. He followed in the path of his father, James Bryan, who founded the facility in 1976 and whose career spanned decades of leadership in the field of alcoholism and addiction treatment. Joe has held all positions at The Beachcomber and is now the owner and CEO. Joe has a degree in business administration from Florida Atlantic University and is currently in school pursuing a degree in nursing.

Joe has been an active advocate for the recovery community and has organized numerous functions to better the community and bring awareness to the horrendous affliction that addiction has on individuals, families, and the community. Joe believes treatment centers have a responsibility to do more than just treat patients; they need to be a positive part of the community and start taking leadership roles. Joe has had numerous positions in the recovery community beginning as treasurer for the local chapter of South Florida Employee Assistant Program in 2001-2002. He also held numerous positions at the Employee Behavioral Health Network of Florida (also known as EAP of Florida), including acting president for 2007–2009 and president from 2009 – 2011. Currently, Joe serves as the vice-president. Joe started a non-profit FATC to help those who have addiction problems and promote the best treatment centers in Florida. Most recently, Joe has offered support by serving on the board of the Care Hope College of Nursing.

Joe has been awarded for his tireless effort to support the recovery community. He received the prestigious Clinician of the Year Award in 2011 for Palm Beach County bestowed by Bob Bozzone, executive director of CARP (Comprehensive Alcoholism Rehabilitation Programs). In January 2019, Joe was awarded the FMHCA award for outstanding community service.

Lui Delgado is the founding director and chairman of the N.O.W. Matters More Foundation. Also known as "The Dope Doctor," he is a certified addiction professional (CAP) and co-host of the Couch Live Radio Show. He's a columnist for Brevard Live Magazine and a treatment service consultant for many clients and patients. He has his own story of twenty-eight years of recovery that he shares on his radio show weekly. He is married and the father of two wonderful girls. As an expert in addiction and recovery, he has been serving the recovery community for many, many years. N.O.W. Matters More, founded in 2011, is an awesome foundation and has helped numerous individuals and families navigate the difficult obstacles and road to recovery.

Philip Dvorak MS, LMHC, is the founder and president of Recovery Church Movement, a network of Recovery Churches reaching and training those in early recovery to grow in their faith and recovery. He started Recovery Church in July 2011 and took on a full-time position as President in 2018. He was a clinical counselor and a pastoral care counselor at the Meier Clinic in Lake Worth, Florida. Phil has a B.S. in Psychology and Religion and a M.S. in Counseling Psychology from Palm Beach Atlantic University. Phil was also the director of the Road to Freedom Treatment Program, as well as the director of spiritual care and senior pastor at a teen treatment center in Lake Worth, Florida, and is still actively involved in the industry. He is ordained by the Christian & Missionary Alliance where he has served thousands of individuals. He was formerly chief operating officer of the Timothy Initiative. Phil is a devoted husband, father, and servant leader.

Dr. Anthony Foster MCAP, CRC, SAP, CADC, RRT is the co-director of the Beachcomber Family Program. He is passionate about helping people overcome alcoholism and addiction. With over 16 years of extensive experience at all levels of care, Dr. Foster has served as a clinical therapist, clinical director, trauma specialist, chief operating officer and chief executive officer. He is the co-founder of the Center for Sobriety, Spirituality & Healing. He is an addiction executive, author, educator, and speaker in family recovery and relapse prevention. He holds a PhD in Counseling from Florida Atlantic University and a dual master's degree in Mental Health and Rehab Counseling, also from FAU. He has been certified nationally as a rehabilitation counselor in Florida, a master certified addiction professional, and an internationally certified alcohol and drug counselor, as well as being an accredited practitioner of rapid trauma resolution. He is a past president and vice president of Employee Behavioral Health Network of Florida (also known as EAP of Florida) and currently serves on their board of directors.

Dr. Karrol-Jo(KJ) Foster LMHC, CAP is the co-director of the Beachcomber Family Program. She is a mental health expert, trauma specialist, clinical therapist, author, and speaker in family recovery and relapse prevention. She is also the founder of Fostering Resilience™ Relapse Prevention and the co-founder of the Center for Sobriety, Spirituality & Healing. In addition to her latest book, The Warrior's Guide to Successful Sobriety, KJ has authored many articles on addiction recovery, and a book chapter on twelve-Step spirituality in the book Spirituality and Religion in Counseling: Competency-Based Strategies for Ethical Practice. KJ lectures locally, nationally, and internationally on the topics of addiction recovery, shame, and spirituality. It is her passion and mission to help individuals and their families recover from addiction and grow into the best and most powerful version of themselves.

Dr. David Jenkins is a psychologist and the director of the MA program in addiction counseling in the Department of Counselor Education and Family Studies at Liberty University, Lynchburg, Virginia. He has served as clinical director of the international board of Christian Counselors of the American Association of Christian Counselors and is on the executive board of the Society for Christian Psychology. Dr. Jenkins also served on the Executive Draft Committee to update the AACC's Code of Ethics for Christian Counselors.

With over 25 years of experience as a clinical psychologist, Dr. Jenkins specializes in the integration of Christian faith and clinical practice. He has worked extensively with addictive, mood, and anxiety disorders in the context of individual, marital, group, and family therapy. Dr. Jenkins has provided education, consultation, supervision, and training for a variety of churches, ministries, and professionals. He is also a renowned author and speaker at conferences, seminars, and retreats.

Douglas Lidwell is campus director and pastor at Faith Farm Ministries, a faith-based recovery program in south Florida. In 2013, he and his wife, Heather, answered the call of God to come to Faith Farm. Their desire is to minister the abundance of grace and the gift of righteousness, to see families restored, and to advance the Kingdom of God by strengthening men in a dynamic way that focuses on their new identity in Christ. Faith Farm ministers to young men. There is no cost to come to the program. The men work on a farm, learn about God and how to conquer their addiction, and live great lives.

Douglas holds degrees in communication and theology from colleges in his home state of Illinois. He was ordained as a pastor at Christ Temple Church in Huntington, West Virginia, after serving as an associate pastor in an urban mission church plant in Pekin, Illinois.

Pasco Manzo is the president and CEO of Teen Challenge New England and New Jersey. Since Pasco's introduction to Teen Challenge over forty years ago, he has been passionately involved in its mission. Under his leadership, many positive changes have taken place. From day one he stressed resident first and that staff are privileged to be able to serve them. A fifth phase was added to the program, offering different tracks for residents to choose from including college, career, ministry, or TC Apprenticeship. Certified life coaching was also implemented to help residents to prepare for their future. Pasco made it a priority to develop and train leaders by instituting an Annual Leadership Management Conference. He established an Adolescent's Girls' Home, a second Women's Home, and an outpatient and short-term program. Through his management of finances, Teen Challenge was able to pay off the inherited seven-million-dollar-plus debt, renovate buildings, build additions and new buildings, including the new corporate headquarters building at a cost of over eight million dollars without borrowing any money. As a result of his efforts, Teen Challenge received six donated real estate properties with an assessed value totaling almost four million dollars.

The "End Addiction Campaign" was established, which proclaimed on billboards and promotional materials such as postcards, T-shirts, and wristbands to be distributed. Teen Challenge staff raises awareness of the drug epidemic in schools through this campaign, keeping TCNE&NJ on the front lines fighting addiction. Under Pasco's leadership, several products have been produced including: Coffee for Change, Tea Challenge, Papa Pasquale's Sauce and Biscuits for Change, Syrup for Change, The Carpenters Shop kitchen wood products, and Changed Lives—Ten True Stories from Addiction to Freedom, a seven-book set.

Pasco's studies have earned him a master of arts in christian ministries distinguished with Summa Cum Laude. He also received a M.Div. equivalency from Assemblies of God Theological Seminary. He taught several years as an adjunct professor, authored two books: Urim and Thummim-Discovering the Will of God and Broken Flowers: A Commentary on the Tragedy of Sex Slavery in America. Pasco has had the honor to minister for Jesus on every populated continent and has traveled to over fifty countries. He gives God all the glory!

Craig Nichols is founder, pastor, and CEO for Washed Clean Ministries in Sioux Falls, Dakota. Craig is a recovering addict who struggled with the demons of addiction for 35 years, dating back to an abusive childhood and carrying over into his own role as a father. He repeatedly failed at twelve-step programs and other attempts to get clean, even finding himself in jail and near death.

Then one day, he heard the call of God. In a flash, Craig realized that real recovery, the kind that goes soul deep, was not possible without the hand of God. He began his recovery that day, never looking back, and for the last three years, he has built a ministry aimed at helping others do the same. Craig is married to beautiful wife, Nikki, who has walked the journey of Washed Clean Ministries with him since its inception in 2017.

Trinity Phillips, AKA "The Dharma Guy" is president of N.O.W. Matters More Foundation, which aspires to change the lives of everyone it touches, help bring more compassion to the world while changing the stigmas associated with addiction, and provide resources and tools necessary to overcome and break free from the bondage of addiction. He is a certified master level trainer, wellness coordinator, spiritual counselor and co-host of "The Couch Live" radio show. He is not in recovery from substance, but used to be addicted to a lifestyle that ruined his life and relationships with friends, family, and loved ones. He and his wife have four amazing children.

Dr. Jared Pingleton is a minister, psychologist, author, and speaker. He is a Christ-follower, husband, father, and grandfather. He is also a credentialed minister and a licensed clinical and consulting psychologist who is passionate about communicating Jesus' love, mercy, and grace to a hurting and conflicted world. A respected leader in the Christian mental health field, Jared has been in professional practice since 1977 offering help, healing, and hope to thousands of individuals, couples, families, churches, ministries, and organizations.

Dually trained in theology and psychology, he has been a professor at several Christian universities and seminaries, served on the pastoral staff of two large churches. He has authored or co-authored eight Christian books addressing topics such as marriage, mental health, recovery, and theology.

Currently Jared serves as the executive vice-president of Choose Grace International and as the director of mental health and ministry of the American Association of Christian Counselors. Prior to that, Jared was the director of counseling services at Focus on the Family and was also in private practice for 36 years. He has appeared as a guest, host, or co-host on hundreds of television and radio programs and many leading print publications. He maintains several professional affiliations, has received five "Who's Who" awards along with several other national recognitions, and is a popular national and international speaker and conference leader.

Kerry Roesser CAP, CRC, SAP, CRRA, LMHC in five states, Kerry is a sober home and treatment center owner, and therapist. Kerry started Foundation Sober Homes for men in south Florida, in June 2012. Foundation is an all-male sober living facility which has a life recovery plan, using goal setting and a relapse prevention strategy. Kerry also owns a medical clinic that provides walk in services for physical and mental health, and a licensed substance abuse clinic.

Mike W. (Anonymous)

Alice H. (Anonymous)

GO TO:
JackAlanLevine.com/ADDICTION

FREE FOR LIFE
OVERCOMING ADDICTION
VIDEO PROGRAM

AVAILBLE ONLINE OR AS DVD

To order visit: JackAlanLevine.com/Addiction

This educational program is groundbreaking and breakthrough. It was designed for addicts and family members, to give them the tools, information and guidance necessary to take immediate steps to overcome any addiction issue including drugs, alcohol and gambling.

Module 1: My Story of Overcoming Addiction.

You will hear the compelling and inspiring story of Jack's own addiction in which he details his personal struggles and his success of overcoming his own addiction and shares the heart-wrenching story of the addiction of his family members and friends. You'll learn what a parent goes through, step-by-step as Jack reveals everything in this life-changing Module.

Module 2: Why Addicts Think and Behave Like They Do.

Jack takes you on a fascinating journey into the addict's mind to see what causes the behavior of the addict. Jack helps us eliminate the hiding places of our own defenses and denial about our addiction. He dissects the thinking that often keeps the addict and often-family members entrapped inside the web of addiction.

Module 3: The Effects of The Addict on the Family.

The addiction has now taken control and the addict's life is now overcome by destructive behavior. In this Module, Jack shows the addict and the family/ friends of the addict how to deal, not only with the external behavior, but also with the loss of self, the emotional bankruptcy, as well as the physical addiction and what to do about it all.

Module 4: Paths to Recovery.

Jack covers everything the addict needs to get onto the road to recovery. Jack covers detox, therapy, rehab, and other less conventional treatments, how they work and how to use them all to your advantage. Jack shares power tips, lifestyle keys and new ways of thinking to help you or your loved one get on the path to recovery and stay on the pathway of freedom for the rest of your life. This module will change your life experience forever.

CHECK OUT

LIVE A LIFE THAT MATTERS FOR GOD

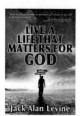

"From a clinical perspective, Live a Life That Matters for God has great value as a teaching and therapeutic tool for the soul. From a spiritual perspective it is a direct hit right to the heart of every Christian. This uplifting book will inspire you no matter what chapter you are reading. I love that you can pick up any chapter, anywhere, in any section in the book and be blessed immediately. Jack covers so many different topics that are relevant and critical to our growth as Christians, our happiness and our desire to walk closer with God. Jack's style is straight to the point and laser focused. Jack doesn't just tell you to do it, he shows you how! "

Julie Woodley,
MA, Division Chair American Assoc. of Christian Counselors

WHERE THE RUBBER MEETS THE ROAD WITH GOD

For every believer who wants to make sure they hear "Well done good and faithful servant."

"A knock out punch for Jesus if there ever was one. Jack Alan Levine's book is the heavyweight champion of the world when it comes to Christians walking a life of faith with God. Read it and make certain you will wear the champion's crown of life for Christ."

Nate "Galaxy Warrior" Campbell,
3x Lightweight Champion Of The World

DON'T BLOW IT WITH GOD

In "Don't Blow It With God", Jack Levine reveals his road map to discovering God's blueprint for living the ultimate Christian life each and every day. Come along for the ride as God teaches Jack life-changing lessons that will help you in your life journey. Jack discovers how to live an abundant Christian life experiencing true joy, peace and happiness and along the way you will discover the formula and the insights about how you can too.

"Jack's unique style of communicating God's plan for an abundant life is a must read for all Christians. This book knocks it out of the park. If you've been striking out and want your life to be the perfect game for God then you need to read this book. "

Chris Hammond, Major League Baseball pitcher

MY ADDICT YOUR ADDICT

This book is about addiction. Author Jack Levine has counseled thousands of people over the years who have gone through addiction, and knows what a torturous life it can be to be caught up in it. It's an awful thing.

He's experienced addiction in his own life and as a parent, as he watched his son struggle with addiction for years (it started when he was 18).

Whether you are in the throes of addiction yourself or seeing a loved one suffer through it, this book can help you. Jack has results and solutions for real-life situations. Each person's situation is different, but the root is the same for everybody. Through his own story, he can tell you what the choices are, the impacts of those choices, the results of those choices, and what sacrifices you'll have to make to get where you want to be.

SUCCESS BLAST

"This is it. A book that finally gives honest, real-world advice on what it takes to work hard, to fight for what you want, and succeed big. I'm already a well-read, successful executive and within the first few pages I simply HAD to start taking notes on all the powerful, creative ideas and inspiring stories that Jack Levine shares in these pages. This book will Blast you up to a whole new level!"

Aaron W. Kassler, Merrill Lynch Vice President & Senior Financial Advisor.

JACK'S OTHER BOOKS...

DOWNLOADING GOD

"Downloading God is the file of information that today's generation needs to click on more than ever. Jack Levine's authentic and transparent self-disclosure rings through in his passionate devotion to his Lord and Savior Jesus Christ. His simple, straightforward, trademark writing style as in his previous books allows the reader to easily absorb, appropriate and apply the word and truth of God in a realistic, revolutionary and redemptive way. 'Downloading God' has short chapters all themed around a clever computer technology motif which makes the timeless truths of God both real and relevant to contemporary culture."

Dr. Jared Pingleton, VP American Association of Christian Counselors,
Clinical Psychologist, Credentialed Minister

TIME GONE

Each year we like to send a holiday letter to our friends and loved ones looking back at the past year and looking forward to the coming one. These letters are extremely personal but also extremely universal. Though written at holiday time, the observations I share are a true reflection of life all year long. In them I share my struggles, joys and thoughts, which like yours, change from year to year and I'm sure mirror many of the same things you go through.

I've left some personal things in here to give you a sense of who I am - a regular person like you with all the normal victories, defeats, happiness, sadness, joy and pain that we all share. Each letter contains reflections, lessons learned, wisdom and insight that God laid on my heart that particular year. I believe these will help you with your life and have great value to you. In these annual holiday letters I ask people to stop, take stock of where they were at, and consider how they were going to move forward. I hope that by sharing these letters with you it will cause you to do the same.

THE MOTIVATED LIFE

What powers your train? You know, some are powered by steam and some by diesel. Some are powered by electricity, and others are powered by battery. Some are even powered by solar energy. But, one thing's for sure. The train needs power to run, and so do you in your life.

So, what powers your train in life? Is it passion and purpose? Is it survival, money, or accomplishment? Is it fear? Perhaps fear of loss? Fear of missing out? It's very important to know what powers you, what motivates you, and what drives you forward each day. And, it's very important to have something that does all of these things. The more powerful your train, the faster and farther you can go and the quicker you can get there.

"It will encourage and accelerate you! Enriches, equips and inspires you to get the most out of every are of your life. I wholeheartedly recommend it."

Peter Lowe
President & Founder Peter Lowe International Get Motivated, Success Seminars

LEARN MORE ABOUT JACK

JackAlanLevine.com